D0626796

INTEREST GROUPS
ON FOUR CONTINENTS

EDITED FOR THE

International
Political Science Association

BY HENRY W. EHRMANN

UNIVERSITY OF PITTSBURGH PRESS

Library of Congress Catalog Card
Number: 58-11146

(c) 1958, UNIVERSITY OF PITTSBURGH PRESS

Second Printing, 1960

Lithoprinted in U.S.A.
EDWARDS BROTHERS, INC.
Ann Arbor, Michigan

FOREWORD

The present volume which is so ably organized and edited by Professor Henry W. Ehrmann is the principal result of a round-table conference held by the International Political Science Association at the University of Pittsburgh, September 9–13, 1957. Meeting for the first time in the United States, it was quite logical that the Executive Committee should have selected the subject of Pressure Groups as a topic for the conference, since considerable study has been given to this important field in America in the past quarter of a century, and more American scholars would be available for participation. The topic proved to be an admirable one, providing as it did for the first time the basis for a broadly international comparative treatment of the subject.

This would not have been possible thirty years ago. There was, in the first place, no International Political Science Association. But also there had been little original research in the field by political scientists. Only in the late twenties did American scholars for the first time begin to give attention to pressure groups. In the earlier books on political parties by Henry Jones Ford, Ostrogorski, Woodburn, Merriam, and Brooks, little reference to the subject is found. By 1927, Professor Sait's book dealt briefly with the subject, and there then appeared a series of pioneering studies by Odegard in 1928, Herring and Childs in 1929, and Schattschneider in 1935. Dr. Herring's book *Group Representation Before Congress*, published in 1929, demonstrated that "groups are rising to a place of increased importance in the community." Spanning the twenty-five year period from Herring's book to Professor David Truman's recent book, and to Professor Hugh Bone's late text in the field of political parties, it is interesting to observe how the subject of pressure groups has become a major emphasis in the United States within the larger field of political parties. As Professor Bone writes; "To a constantly increasing extent American Politics is the politics of organized groups."

Outside the United States, however, until recently, definitive studies have been lacking. When I was a fellow of the Social Science Research Council in Europe in 1927, 1928, and 1929, I found no awareness of the importance of the subject. To an early article of my own on British interest groups published in 1931, I gave the hesitant title "Auxiliary and Non-Party Groups in Britain." Jumping the twenty-five years from my own book, *Money and Politics Abroad*, which appeared in 1932, to a recent German study on pressure groups by Breitling, one finds as many as 233 German groups listed in Breitling's book. A bibliography compiled for a preparatory conference at the University of Michigan in February, 1957 on European Pressure Groups, and utilized by this Pittsburgh conference, lists a number of recent studies in Britain, France, and Germany.

The time was therefore right to discuss pressure groups comparatively, the setting was very appropriate, and best of all the participants, twenty-nine in all, represented fourteen countries. Leading authorities from all of these countries prepared papers on the subject, and the discussions were centered around these multi-national contributions pointed up and integrated by a working paper prepared by our efficient rapporteur-general, Professor Henry Ehrmann. Thanks to the generosity of the University of Pittsburgh and the Falk Foundation it is now possible to publish the major papers with the carefully edited proceedings of the conference. With several of the pioneers in this field of political science research joining colleagues from fourteen countries, and with the newer and more refined techniques of research represented by younger scholars in the field, the pages of this book provide a high level of achievement for international political science.

The holding of the conference, in the first place, was made possible by generous grants from the Ford Foundation, the University of Pittsburgh, and the Falk Foundation. Our great appreciation for this assistance has already been expressed but deserves repetition here. Chancellor Edward H. Litchfield and his able assistants at the University of Pittsburgh made the whole conference a most pleasant experience for all of the participants. Thanks also should be given to Unesco for its continuing interest and support of the International Association. Finally, special tribute should be paid to Professor Ehrmann without whose devoted efforts this volume would not have appeared, and to Professor Albert Martin and the University of Pittsburgh Press for their indispensable assistance.

JAMES K. POLLOCK
President of the International Political Science Association, Murfin Professor of Political Science, and Chairman of the Department of Political Science, University of Michigan.

Ann Arbor
February 10, 1958

EDITOR'S PREFACE

Well over a century ago that most perspicacious of all foreign visitors to these shores reserved highest praise for the perfection which Americans had reached in the "art" of forming numerous and vigorous associations. In exuberant terms de Tocqueville described this art as the mother of action and of science. He believed that on its progress rested all democratic advancement. Accustomed as he was to the exercise of comparing political institutions, the French nobleman suggested that there was a connection between the principles of association and equality, and that in the New World associations stood in lieu of those powerful private individuals whom the equality of conditions had swept away.

How fitting, therefore, that when the International Political Association convened for the first time in the United States, it invited scholars from many lands (disciples all of the Comte de Tocqueville) to discuss the "civil associations" of our time—the modern interest groups.

Since Tocqueville's travels the "new science" has spread far and wide. In the United States as well as in other countries the French observer's sagacious remark that the enjoyment of the "dangerous freedom" of association might render "the dangers of freedom less formidable" has proven on the whole a correct insight into the workings of democratic government. While at the time he wrote he was able to discern but dimly the perils that may arise from the existence of groups for the cohesion of society and the efficacy of government, the reports and debates published in this volume carefully weigh both opportunities and threats connected with the pressure of interests and with the group process as a whole.

Until recently the anatomy and physiology of interest groups have been examined systematically only in the United States. During the past few years, however, political scientists have been increasingly concerned with pressure groups in many countries, especially—but not solely—in England and in continental Europe. On both sides of the Atlantic the study of group activities is now judged important for a realistic understanding of the political process and, possibly, for the formulation of desirable policies. Such widening of the geographical scope of our inquiries has naturally led to the query whether a comparative study of interest groups would not permit sharpening the focus of our observations. "Il n'y a rien," noted the *Encyclopédie,* "que l'esprit humain fasse si souvent que des comparaisons." To add comparative investigations of pressure groups to those of parties and public opinion does not mean that here an alternative—and even less a single alternative—to the traditional emphasis on formal governmental institutions is suggested.[1] But we can expect that as our studies become truly comparative, our increased knowledge of the significance of interest groups will lead to a more complete understanding of political dynamics and ultimately, it is hoped, to a more adequate conceptual framework for the analysis of politics in general.

The careful empirical studies brought together in this volume, and their elaboration in the debates at the Round-Table as well, illustrate why pressure groups furnish excellent material for comparative consideration. The interests which groups defend in their respective countries are similar even where the political regime or the party system differ widely. The conflicts that arise between the various interests have an equal similarity, although the forms in which the conflicts are resolved will be shaped by the general socio-economic and political milieu. Everywhere the groups seem to rival political parties in becoming the link between the citizen (mostly, but not only, as a *homo economicus*) and the government. Everywhere, too, there will be a phase where the concerns of conflicting interests, whether organized or not, are dealt with in the interstices of political society. In a brilliant presidential address in New York a few days before the international gathering opened at Pittsburgh, E. E. Schattschneider suggested that "a look at the literature of American politics reveals that there is an eternal struggle between the conflicting tendencies toward the privatization and socialization of conflict." And he concluded, "The important point about pressure politics is not that it is a conflict of private interests, but the fact that private conflicts are taken into the public domain. Pressure politics is therefore a stage in the socialization of conflict; it represents the breakdown of the attempt to privatize conflict."[2]

The general validity of such an analysis beyond American politics is evidenced amply throughout the present volume. It seems added proof that our studies are able to isolate variables in a way that may be particularly productive of meaningful comparisons. It has also become clear that we have here a field where the one-sidedness of the institutional and of the behavioral approaches can be overcome.

[1] See the remarks on this point by Gabriel A. Almond in *The American Political Science Review*, vol. LII (1958), p. 271, "A Comparative Study of Interest Groups and the Political Process" (1957), p. 5. That report was written under the auspices of the Committee on Comparative Politics of the Social Science Research Council which, in a parallel effort to that of the I. P. S. A., is also exploring the opportunities which the study of groups offers to the field of comparative politics.

[2] See E. E. Schattschneider, "Intensity, Visibility, Direction and Scope," *The American Political Science Review*, Vol. LI (1957), pp. 953–954.

The groups recruit feelings and opinions (even if they do not always "enlarge the heart," as de Tocqueville hoped they would.) Through them individual and organized behavior has its effect on governmental institutions just as the forms of authoritative decision-making determine group structure and strategy. Demands and responses to demands, as well as the effects which the enactment of the responses has on the administration of the *res publica* and on the degree of consensus obtained among the citizenry, are the subjects of our investigations. To conduct them successfully neither a mere study of governmental institutions nor a one-sided behavioral analysis will suffice.

After a highly successful meeting on "The Comparative Study of European Pressure Groups" which was organized by his department at the University of Michigan, Professor James K. Pollock asked me to take a hand in preparing the Annual Roundtable of the International Political Science Association. Needless to say that I appreciated the opportunity to hear problems that have preoccupied me for a number of years discussed by distinguished colleagues from abroad. The constant advice and vigorous assistance of Professor Pollock were indispensable to me in selecting rapporteurs and participants and in deciding on the topics for discussion. I wish to express to him my sincere gratitude for what turned out to be one of the most rewarding experiences of my professional life.

Mr. John Goormaghtigh prodded me into drafting the working paper which now introduces this volume and which was circulated among the rapporteurs well ahead of the meeting in order to prepare for the papers and the discussion. The Executive Committee of the International Political Science Association was generous enough to invite me, after I had served as rapporteur at the Roundtable, to become the editor of the reports and proceedings. But we would never have been able to submit this record of our meetings to a wider public without the painstaking editing of their reports and remarks by almost all participants. If I have taken the responsibility for the final form and have revamped rather drastically the reports that were translated, I have done so reluctantly and in the hope that I have not distorted any essential thoughts in either the reports or the debates. The bibliographical notes were prepared by the authors of the reports, although in some cases they were enlarged upon by me. It is hoped that they may form the basis for an early complete bibliography of pressure group studies the world over.

Indispensable for the preparation of this volume was the assistance which was tendered both during the Pittsburgh meeting and subsequently in most generous fashion by Professor Albert Martin, chairman of the Political Science Department at the University of Pittsburgh, and by Mrs. Agnes Starrett of the University of Pittsburgh Press. Mrs. Betty Brandenburg, secretary of the Laboratory of the Social Sciences at the University of Colorado, doggedly typed and retyped the manuscript. She never tired of editing the editor.

Boulder, Colorado
March 21, 1958

Henry W. Ehrmann
Professor of Political Science,
University of Colorado

LIST OF PARTICIPANTS

PROFESSOR BENJAMIN AKZIN
The Hebrew University
Jerusalem, Israel

PROFESSOR GABRIEL ALMOND
Princeton University
Princeton, New Jersey, USA

PROFESSOR SAMUEL BEER
Harvard University
Cambridge, Massachusetts, USA

PROFESSOR DONALD BLAISDELL
City College of New York
New York, New York, USA

PROFESSOR TH. BRANDAO CAV-
ALCANTI
University of Brazil
Rio De Janeiro, Brazil

PROFESSOR NORMAN CHESTER
Nuffield College
Oxford, England

PROFESSOR TAYLOR COLE
Duke University
Durham, North Carolina, USA

PROFESSOR JOVAN DJORDJEVIC
University of Beograd
Beograd, Yugoslavia

PROFESSOR HENRY W. EHRMANN
University of Colorado
Boulder, Colorado, USA

PROFESSOR SAM ELDERSVELD
University of Michigan
Ann Arbor, Michigan, USA

PROFESSOR S. E. FINER
University College of North Stafford-
shire
Keele, England

MR. JOHN GOORMAGHTIGH
Secretary General of the International
Political Science Association
Geneva, Switzerland

PROFESSOR GUNNAR HECKSCHER
The Swedish Institute
Stockholm, Sweden

DR. PENDLETON HERRING, PRESI-
DENT
Social Science Research Council
New York, New York, USA

PROFESSOR WOLFGANG HIRSCH-
WEBER
Institut für Politische Wissenschaft
Berlin-Dahlem, Germany

PROFESSOR MASAMICHI INOKI
University of Kyoto
Kyoto, Japan

PROFESSOR KENKICHIRO IWA-
NAGA
University of Tokyo
Tokyo, Japan

PROFESSOR LOLO KRUSIUS-AHREN-
BERG
Swedish School of Economics
Helsinki, Finland

PROFESSOR GEORGE LAVAU
University of Grenoble
Grenoble, France

PROFESSOR AVERY LEISERSON
Vanderbilt University
Nashville, Tennessee, USA

PROFESSOR EDWARD LITCHFIELD
Chancellor, University of Pittsburgh
Pittsburgh, Pennsylvania, USA

LIST OF PARTICIPANTS

PROFESSOR C. B. MACPHERSON
University of Toronto
Toronto, Canada

PROFESSOR DAYTON MCKEAN
University of Colorado
Boulder, Colorado, USA

PROFESSOR ROBERT MACKENZIE
The London School of Economics and
   Political Science
London, England

PROFESSOR MARCEL MERLE
University of Bordeaux
Bordeaux, France

PROFESSOR SIGMUND NEUMANN
Wesleyan University
Middletown, Connecticut, USA

PROFESSOR JAMES K. POLLOCK
President of the International Political
   Science Association
University of Michigan
Ann Arbor, Michigan, USA

MR. KENNETH THOMPSON
The Rockefeller Foundation
New York, New York, USA

PROFESSOR W. A. TOWNSLEY
University of Tasmania
Tasmania, Australia

PROFESSOR FRANCESCO VITO
Catholic University of the Sacred Heart
Milan, Italy

PROFESSOR CHISOLM WEBB
Australian National University
Canberra, Australia

CONTENTS

CONTENTS

I. A WORKING PAPER

THE COMPARATIVE STUDY OF INTEREST GROUPS

HENRY W. EHRMANN

This paper intends to highlight some of the problems and approaches which in the past have proven useful for a discussion of interest group activities. In order to obtain for our discussion the kind of data which would make possible a genuinely comparative consideration, it is suggested that the national rapporteurs direct their attention to the points here raised. On the other hand, the present paper should in no way be regarded as a straight jacket. The rapporteurs should feel free to demolish some or all of its assumptions; they may want to treat aspects not covered here or neglect those which are of little importance in the political process of their countries.

* * * *

In his helpful attempt at classifying the factors which give interest groups effective access to the institutions of government, David Truman distinguishes (1) factors relating to a group's strategic position in society, (2) factors associated with the internal characteristics of the group, and (3) factors peculiar to the governmental institutions themselves.[1] To these there must be added such environmental factors as a given country's economic and social conditions. The political system, as well as the social structure, will often decide whether claims raised in the name of special interests will be successful or not; it may determine the "style" used by pressure groups when raising their demands.

It is suggested that such a classification, although formulated in regard to American politics, has its place in a cross-national or even cross-cultural consideration of group activities; it remains to be determined,

[1] David B. Truman, *The Governmental Process*, New York, 1951. My thinking on the problems discussed in this working paper owes much to Mr. Truman's book. In addition the article by Oliver Garceau, "Research in the Political Process", *The American Political Science Review*, XLV (1951), pp. 69–85, and the report prepared by Gabriel A. Almond for the Social Science Research Council's Committee on Comparative Politics, now published as *A comparative Study of Interest Groups and the Political Process*, *ibid.*, LII (1958), pp. 270–282, have proven extremely valuable.

it is true, whether (and which) other factors are particularly important in non-Western countries.

IDENTIFICATION AND GENERAL DESCRIPTION OF INTEREST GROUPS

It may be useful to start with an identification of the major interest groups active in various countries, and to classify them according to the kind of interests they represent and the membership they seek to attract, and to differentiate them as far as possible from other politically active organizations, such as parties, status groups, the Army, social cliques, and the like. Although there is no need for overly rigid classification, the existence or absence of public (civic) interest groups, as distinguished from groups representing special interests, appears to be a significant factor. Which non-economic interests are represented? What is the frequency of *ad-hoc* groups in relation to more permanent organizations? How high is the density of interest representation? Which interests are as yet unorganized but potential groups of the future? In general the relationship between latent and manifest interests needs attention, among other reasons because in non-Western countries interests will frequently be less articulated and still dormant. Where specialization of representation is driven rather far, the existence of specialized groups may be supplemented by the formation of more or less impressive confederations, broad coalitions, or "fronts".

As to the internal life of organized groups, important differences will often be observed between the formal pattern of organization and the methods by which decisions are actually reached. Behind a structure seemingly indicative of intensive membership participation, authoritarian decision-making may take place. Other groups, or important subgroups, are frankly elitist, just as some derive their influence from a deliberately shapeless structure in which membership initiative—possibly through such devices as referenda—plays an actual role. Widely varying practices will be observed in regard to the role played by the active minority, the formal officialdom, and the rank and file members. The social origin and the training of leadership and of professional staffs will have an important bearing on group activities. However, at present the study of interest group leaders is but a little-explored field.

How does the individual member preceive his group membership and the purposes of his group? How much discipline is expected from him and what are the sanctions following infractions of established rules? The phenomenon of over-lapping membership and of its over-all effects is worth observing and comparing. In some cases conflicting loyalties are known to seriously infringe on group cohesion and the effectiveness of sanctions; in others multiple membership has accentuated the paralyzing influence which pressure groups may exercize on the governmental process. Why the difference?

The age-old problem of "money in politics" lends itself to muckraking exposés rather than to serious scholarly inquiry. However, a comparative analysis of the sources and methods of group financing could be useful and not altogether impossible. In this connection we may wish to examine the effectiveness of legislative attempts to give more publicity to lobbying activities and to the sources from which groups derive financial support.

INTEREST GROUPS AND THE POLITICAL PROCESS

Although we may never have means of measuring political power accurately, it is by now generally recognized that interest groups wield a significant amount of power in the most varied political systems. The constitution of the Union of Soviet Republics specifically assigns (in its Article 126) to such groups a role of political participation. While the "tactics of influence" will vary with the characteristics of governmental institutions, almost everywhere the relationships between groups and parties and between groups, the legislatures and the executive branch must be investigated in order to arrive at a realistic appraisal of the political process. Our discussions may be focused on the different ways in which interest groups transmit the unaggregated demands present in a given society to the centers of authoritative decision-making. In order to understand the role of organized groups in relation to public policy it will also be necessary to study the efforts which interest groups are making to win a favorable audience with the public at large.

Intergroup relations deserve attention for the effect they have on both the governmental process and on public opinion. In which areas of policy do the principal organized groups cooperate, compete, or remain neutral or indifferent? Can a consistent pattern of intergroup relationships be detected? Is the effectiveness of group action a function of certain alignments? Does their absence have a foreseeable impact?

INTEREST GROUPS AND PUBLIC OPINION

It has been said that group leaders—whatever else they may neglect—cannot afford to be ignorant of widely-held attitudes which have a bearing upon the prestige and the objectives of their organization. The feelings of the community toward particular interests, such as large or small business, farming, church organizations, etc., will often be indicative of a significant behaviour pattern. The feelings and the forms in which they are expressed may shed light on the amount of consensus or, conversely, the fragmentation prevalent in a political culture.

Different groups will develop different propaganda activities either to win support or at least to neutralize opponents. While in one country a group may not hesitate to engage in a boastful "public relations" campaign, the same group in another country—possibly with a similar political system—may be thoroughly convinced that it can never win widespread support and will therefore concentrate its energies and financial means on covert, rather than overt, activities. What audiences do the groups strive to reach and what are the characteristics of their appeal? Are they willing and able to recognize and formulate long-range objectives, or is it true that pressure groups are "structurally" incapable of doing so in fact even when they try to accredit themselves as defenders of a nebulous "general interest"? Interesting are also such more technical but connected questions as the relationship of interest groups to press, to radio, and to the educational system at various levels.

Interest Groups and Political Parties

The influence which pressure groups bring to bear on political parties is generally considered as the most legitimate of the activities in which organized interests may engage. It is also easily of critical importance since, at least where the party system is fully developed, the political party stands between the special "unaggregated" demands of the interest groups and the authoritative decision-making of parliament and bureaucracy.

The various forms which the interaction between parties and pressure groups might take could lead to a useful typology of political systems. Obviously the relationship between groups and parties will be different where there exist one, two or several parties; the prevailing electoral system may also shape group tactics. However, there are other possibly more significant factors: the amount of discipline which a party exacts from its representatives inside and outside of parliament and from its membership; the allegiance of the party to a well-defined program or merely to a set of highly flexible principles. Only a comparative analysis can discover what kind of party and what kind of party system will provide the more effective screen between the special interests and the final political decision.

In some countries an entire political party may consist mainly of one interest group; elsewhere the fact that the special interests have a foothold in a number of parties will give them a particularly powerful lever. Sometimes party or group may use the other as an instrument for the attainment of its objectives. In those non-Western countries where neither parties nor groups are fully integrated, the effect may again be significantly different.

Worthy of study is also the overlapping of membership and officers in parties and groups. Does a party, especially during election campaigns, rely on interest groups for personnel and leadership or does it have a membership reservoir of its own? What role, if any, do interest groups play in determining the composition of the party leadership, in nominating candidates for elective office and, thereby, in the shaping of party policies? Do the groups provide financial support to parties either permanently or at least at election time, and how is such support given? Obviously the relationship between parties and groups will frequently be connected with the techniques which the groups employ to mold public opinion and with the prestige of a given group in society. Since the relationship will frequently change even in the same country, meaningful comparisons can be drawn by observing it in a given political system at different periods.

Interest Groups and the Legislative Process

The methods by which pressure groups penetrate parliament will in part be conditioned by the nature of the constitutional processes; a parliamentary system, a system in which the separation of powers prevails, a federal system, and a unitarian system will of necessity place the organized interests in a different position. However, the flow of communications from the groups to the individual legislators or to the party in parliament will be determined by many other factors as well. If pressure group officials are members of parliament, what is their role in the party to which they belong and in the legislative process? Are there other members of parliament who, while they have no official tie with an interest group, are generally considered or openly acting as the "spokesmen" of special interests? Which form does "lobbying" proper take? Can a line be drawn between the hearing to which the special interests have a claim and between outright pressures or even intimidation? Are the representatives able to ward off an intervention where the party organization is fuzzy, where they have been elected with slim majorities, and where the interest groups have a numerous clientele among the constituents? Are there subtler ways of influencing members of parliament such as providing technical information or help in the drafting of bills?

Altogether the "style" of interest group intervention will frequently best be observed where the target of group activities is the legislative process. Differences in style, however, will frequently be conditioned not only by the particularities of the party system and parliamentary methods but by the mores of the community, the mutual feeling of groups towards each other, and the knowledge that either moderation or immoderation promises success.

In those legislatures in which committee work is important, the role which groups are able to play in committee deliberations are well worth observing. It is said that in some countries the committees have become nothing more than the institutional facade for almost unchecked group activities. In a parliamentary system the groups may play an important part in bringing about a cabinet crisis and in solving it; either specific groups or coalitions of such groups may take a hand in proposing candidates for the new cabinet. In bi-cameral systems any preference which the groups show in trying to win access to one or the other chamber deserves analysis. Their methods may significantly change in regard to the lower and to the upper house.

A special situation arises where major economic interests are given formal representation in an Economic Council or some such similar body. That, with a few exceptions, these "corporatist" parliaments seem to play a negligible role in shaping legislation is in itself significant. On the other hand, the demeanor of group representatives in such bodies can often provide an insight into the methods and the philosophy of interest groups.

INTEREST GROUPS AND THE EXECUTIVE

Groups will concentrate their best efforts on those organs of governments which are responsible for decisions affecting most directly their clientele. The rapid accretion of executive functions in the modern state will naturally drive the organized interests to seek access to the executive. In countries where the cabinet is clearly dominant over parliament and has the initiative in legislation, group activities which in other countries take place in parliament, will be directed toward the members of the cabinet.

Everywhere the bureaucracy will be an important target for interest groups, though some groups will feel drawn more to the civil service than others. The central problem seems to be to what extent the bureaucracy has preserved its "neutrality" where traditions of neutrality exist or has acquired such an attitude where in the past partisan orientation had been an admitted pattern. The permeability of the civil service will frequently be determined by its internal cohesiveness; often, too, by the effectiveness of central control. But also the social composition, the recruitment, the training pattern, and the prestige of civil servants will account for notable differences in the results of group actions. Is it everywhere true, as has been said about the United States, that the bureaucracy will be able to "hold the line" if parliament shows sufficient resistance against pressure group demands?

The influence exercised by groups on the administrative process can probably be considered on a continuum. On the one end there exist in many countries officially sanctioned institutions described sometimes as organs of "administrative pluralism", i.e., boards and committees which are merely supposed to provide expert advice to the administration, especially in economic and social matters. On the other end we find situations where public and private "managers", the civil servants and the staff of interest groups, are working so closely together that to speak of pressures applied "from the outside" is no longer an adequate description. Here the administrative process may have been "colonized" by the representatives of the interest groups to an extent that the dividing line between state and society has all but disappeared. The conditions which facilitate such a constellation and its consequences have to be investigated as well. How great is the ideological and social affinity of bureaucrats and pressure group officials? Such affinity must be examined, not only as regards the frequently-discussed relationship between administrators and big business, but also between the labor inspectorate and trade-unions, the local or regional representatives of ministries of agriculture and the farm groups, etc.

Because of the great importance which administrative decisions have in the broad area of economic growth and development, the ways in which groups affect policies in those fields deserve particular attention. The interaction between groups and administrative action may have much to do with the integration or the dissatisfaction of the citizenry, and may decide whether the administration of the *res publica* is characterized by dynamic stability or by frustrating stagnation.

Need for a "Conceptual Framework"?

It may be assumed that all reports will, in one way or the other, indicate how the intensive and comparative study of pressure groups can contribute to a realistic understanding of the dynamics of politics. However, can more be done to give to a consistent conception of the role of interest groups in the political process not only empirical and historical significance but also theoretical depth? Can we develop a general theory of political groups or, at least, a set of hypotheses about the characteristics and consequences of the main types of interest group systems? One of our British colleagues has remarked that unless we are content with using the concept of interest groups merely as a convenient shorthand term, we should be aware that in our judgments of pressure group activities very fundamental issues of political theory are involved[2]. It is quite true that many of the terms such as "access", "claims", and "interests", used by us when we discuss pressure politics, are usually loosely defined even if they are carefully exemplified. This may have much to do with the inarticulateness of our conceptual scheme of the political process in general. Is there at the bottom of our evaluations some normative commitment to an imprecise "equilibrium" theory which could either be confirmed or exploded by being made explicit? Will the quest for greater theoretical clarity merely lead to "variations on the pluralist theme"? Or will a concentration on a study of the political functions of groups enable us to test to what extent generalizations derived from one political culture will hold true in another?

The national reports as well as our roundtable discussions may wish to add to our empirical investigations some reflections on the contribution which a comparative study of this kind could make to the advancement of political theory. It would certainly be useful if the rapporteurs were to appraise the efforts made in that direction in their respective countries.

[2] W. J. M. Mackenzie, "Pressure Groups: The Conceptual Framework", *Political Studies*, III (1955), pp. 247 ff.

II. COUNTRY REPORTS

PRESSURE GROUPS IN AUSTRALIA

W. A. TOWNSLEY

In Australia teaching and research in Political Science have in the main developed only since 1945, and chairs in Government or Political Science have been established in six of the ten Universities only since 1949. It is necessary to understand at the outset therefore that Australian scholars in this field are only in the pioneering stage, though much good work is now being done on the subject of political parties. On the subject of pressure groups, as distinct from parties, the first studies have yet to be made. Trade unions have received most attention because of their close link with the Australian Labour Party.

THE ECONOMIC AND SOCIAL STRUCTURE

As elsewhere the economic and social structure of Australia determines the nature and functioning of interest groups within it. The country has a size equivalent to that of the United States and a population of 9½ million. The people are heavily concentrated in the cities and towns on the eastern and southern coasts. Nearly one third of all Australians live in Sydney and Melbourne. Yet up to the depression of the 30's the national economy was largely built upon rural interests, wool, wheat, meat, sugar and fruits. These interests still dominate the export market, but since the census of 1933 there has been a marked shift of workers into secondary and tertiary industries. The rapid industrialization is concentrated in the states of New South Wales, Victoria and South Australia, the first two of which could properly be described as economically dominant. Yet there is not, and has not been for a long time, any significant difference in the standard of living between the six states of the Commonwealth. A striking feature of the post-war industrialization has been the rapid influx of migrants. The population which was 98 per cent British in origin has been modified by official immigration of Dutch, Polish, Italian, Hungarian, Yugo-Slav and other European people. What is unofficially called the "White Australia Policy" bars from Australia non-white immigrants even on a quota basis. One result of this wave of immigration, which is relatively higher than the highest wave achieved in the U.S., is that the average age of the population is revealing a downswing. Another is that pockets of migrants are appearing, and new social tensions are in the making. The "new Australians" provide a special field for pressure group work for political parties, for the churches, particularly the Roman Catholic church, and for such citizen organizations as Good Neighbour Councils and Citizenship Conventions.

Social history covering more than one hundred years has revealed the development of a peculiarly Australian egalitarianism, which while differing from the American, distinguishes the Australian from his British cousin. This strong dislike of privilege in any form makes the open espousal of particular interests difficult so that most pressure group activity is "under cover" and is regarded as insidious. But trade union activity in and outside the Labour Party and the pushing of farming interests in and outside the Country Party is openly interpreted as the defence of natural rights or legitimate interests. By contrast it would be thought irregular for a member of Parliament openly to espouse a particular interest in parliamentary debate. This refusal to acknowledge the facts of the economic and political world seems hypocritical, but it derives from the presuppositions of an egalitarian democracy that developed within a rural economy during the 19th century. The fact is, of course, that all major interests—farming, labour, and business—have used their influence quite selfishly, particularly during the post-war boom, which has been marked by full employment, rapid inflation, and relatively inadequate services. This has left the unorganized sections of the community—the pensioners, and particularly the housewives—the only real "exploited class." Women are only slowly being organized in this country. "Housewives Associations" are at last in being and the "National Council of Women" have petitioned in the national capital on behalf of women's rights, while the "Country Women's Associations" have for years operated in several states to mitigate some of the harshness and isolation of rural life. Occasional publicity has been given to complaints of the consumers, who are not organized, through the daily press. The strongest action, however, has been taken by the trade unions. For one of the serious effects of inflation has been the reduction in the margins paid to skilled workers, and professional men, especially teachers and engineers. It has created a major problem in education at a time when school population is rapidly increasing, and has left the country with inadequate technological resources to meet the needs of defence and national development.

The size of the country and the smallness of the population have made the development of natural resources an urgent and formidable problem. Despite excellent air services the people of Western Australia, concentrated in Perth, feel relatively isolated, being 1500 miles from the nearest city, Adelaide, while people in Brisbane (Queensland) are nearer to Hobart (Tasmania) in the "far south" than to some Queenslanders who live in the "tropical north." Difficulties of communication, particularly with the "outback" still determine the Australian economy, but the national psychology is such that no distance deters. Many Australians think nothing of driving 100 miles on a Saturday for a game of tennis or bowls. Difficulties of communication have however affected the attitude of Australians to the national capital, Canberra, a modern, planned city (the Federal capital since 1927 and now having a population of 35,000). By most it is considered "remote" and this fact alone is not without its effect on pressure groups.

Given such an economy and such social attitudes certain groups occupy strategic positions from which they exert pressure on governments. Traditionally wool growers claim that Australian economy "rides on the sheep's back," and after a succession of good seasons (the periodical drought has not struck since the war) and high world prices, wool growers have been so prosperous that, except on occasion, such as when the Menzies government held back 20 per cent of the wool cheque in the interests of economic stabilization, they have not felt the need to exert undue pressure. But those farming groups, whose interests are in wheat, meat, dairy products, potatoes and fruit, make full and constant use of their strategic position. They operate on all parties, but particularly on the Country Party at both state and federal levels. Against them stands the largest organized labour force, the Australian Workers Union; between it and the shearers and the graziers, there have been since the late 19th century a number of long and bitter struggles. The interests that produce and distribute power—coal, gas, electricity, oil—are well organized, and many interruptions of community life between 1945 and 1951 were a result of friction between coal owners and the Miners' Federation in the key state of New South Wales. Almost equally influential are transport interests. The railways are state owned and controlled but the Australian Railways Union has been, like the Miners' Federation and the Waterside Workers' Federation (Dockers) directed by communist officials. The W.W.F. has been in a constant state of friction with shipping interests, which are part of a large overseas (British) combine. Communications and transport being Australia's "Achilles' heel" these groups have exercised quite ruthless pressure both before and particularly since the war and have contributed largely to the increasing costs that mar Australia's economy. Well placed within the new industrialized society are various manufacturing interests, which when organized in the Associated Chambers of Manufacturers provide possibly the strongest single lobby in the national capital. Well behind them, in terms of power and influence, come the Chambers of Commerce. But the industrial giant is Broken Hill Proprietory Ltd. which, through the development of a large and competitive steel industry, has provided the basis for the industrialization of Australia. In the industrial field workers have organized in every state and unions are co-ordinated at a federal level in the Australian Council of Trade Unions. Only the A.W.U. among influential trade union bodies remains outside. The rapid development of secondary industry and the continued prosperity of primary industry has led to increased capital investment. Banks and insurance companies have shown a corresponding growth in influence and power. Higher purchase has attained significance in the national economy only in the present decade. It has led old established banks, such as the Bank of New South Wales, to obtain a major control over this sort of business. Australia has had a central bank, known as the Commonwealth Bank, since 1912. Relations between this central bank and the national government are quite close, while relations between the Commonwealth Bank which embraces the Commonwealth Trading Bank and the private trading banks continue to provide the political parties with contentious issues. Since 1945 there have been three important Banking Acts and at present (1957) the fourth has just been defeated by Labour opposition in the Senate. The Act of 1947, which sought to nationalize the banks, (but which was found invalid by the High Court), gave rise to feverish pressure group activity and incidentally led to the defeat of one State government. Less need be said about professional associations like the British Medical Association and the Teachers' Federation which occupy strategic positions on narrower fronts. Moreover, it would be mistaken to overlook the special part played by Public Service Associations throughout the Commonwealth, and especially in Canberra, as well as in the six states. All these bodies and groups, associations and unions play key roles in the economic and social life of the people.

POLITICAL INSTITUTIONS

The activities of interest groups are conditioned by the configuration of the country's political institutions and even more by the conventions which govern political practice. Australia has a federal constitution. This constitution (1900) lists the heads of power under which the Commonwealth Parliament (House of Representatives and Senate) can make law. The legislatures of the States have residual sovereign powers. Much political activity resolves itself around the financial relations between the Commonwealth and the States. Since a High Court judgment (1942) gave the Commonwealth virtually exclusive power in the field of income and corporate taxation, the States have become more dependent. This has inevitably led to the concentration of heavy group pressure on the Commonwealth government and Parliament, to which real power has shifted. Nevertheless groups still try to play States and Commonwealth off against each other, particularly in New South Wales and Victoria or when the opposed parties wield power at the different levels of government. Moreover, in four states the Upper Houses (Legislative Councils), elected on a restricted franchise, have for a long time acted in the interests of conservative and even reactionary groups, representing landed or corporate estate. For example, the attempt made by Dr. Evatt to have more powers transferred from the States to the Commonwealth was defeated by the action of the Legislative Council of Tasmania. The subsequent move to amend the Constitution by referendum was rejected by the people. The States are also represented equally in the Federal Senate, and this to some extent counters the strongest pressure groups centered in Melbourne and Sydney which are heavily represented on a population basis in the Lower House. However, the Senate has never realized the aims of the fathers of the constitution and its members are by and large subject to the decisions of the parliamentary parties. In the less disciplined Liberal Party it is not uncommon for Queensland senators, representing the sugar industry, to clash with Tasmanian senators who think primarily in terms of fruit and jam manufactures.

Although operating within a federal structure real political power, at the State and Commonwealth levels, is centered in the Cabinet. The normal approach of groups is therefore not to the legislators but to ministers. And the fact that cabinet decisions are secret makes it all the more difficult to uncover the weight, the place and the timing of pressure group activity. The nature of the three political parties and their attitude to cabinet building affects in some degree the approach of pressure groups. The Leader of the Labour Party (Curtin, Chifley) has the members of his cabinet team picked for him by secret ballot by the parliamentary Labour Party. The Leader of a Liberal government (Menzies) can pick his own team, except insofar as he has to accept limitations imposed by the Liberals' alliance with the Country Party, which usually drives a hard bargain in terms of cabinet seats and the legislative programme. One other convention of cabinet practice is pertinent. Every Prime Minister finds it necessary to include in his cabinet at least one member from each state. If he is wise he keeps an even balance between the rival interests of Victoria and New South Wales.

Interest groups are usually classified according to their social function. The method has the virtue of simplicity and provides easily recognized standards of comparison. Active groups in Australia could be arranged in the following pattern:

Farmers' Groups

The Wheat Growers' Federation exercises strong influence in four mainland states, and the growers have been known often to decide the fate of a number of seats in the wheat belt. In the state elections in South and Western Australia the electoral system is biased strongly in favour of these country interests. The National Farmers' Union is a strong pressure group and exploits to the full its influence on the Australian Country Party. The Graziers' Federal Council, under which operate a number of graziers organizations, has rarely found it necessary to put on pressure during the prosperous years since the War. However, it has been estimated that the graziers caused the Menzies-Fadden coalition government to lose two seats in the 1951 election out of resentment against the government's action in holding back 20 per cent of wool cheques under a tax-pre-payment plan. The Sugar growers and particularly the Colonial Sugar Refining Company are another influential group in Queensland.

Workers

Since late in the 19th century workers have been well organized and have steadily improved wages and conditions of labour. On the basis of trade union organization the Australian Labour Party was formed in every state and was federally organized. The trade union organization itself is organized within each state and co-ordinated at the federal level in the Australian Council of Trade Unions. These unions are affiliated with the Australian Labour Party, help to finance it, and exercise strong, sometimes decisive, control over its policies and decisions. Both the party and the unions officially support the arbitration system, from which the workers have over 50 years gained much. Pressure takes often the form of advocacy before the Arbitration Court, where unions and employers' organizations, both represented by legal counsel, plead their cause. In years immediately after the War, 1945–50, key trade unions—miners, seamen, waterside workers, railwaymen—were controlled by communist officials who exploited the full employment policy of the Labour government in a situation marked by shortages to foment industrial upheaval for political purposes. The attacks were designed to undermine the arbitration system and culminated in 1949 on the coal fields of New South Wales where the Communist leaders challenged the government in widespread strikes. The Prime Minister, Ben Chifley, appealed to public opinion, and then broke the strike by putting troops into the minefields. From 1950 anti-communist Industrial Groups formed within the Unions and wrested the leadership from the communists in many key unions. These groups worked closely with the Catholic Movement which openly sponsored Catholic social doctrine through weekly periodicals and more secretly penetrated to the offices of the Executive of the Labour Party. In 1954, however, Dr. Evatt, the leader of the Party, denounced "the party within the party" and identified it with Catholic Action and particularly with Mr. Santamaria, influential organizer and propagandist in Melbourne. Thus began a schism in the Labour Party which led to the formation of a "breakaway" party, the Anti-Communist Labour Party, which at present through its two members holds the balance of power in the Federal Senate. Meantime "groupers" were driven from official positions on State Executives and the Industrial Groups were weakened, to the advantage of the communists, in the unions. During recent years the Menzies Liberal Government, thus freed from the challenge of organized labour, has by legislation introduced secret ballots into union affairs and improved the machinery of arbitration. A close understanding has developed between the President of the Australian Council of Trade Unions, Albert Monk, and the Minister for Labour, Harold Holt.

Business

The most powerful lobby in Canberra is the *Associated Chambers of Manufactures*. It has permanent headquarters in the capital with a full-time secretariat. It operates daily on ministers, on members, through the press and over the radio. Its real centre is Melbourne and its strongest interest is in the tariff. From the 1920's till 1939 it campaigned with great success for the protection of secondary industries against British manufactured imports. Today these industries are entrenched behind high tariff walls. The Labour Party has for years been committed to a high tariff policy and when it came to power in 1929 industrial, trade union and social pressure was put on it. The foundations of many modern secondary industries were then laid. The greatest single industrial undertaking is the Broken Hill Proprietary Limited, which has built up a modern steel industry at Newcastle and Port Kembla N.S.W., and at Whyalla in S.A. General Motors Holden Limited has also established itself in the domestic market. There are other subsidiary, yet powerful manufacturing groups, such as the Australian Consolidated Industries, the Cotton and Rayon Spinners and Weavers Association and the Australian Woollen and Worsted Textile Association. The strength and the methods of the manufacturing interest are now being shown in reaction to the recently concluded Australian-Japanese trade treaty. Representatives of the Graziers Federal Council, the Wheat Board and the Meat Board expressed openly their satisfaction. But the Chambers of Manufactures spokesmen have attacked the treaty daily in the Press and these sentiments have been re-echoed in Parliamentary debate by members of the Labour Party.

Commerce and Trade

The Australian economy depends heavily on export earnings. The trading interests, organized in each state as Chambers of Commerce and co-ordinated at the federal level, provide an important pressure group, though much less powerful than the manufacturers. Their interests lie in the liberalization of trade and over recent years they have pressed hard for the relaxation and removal of import restrictions. In this category must be placed too the extensive shipping interests—a large British combine. Labour governments' attempts to establish a Commonwealth Shipping Line have been matched by the combine's efforts to buy it out.

Banking and Insurance

For many years the private banks openly fought each other and failed to agree on a general line of policy in face of the growth of the Commonwealth Bank. In the depressed 30's the Bank of New South Wales exercised special influence with the Central Bank and thereby aroused the jealousy of other trading banks. Only when Chifley moved to nationalize the banks in 1947 did they show a capacity of unified action. They fought a bitter campaign against the Banking Act, which the High Court declared invalid. Pressure by banking and other interests led the Menzies Government in 1951 to establish the Commonwealth Bank Board, thereby giving the Bank a greater measure of independence of the Treasury. In 1957 a further Bank Bill was introduced designed among other things to separate the Commonwealth Trading Bank from the Central Bank. In this instance pressure had been exerted on the Cabinet by a number of Liberal private members, who were responding to a pledge given some years ago to the private trading banks. The Australian Labour Party opposed the measure most bitterly and it was rejected by one vote in the Senate. In the debate Labour members' assertions that the private banks had heavily subsidized the Liberal Party's electoral campaign in 1949 were not challenged. Also fully revealed were the interlocking interests of directors of private banks with manufacturing, shipping and insurance companies, breweries and the press. Labour members continue to warn against efforts made by private interests to destroy government enterprises such as the Commonwealth Bank and Trans Australia Airlines as they have already destroyed the Commonwealth's interests in Commonwealth Oil Refineries Ltd., and Amalgamated Wireless (Australia) Ltd.

Professional Organizations

Organizations such as the British Medical Association, the Australian Dental Association, the Teachers' Federation, are active constantly in defence of special interests, particularly with reference to standards and remuneration, recruitment and training. Engineers and chemists have similar bodies. The British Medical Association is very powerful and worked against the plans of the Chifly Labour Government for a nationalized medical scheme. The present system, sponsored by the Menzies Liberal Government, of hospital, medical, and pharmaceutical benefits, was set up in conjunction with the professional interests involved.

Academic, Cultural, and Scientific

The most important among these are the Universities of which there are ten. Two of these are in Canberra and are supported by the Commonwealth Government. The rest are dependent almost entirely on State financial support. The Federal Council of University Staff Associations has developed recently, particularly with the object of a concerted attack on separate State governments to raise salaries which lagged behind during successive years of inflation. The Universities act in concert also through the Vice-Chancellors' Committee. In 1957, following pressure from these groups, the Commonwealth Government set up a Committee to inquire into University needs and accepted its recommendations for development, including the establishment of a Universities Grants Committee on the British model. The Commonwealth Scientific and Industrial Organization, a federal body, has been able to keep its standards of remuneration ahead of those of the Universities primarily because of its Commonwealth links. Cultural bodies that exercize a continuing influence include the Australian Broadcasting Commission, the Commercial Radio Proprietors, the Film Distributors, and recently created the Elizabethan Theatre Trust, which aims to support and develop a national theatre and opera company.

Veterans' or Returned Servicemen's Organizations

The oldest and most powerful is the Returned Servicemen's League. Formed after the First World War on a non-political basis it exercised immense influence in community life, and no politician thought it worth his while to flout it. It kept hallowed "the spirit of Gallipoli" and exalted a sense of nationhood. In material ways the League pressed successfully for a policy of "first preference" for ex-servicemen in employment, and the rapidly growing Civil Service after 1920 was recruited largely in this way. It watched over repatriation hospitals and medical benefits and pensions, and after World War II over the much more extensive Reconstruction, Training and Rehabilitation schemes. So influential and so critical were these Veterans' organizations that more than one Minister for Repatriation lost not merely his cabinet rank but his parliamentary seat.

Special Interests

Special interests of all kinds include the Pensioners' Association; migrant organizations as different as the Good Neighbour Councils (for New Australians) and national minority group organizations such as the Polish Association; a number of Women's organizations, such as Housewives' Associations, Country Women's Associations and the National Council of Women. And to these may be added the Taxpayers' Association, the Constitutional League, the Temperance Alliance, etc.

Religious Organizations

Between 20 and 25 per cent of Australians are Roman Catholics and with migration this ratio is becoming higher. Traditionally the Irish Catholics in Australia have been from the 19th century, in the main, supporters of the Labour Party. In recent years they have helped to form the most compact organization (Industrial Groups) fighting the communists in the trade unions. In the Labour Party they have striven to "water down" the socialist creed in accordance with Catholic social doctrine. During the referendum campaign on the question of Commonwealth power to dissolve the Communist Party many Catholics voted Yes (in support of the Liberal Government) while the Labour Party called for a No vote. Roman Catholic Archbishops have from time to time actively supported certain policies, though the Catholic hierarchy has in general maintained a neutral attitude. Prime Minister William Hughes threatened to deport Archbishop Mannix of Melbourne on account of his pro-Irish opinions in 1920. Archbishop Duhig of Brisbane materially helped the Liberals' return to power in 1949. A live political issue is the question of state aid for private schools in favor of which Catholics campaign most vigorously, though, so far, without much success.

The Protestant majority is less well organized. However, the World Council of Churches can, when it acts as a concerted body, which is not often, exert strong influence. This has been shown particularly in its campaign against the extension of liquor trading hours when the question has been put to a referendum. All attempts to change the law of "six o'clock closing" in Victoria have been defeated by the combined churches. Many Protestant clergymen openly campaigned for the rejection of the referendum in 1951 "in defence of civil liberties," but the Churches as such were not involved. More rabidly sectarian is the Protestant Federation, which throws its weight and influence against all Roman Catholic candidates of whatever party at every election. The Jewish community is small, but well organized.

Regional Groups

These are active in particular areas or states. Of some importance is the new State movement. By far the most powerful branch of this is in New England, New South Wales, from where pressure is exercised on Sydney; interests in the capital have been ready to grant concessions to New England, if only to keep it quiet (e.g., a University has been founded there). A similar movement, though as yet less influential, is going on in North Queensland. But much more important is the Northern Territory, for which the Minister for Territories is responsible to the Commonwealth Parliament. Apart from the demand for responsible institutions, which have been granted and located at Darwin, it is not unusual for large grazier interests to use "stand over" tactics in Canberra, and under unrelenting pressure Ministers have been known to give way. All states know local pressure groups. Even in the smallest state, Tasmania, northern interests organize to get the maximum of concessions from the capital, Hobart, which is located in the South.

INTEREST GROUPS AND MASS MEDIA

Nothing has so far been said about the press, radio or other mass media of communication and to what extent they constitute pressure groups in themselves. It is difficult to estimate the influence on politics of the Australian press, though it must be considerable. There is no national newspaper. Each of the capital cities runs one or more newspaper and several of the provincial towns have their own. Outside Sydney and Melbourne there operates a virtual monopoly, though this is being challenged in some places as communications, particularly by air, have improved. For instance, Melbourne "evening" newspapers are flown to Hobart (400 miles) where the proprietors of the "Mercury" have a monopoly. There is no "Labour" newspaper, and, while the press remains uncommitted to any political party, it is inclined to be more critical of Labour than of its political opponents. The average Australian is skeptical and openly boasts of his distrust of news and comment. There is reason to believe, however, that he is little more immune than most other peoples to the modern practice of subtle censorship or the effects of quiet but persistent emphasis. Some Ministers have been subjected to campaigns of abuse and even calumny. The worst offenders in this respect have been part of the Sydney press against which the Labour government of New South Wales have been known to take legislative action, empowering the Attorney-General to organize an investigation to discover sources of information from editors and press correspondents. This attack on the freedom of the press, arising from the abuse of it, has, however, not been pushed far. The Australian press has to operate subject more to the law of libel and contempt of Parliament than has the American press.

Radio transmission is controlled by the Government instrumentality, the Australian Broadcasting Commission and by several commercial networks. This dual system is also subject, in a loose general sense, to the Australian Broadcasting Board. Television is still in its infancy and has appeared only in Sydney and Melbourne. The A.B.C. news service has a high reputation for impartiality and is more trusted than the newspapers, although its coverage is much less and its effects less lasting. All parties, but especially the Labour Party, use radio for propaganda purposes. It is not much used by other interest groups, except for commercial purposes.

Although the controllers of mass media, in particular the press, may have only indifferent success with the Australian public, there is no doubt that pressure groups operate regularly through the media. Press statements by spokesmen of associations, by leaders of trade unions, by politicians, are regular features. Sometimes there is recourse to advertisement. Political parties use this method during election campaigns. Even the Commonwealth government resorted to full page advertisements in the daily press in the form of a statement over the Prime Minister's name, when in 1949 Ben Chifley sought public support of his moves to break the coal strike which was paralysing national industry.

INTEREST GROUPS AND POLITICAL PARTIES

By and large the three political parties were founded and continue to work in support of interest groups. The clearest example of this is, of course, the trade union basis of the Australian Labour Party (A.L.P.). Trade unions are affiliated with the party, so that trade unionists are indirectly members of the party, contribute to its financial strength, and are represented on its councils. All trade unionists pay a political levy, and there is no arrangement for contracting out. Quite recently two members of the Waterside Workers' Federation refused to pay the levy on the ground that they supported the Labour Party (Anti-Communist), which broke away from the A.L.P. They were expelled from their union, and there may be an appeal to the courts. Trade unions, and more particularly the Australian Council of Trade Unions and the Australian Workers' Union, put pressure on the government. The President, Secretary and Federal Executive of these two trade union bodies exert constant pressure, though they also act as a restraining influence on individual unions. The pattern is repeated through Trade and Labour Councils in their relations with state governments.

The various agrarian groups referred to above do not link themselves so directly with the Australian Country Party, but there can be no doubt that they support it indirectly, or more properly they put heavy pressure on it. The rest of the groups,—manufacturing, trading, professional, etc.,—do not link their fortunes with any party, leaving themselves free to give their support or put on pressure as their interests suggest. The private trading banks do, however, quietly and unobtrusively, support the Liberal Party. The Churches are not committed to any party, although a large majority of Roman Catholics (chiefly Irish and developing strong attitudes from the 1880's) have traditionally supported the Labour Party. But with the present schism in the Party the traditional attitude is subject to new influences.

The Australian Labour Party

The constitution of the A.L.P. gives a large measure of control and considerable influence to the trade unions. However, unions have, except during critical years in the history of the A.L.P., occupied themselves by and large with industrial matters. As a result there has always been a certain suspicion of the politicians, i.e., the parliamentary members of the Party and even of the leadership. The relations between the Executive of the Party (on which the industrial "left wing" has a growing, if not a decisive influence) and the Parliamentary Party are now, at both Federal and State levels, so obscure that the independence of parliamentary members from the pressure of "an outside body" not responsible to the electorate is extremely doubtful. The Federal Executive of the Party directed Chifley and the Parliamentary Labour Party to reverse their attitude to the Communist Party Dissolution Bill in Parliament in 1951. In April 1957 the Queensland State Executive expelled the Labour Premier of the State and all his ministers but one from the Party for refusing to accept its directives.

The constitution of the A.L.P. makes for centralized, oligarchial control which facilitates pressure on key personnel. The platform commits the party to the strengthening of Commonwealth powers at the expense of the states, and those interests, chiefly manufacturing, which see little to lose in a process of unification are apt to support Labour. The stricter discipline that rules in the A.L.P. ensures that if leaders can be won over to a policy there is less chance of a revolt of back-benchers inside the party room, and, more important, outside it. The rules of the A.L.P. also tie the hands of a Labour Prime Minister (or Premier) as all Cabinet posts are filled by secret ballots. All major sections of the party thereby get representation, and this fact has been known to provide sectional interests with advantages.

The most important developments within the A.L.P. since Chifley lost the Federal election of 1949 have been in turn the growth of influence of the Industrial Groups in unions at the expense of the communists, and of Catholic Action within the A.L.P.; and the denunciation by the present Leader, H. V. Evatt, of "clerical influence" and his repudiation of "the party within the party." Since 1954 there has been internecine war within the A.L.P. which has left the Party shattered and impotent in the Federal Parliament, and has destroyed State Labour governments in Victoria (1955) and in Queensland (1957). The schism has in fact extended to every state except South Australia, where Labour is more radical and the Catholic population less numerous.

Doctrinally weak, the A.L.P. decided in March 1957 to re-state its doctrine in terms of "democratic socialism." It is likely, however, that in the future as in the past the Party will concentrate its energies on immediate issues, such as industrial discontent and social injustice. Only when it has appeared as representing national public opinion as distinct from sectional interests, has the A.L.P. won and maintained itself in power.

The Liberal Party of Australia

This party approximates what Maurice Duverger calls a 'bourgeois' party. Though reconstituted in 1945 and given a broader and more democratic base, its antecedents go back to those 19th century parties wich adopted "fusion" in 1910 against the A.L.P. The party has little doctrine, though traditionally it stands for the imperial connection and for freedom from socialist controls. Ideologically the party is committed to private enterprise (and opposes monopoly); and in consequence interests think themselves justified in pressing Liberal M.P.'s to remove restrictions to trade and enterprise. However, the strong protectionist wing of the party—part of the fusion of 1910 and strongest in Victoria—fights unremittingly for the maintenance of a high protective tariff. The Australian-Japanese trade treaty (1957) concluded by the Menzies Liberal Government is regarded by these interests as a "betrayal." The reconstitution of the Liberal Party (1945) sprang from the fact that the old Nationalist Party had become discredited, not least because it had been intimately connected with business interests, centered particularly in Collins Street, Melbourne. The party before the World War II was controlled by a narrow but financially powerful oligarchy, which had insisted that as it paid the piper it would call the tune. It was known to refuse endorsement to local candidates at elections. The present Liberal Party claims that it is not subject to control by any financial interest and that donations to party funds can be received only from individuals and not from corporate bodies. Certainly the spirit developed in the constituency branches helped to bring electoral victory in 1949, 1951, 1954 and 1955, but with the Labour opposition in disarray, it is no secret that a gulf has developed between the top echelons of the party (Prime Minister Menzies is the dominant personality) on the one hand and private members and active branch members on the other. The fact that the Liberal Party, unlike the two other parties, is uncommitted to major pressure groups signifies to some that it is all the more open to pressure from all quarters. The Deputy Leader, Harold Holt, as Minister for Labour has established an effective working relationship with the President of the A.C.T.U., Albert Monk leading inter alia to amendments to the Arbitration and the Stevedoring Acts. The coalition with the Country Party has entailed certain acts of policy, e.g., the trade treaty with Japan, and the refusal to modify the exchange rate, which have cause heart burnings in sections of the party. Pressure by the trading banks on private members is now (1957) forcing ministers to bring in a new Banking Act. The less rigid rules of discipline have permitted private members to revolt occasionally against the leadership. Liberal Senators too are known to clash with each other as, for instance, those from Queensland support the State's sugar industry and those from Tasmania their State's interests in fruit canning, jam and cordial manufactures.

The Australian Country Party

A.C.P. owes its origin and *raison d'être* to the need to protect rural and, above all, wheat and grazing interests against organized labor and the city maunfacturing and trading interests. The A.C.P. is primarily a sectional interest. Though it operates in four states it is in no way a national party, though members and supporters readily point to the dependence of the national economy on the primary industry. In coalition with the Liberal Party it can, and does, drive a hard bargain in terms of cabinet seats and the legislative program. The financial needs of the party make it dependent on rural interests and these can and do, on occasion, use 'stand over' tactics. Leaders of the Country Party, Sir Earle Page and Sir Arthur Fadden, at present Commonwealth Treasurer and Acting Prime Minister, have since the 1920's played an influential role in the making and breaking of cabinets. The Country Party stubbornly resists all proposals to restore the Australian pound to parity with the sterling, it insists on taxation rebates and acclaims trade treaties which are advantageous to wheat and wool. In certain states, e.g., Victoria, the A.C.P. is not in coalition with the Liberals, but often bitterly opposed to them. Only a few years ago a minority government of A.C.P. held power with the conditional support of the Labour Party.

INTERESTS GROUPS AND THE LEGISLATURE

Interest groups not only attempt to influence parties and determine party policy but also work on parliamentary members and the leaders in Parliament. No leader, however, has been foisted on to a party by an outside pressure group. There may be factions within Parliamentary parties, but the members decide the leadership of their party. Groups do give financial support to parties, and if they are influential, as the Australian Workers Union is in several State Labour Parties or as "the Collins Street junta" was in the old Nationalist Party, such groups can, by granting or withholding their assent to the endorsement of a candidate, decide in part the composition of the legislature. Certain rural interests have been known to give their support to and even to campaign for a particular candidate. This is, however, more the exception than the rule. If a candidate keeps his election expenses within the limits prescribed by law there is no means of knowing whether he has received financial support from a particular interest group. What is known is that no M.P. appears in Parliament as the spokesman for an interest group, except, of course, that Labour Party members give general support to unions and Country Party members can be relied upon to push the interests of primary industries. An odd member may be known to act at all times as advocate for the pensioners, but this makes him a curiosity. The few women members rarely talk about women and M.P.'s rarely give cause for anyone to dub them as spokesmen of particular interests. Nothing is frowned on more than expressions of class, sectarian or even regional prejudice. Coming from the separate states M.P.'s in the Federal Parliament are very conscious of the fact that they represent the nation and they are never slow to remind critics from their own state or from their own party of that fact. While in the interests of self-preservation they do what they can for their constituency, there is nothing in Australia comparable to the pork-barrel in American politics. There are few members who would not openly resist outright pressure and they would treat intimidation as contempt of Parliament.

The electoral system determines to some extent the nature of the pressure and the point where it is applied. Various systems operate in Australia. For the Federal House and for most state parliaments there are single member electorates and preferential voting. The Federal Senate (10 seats to each state) is elected on a proportional representation basis with preferential voting. In Tasmania there is a more intricate P.R. system with a single transferable vote, each of five electorates returning six members. In Queensland elections are decided on a simple majority with no transferable vote in single member constituencies. Powerful pressure groups, such as trade unionists on the Labour Party Executive, have been able to exploit the P.R. method in the Senate in favor of particular candidates. By contrast the Tasmanian system provides no safe seats for party hacks or stooges of particular interests. Equally important is the method of pre-selection of candidates. In most states the Labour Party chooses its candidates at the Conference where all interests are represented and where pressure and counter pressure is normal, and in recent years, due to sectarian and ideological differences, extremely bitter. Where a small oligarchy controls the party machine interests groups adapt their methods to suit.

All groups, large and small, work actively at some time for the passing or repeal of legislation or for a change of the constitution by referendum. Two instances in recent years must suffice. In 1947 the Chifley Labour Government which controlled both the House and the Senate introduced a Banking Bill designed to nationalize the trading banks. Opposition was organized throughout every state. Mass petitions were addressed to the Governor-General, to the Speaker and to members. Individual petitions, letters and telegrams poured into Canberra threatening to disrupt the postal service there. Public opinion polls were taken and showed consistently that about 63 per cent of the electorate opposed nationalization, about 23 per cent supported it, with the rest undecided. Chifley refused to be deterred. An organization of bank employees, separate from the official organization, was set up to campaign against the bill. There were public debates and rowdy meetings. The banks financed a campaign in the press and had distributed thousands of leaflets. Apart from certain churchmen the churches decided that the issue was secular and for individual decision. The Liberal governments of Western Australia and South Australia announced that they would challenge the validity of the legislation in the High Court. Finally in Victoria the Upper House rejected the budget, thereby forcing the state Labour Government to an election which was fought on a federal issue and resulted in the defeat of the Labour Government. In face of this intense barrage Chifley persisted, the bill became law, but on being challenged in the High Court, it was declared invalid.

In 1951 the Menzies Liberal Government, after its Communist Party Dissolution Act had been declared invalid by the High Court, sought constitutional powers by referendum to dissolve the Communist Party. The Liberal and Country Parties campaigned for a Yes vote and Dr. Evatt led the A.L.P. in favour of a No vote. The campaign was bitter and divided the country. The referendum was lost by little more than 50,000 votes and by the fact that only three of the six states, viz., Queensland, Western Australia and Tasmania, approved it. An interesting alignment of group forces was revealed. Both sides used the press for advertisements. Press news and comment was fairly evenly distributed in Sydney and Melbourne (where the "Argus" came out strongly in favour of a No vote), but the provincial press showed decided preference for the Yes vote. Both sides made full use of radio, both national and commercial. The A.L.P. and the Communist Party made greater use of leaflets, posters and how-to-vote cards than the Liberal and Country Parties. The government parties found it more difficult to raise funds than did the Opposition, which received considerable financial and active campaign support from certain trade unions, especially those with communist officials. Two Universities, Melbourne and Sydney, took an active part in the campaign, and the articulate members of the staff and student body were strongly in favor of rejection. More prominent was the role played by leading churchmen of all denominations. One Anglican Bishop, while advocating a No vote, declared that the Roman Catholic Church sought to extend its power by supporting the Menzies Government's attack on civil liberties. Two Roman Catholic prelates replied in terms which suggested that the Church gave no direction but left the decision to the Catholic conscience. The Catholic Archbishop of Brisbane announced that he would vote Yes, and thought the people needed guidance. Anglican leaders were divided, but the Church itself gave no direction. A Public Opinion poll revealed that most Protestants, particularly Presbyterians, intended to vote Yes, while Roman Catholics were equally divided. The schism developing in the A.L.P., above all on the Victorian State Executive, revealed the crisis of conscience faced by good Catholic members of the Party.

Pressure on the Cabinet

Government in both the Commonwealth and the states of Australia is cabinet government. The power vested in cabinet has increased and is increasing and the executive has physically invaded Parliament House in Canberra, where Ministers occupy the best "suites." And as the Cabinet has the power interest groups tend to concentrate their energies on Ministers. If the Cabinet hangs together even the strongest pressure can be resisted. But more than twenty ministers, some of whose departments are located still in Melbourne and Sydney, cannot know each other's minds all the time, even if there were homogeneity and there rarely is. One of the worst features of certain ministries has been the amount of leakage of information to the press, and nothing is more calculated to destroy harmony within a Cabinet.

Strong pressure groups have been known to give active support to some ministries, e.g., the manufacturers backed Scullin's tariff policy in 1929. Often they have worked against a ministry, e.g., the shipping interest against Hughes in 1920. Group pressure takes various forms. Some time ago the Australian National Airlines used a man stationed in Canberra ostensibly as local manager. He was a distinguished Royal Australian Air Force type, a good mixer and a very shrewd operator with an unlimited expense account for purposes of entertainment. The shipping combine have used similar tactics against Ministers in the Hotel Canberra. Some pressure too was used by oil companies in inducing state governments to abandon price controls on motor spirit. Another example is the way in which manufacturers expressed their resentment to persuade the Federal Government to allow the Defense Preparations Act (1951) to lapse.

Groups are known to give rewards for services rendered and to take reprisals when left unsatisfied. By the nature of things rewards are not clearly discernible, and they take many forms, e.g., the sale of yachts and the lease of race-horses. At least it is freely stated that many Ministers have benefited financially by representing the interests of a firm. Pressure is indirect rather than overt even when it comes to reprisals. For instance, certain established newspapers, incensed because a cabinet minister had granted a newsprint license to a newcomer, ran what they called "new blood" candidates in his constituency.

Pressure has been known to result in a cabinet crisis. Local importers, the retail trade generally, pressed for a revaluation of the pound. Country Party interests were flatly opposed to the change and threatened to leave the Government. The Country Party won. Revaluation was abandoned. Within the Liberal Party, the two biggest interests are the manufacturers and the importers and the clash between them almost led to the defeat of the Menzies Government in 1954 when manufacturers were still resenting the abolition of import controls. Similar resentment is again building up over the trade treaty with Japan. The Roman Catholic Church exerted much pressure on the Labour Government during the war; in the Menzies Cabinet it works through a Minister who by threatening to resign unless his colleagues agreed to aid denominational schools nearly precipitated a cabinet crisis.

The best clinical example of group pressure is provided when a Labour government is in power. Prime Minister Hughes once said: "When trying to forecast members of a Labour Cabinet, don't look at the men, look at the union behind them." The more powerful the union the more it will influence men and events. Hughes himself rose to power with the backing of the Waterside Workers. Curtin was an Australian Workers Union man, so were many of his Ministers, excepting Chifley and Drakeford, who were locomotive engine men.

The press has occasionally scored some notable successes against cabinets. The press was instrumental in killing the Scullin Government (1929–31), though other forces, including the banks, played a major part also. The press attitude was closely related to that of the banks. The same forces combined to kill the Lang Government in New South Wales about the same time.

Finally it should be remembered that Ministers are subject to the same electoral pressures as private members of Parliament. They are under the close scrutiny of the local press and their offices are inundated with all sorts of printed material as well as with letters and telegrams. Moreover more than private members, they have to run the gauntlet of endless cocktail parties. The Hotel Canberra is one of the biggest centers of group pressure, if only because the Ministers stay there.

PRESSURE ON THE PUBLIC SERVICE

Most group leaders have good personal contacts with key men in government departments. Pressure is applied indirectly. There are many parties in Canberra where top public servants are wined and dined. However, the Commonwealth Public Service is reputed to have a high standard of integrity. There are weak reeds, and pressure groups are capable of conducting campaigns against uncooperative public servants. It is known that some senior public servants, who have antagonized representatives of industry, have been busily "white-anted" with their Ministers and with other Ministers. Administrative Boards and Commissions, such as the Tariff Board, have generally shown themselves resistant to such pressures, though there have been cases of graft revealed in relation to government contract boards. On the whole public servants know when, at the bidding of their Ministers, they are asked to do some work in the interests of some pressure group. Some have said privately that when Labour Ministers asked them to do exacting preparatory work it was more likely intended for a Trade Union Conference than for Parliament.

CONCEPTUAL FRAMEWORK

Scientific study of political phenomena has only recently begun in Australia and any theorizing has been incidental. The most fruitful field of investigation has been that of electoral behaviours, but this has been concerned principally with political parties on which a number of studies have or are being made. Case studies of interest groups such as the Chamber of Manufactures, the National Farmers Union, the Waterside Workers Federation or the British Medical Association simply do not exist. And until a number of pilot studies is made it is more than likely that Australian political scientists will borrow their conceptual framework from elsewhere. However, it may well be that out of the context of Australian society a new approach to the problem of interest groups may be developed.

For the time being all too little is known about the nature and workings of these groups, and though they are known to exist and indeed to be quite influential, there lingers in the minds of Australians, whether professional politicians or ordinary citizens, the sense of embarrassment common to those of us who do not like to acknowledge disreputable relations. A large section of public opinion still maintains an attitude of criticism toward the trade unions and this sharpens with the slightest wave of militancy. Less visible to the general public are the pressures exerted by bankers, manufacturers, traders, farmers, brewers, the shipping combine or the medical profession. Many people know these exist, but they are more insidious, and come into the open only when an opportunity presents itself to swing the public in their favour. But we know nothing of how business organizations make their decisions, how they are financed, what conflicts exist within and how they are resolved. By contrast, the trade unions, suspicious though they are of even academic investigations from without, do wash much of their dirty linen in public.

To the outsider any evaluation of the Australian political scene must stress the strong sense of nationality. The Australian has perforce to depend on foreign capital, intellectual and otherwise, but he is busy developing his own. His political attitudes, less subtle and less concerned with doctrine than the European's, have been moulded largely by British empiricism and to a lesser degree by American pragmatism, but remain above all the product of Australian environment. His is the genius of improvisation. His eyes are used to long vistas and his tempo is that of his "timeless land". Even amid the mechanisation of life in his cities he has not become obsessed, like so many Europeans, with the problem of power. And, though he is law-abiding, he is not too rigidly bound by notions of legality as his English cousin is in his neat little island, being inclined to separate in rough and ready fashion justice from law, and to seek the former, without recourse to metaphysical idealism, in what he readily measures as a "fair go" for one and all.

This being so, there are limits beyond which interest groups cannot go with impunity. They must not completely ignore the philosophy of "a fair go", and they cannot run counter to what is conceived to be the national or public interest. However inbred their individualism Australians have learned, in a land remote and isolated from Europe and in which nature, if not subdued can be the enemy of all, to give meaning to the principle *salus populi suprema lex*.

Democratic theory presupposes both the nation and the states; it shows much less regard for interest groups. The first creative period of Australian political thinking, between 1850 and 1880, was strongly influenced by the prevailing utilitarian philosophy, and something of the Benthamite distrust of "sinister interests" has persisted to this day. The second creative period, between 1880 and 1900, saw the emergence of the manufacturing interest and of organized labor, both of which contributed to the growth of national sentiment and the federal movement. In the twentieth century under the Commonwealth there has been a struggle between rival interest groups and between the Commonwealth and the separate states. Today, although new tensions are emerging, an equilibrium has been reached. In an egalitarian democracy, where individual liberties are prized and most citizens own their own homes, where social justice is sought after and social controls are distrusted, the decisive factor is still national sentiment. As long as interest groups can reconcile their claims with the public interest they may prosper and their legitimate rights will be protected in law, but comes the day when they stake their claims unheeding all other interests, the national will knows how to reassert itself. Whatever the principles and programs or the sectional interests that make up or divide them, each of the major parties knows that it can win and hold power only by convincing a majority of the people that it is truly the "national" party.

Selected Bibliography

A very complete bibliographical article has been presented recently by Josephine F. Milburn and Taylor Cole, "Bibliographical Material on Political Parties and Pressure Groups in Australia, New Zealand, and South Africa," *The American Political Science Review*, vol. LI (1957) pp. 199–219. The following works may be specially mentioned:

A good general introduction is presented by G. Greenwood (ed.), *Australia*, Sydney, 1955; and by G. Sawer, *Australian Federal Politics and Law, 1901–1929*, Melbourne, 1956. A second volume, covering the post-1929 period, is in preparation. On the party system there are: L. Overacker, *The Australian Party System*, New Haven, 1952; S. R. Davis *et al*, *The Australian Political Party System*, Sydney, 1954; J. D. B. Miller, *Australian Government and Politics*, London, 1954.

Among single parties the Labour Party has been most studied, e.g. L. F. Crisp, *The Australian Federal Labour Party, 1901–1951*, London, 1955; W. Denning, *Caucus Crisis*, Parramatta, 1937; D. W. Rawson, *The Organisation of the Australian Labour Party, 1916–1941*, University of Melbourne PhD. Thesis, 1954; T. C. Truman, *The Pressure Groups, Parties and Policies of the Australian Labour Movement*, University of Queensland, M.A. Thesis, 1953; A. Davies and G. Serle (eds.), *Policies for Progress*, Melbourne, n.d. The most recent political biography of importance is W. F. Whyte, *William Morris Hughes*, Sydney 1957.

The best study on the Liberal Party is F. W. Eggleston, *Reflections of an Australian Liberal*, Melbourne 1953. On Communism there is L. Webb, *Communism and Democracy in Australia*, New York 1955; and on Catholicism in politics, A. W. Sheppard, *Catholic Action and Australian Labor*, Sydney 1955.

Election studies include D. W. Rawson and S. Holtzinger, *Politics in Eden-Monaro, 1955–56*, Canberra 1956; and H. Meyer and J. Rydon, *The Gwydir By-Election, 1953*, Aust. Nat. Univ. 1954. Employers associations are treated in K. F. Walker, *Industrial Relations in Australia*, Cambridge, Mass. 1956. Shortly there will be published S. R. Davis (ed.) *State Government in Australia*, London 1958.

Periodical literature includes the following: A useful coverage of political developments at both the Commonwealth and State levels is presented in the section "Australian Political Chronicle" of the *Australian Journal of Politics and History*, published twice a year since November 1955. Of interest are also the following articles R. D. Horne, "A Breathing Space for the Press," *Australian Quarterly*, vol. 21 (Sept. 1949); E. L. Wheelright, "Trade Unions and the State," *ibid.*, vol. 25 (June 1953); M. R. Hill, "The Basic Wage, 1907–1953," *ibid.*, vol. 25 (Dec. 1953); K. Henderson, "Employer-Employee Relations—the Irrational Factors," *ibid.*, vol. 26 (June 1954); D. W. Rawson, "A.L.P. Industrial Groups," *ibid.*, vol. 26 (Dec. 1954); Dean E. McHenry, "The Australian General Election of 1954," *ibid.*, vol. 27 (March 1955); W. A. Townsley, "The Labour Party in a Changing Society," *ibid.*; R. G. Neale, "The New England New State," *ibid.*, vol. 27 (Sept. 1955); W. P. Hogan, "The Banking Deal," *ibid.*, vol. 29 (Dec. 1957). An interesting and recent article is Lloyd Ross, "Problems of Trade Unionism," *Quadrant, an Australian Quarterly Review*, No. 5 (Dec. 1957).

THE POLITICAL POWER OF ECONOMIC AND LABOR-MARKET ORGANIZATIONS: A DILEMMA OF FINNISH DEMOCRACY*

LOLO KRUSIUS-AHRENBERG

INTRODUCTION

Although political parties in Finland—a country of proportional representation—are closely connected with definite interests and social groups, linguistically a clear distinction is made between the concepts of "party" and "interest organization". While parties are operating in the general field of politics and open to the entire electorate, one designates as interest organization the vast network of specialized organizations devoted to their own particular ends and which exist in the modern community for nearly every kind of idealistic or material interest. Individuals group together to engage in similar activities for the best attainment of the aims they have in common. The Finnish interest organizations do not, as a rule, recruit their members along partisan lines, for, if they did, they would endanger their own organizational ends which require them to aim at the widest possible membership within their proper field of interest. Regardless of what happens in fact, it is a characteristic of interest organizations in Finland that they are formally neutral where party politics are concerned.

This, of course, does not mean that the organizations do not link up closely with certain parties or take up very definite stands concerning the problems of day-to-day politics. Actually their participation in the political life of the nation as more or less effective pressure groups represents a paramount characteristic and a necessary element of modern democracy. However, pressure group activity, while essential, also constitutes a problem within the orderly democratic process. The emergence of this problem is in Finland—as elsewhere—directly related to the structure of government and of the party system as well as to the greatly enlarged functions of the modern state, particularly in the fields of social and economic policy. Party headquarters and governmental bodies cannot dispense with the cooperation of the great interest groups.

* Translated from the original.

Government authorities are, as far as Finland is concerned, bound to consider the specialized knowledge represented, for instance, by the big industrial and commercial federations, the trade union federations, and the associations of agricultural producers. The important economic interests which these organizations represent could easily be harmed if decisions concerning them were left to the mere decisions of the political and administrative organs. On the other hand, the question as to what form the political collaboration of the interest organizations ought to take and to what point it should be allowed to develop, seems to give rise to difficulties everywhere. The answer obviously involves a theoretical and value commitment. The fact remains that so far, at least in Finland, no truly satisfactory forms for this collaboration between the interest groups and the corresponding political authorities have evolved.

The basic problem—the need for an improved coordination—raises another issue: how can the activity of strong pressure groups be kept within the bounds of democratic control? The idea and technique of democracy are based on the principle that the exercise of political power must be subject to controls and responsibility. This control is, according to classic democratic theory, in the last instance vested in the electorate. Where do the interest groups, which are never subject to popular vote, fit in with the scheme? The answer must be—and is—that those who hold legitimate governmental power (and the parties as the channels of the popular will) are responsible for the final decisions, whatever may have been the share of the interest groups in the process of policy making. As long as the parties in power and the decision-making authorities are strong enough to withstand the pressure to which the interest organizations subject them, the problem of the irresponsibility of groups remains latent. However, when the authorities have to admit that they cannot resist the pressure of interest organizations or when the latter use ultimatums or force the government into a tight corner by other means, then the activities of organized interest become an acute problem for the democratic community.

I. The Principal Pressure Groups and the Political Setting

The above remarks have brought us to the core of the Finnish dilemma. Because of the difficulties created by the attitude of certain large, centralized organizations toward the foci of political decision-making, Finland presents a very fruitful field for observing the disturbances of the functioning of democracy which may arise from a disproportionate exercise of interest pressure. The most serious of these disturbances generate in the sphere of economics where organizations can use economic weapons in order to make persuasion effective. This report is chiefly concerned with these disturbances, and it must be stressed that it deals with the sharp forms of pressure rather than with the daily routine of friendly contacts and confidential consultations, about which very little is known but which form the bulk of the relationship between groups and government.

Finland aims at the creation of a welfare state as all-encompassing as that envisaged in the other Scandinavian countries; but the crippling economic efforts made necessary by the war, the territorial losses to the Soviet Union, and the heavy reparation payments have resulted in Finland in a far greater degree of economic regulation by the State than in other Scandinavian countries. Herein lies an important reason for the high degree of activity on the part of the economic interest groups in Finland. In spite of their relatively restricted membership, they are highly centralized and on the whole have no rivals in their sectors of economic life, a situation which is quite characteristic of the oligopolistic organizational structure of Scandinavia in general. However, whatever the political importance of these organizations in general, there is a clear difference in their ability to exert pressure. The central organizations in the main branches of industry and commerce (e.g., the "Central Union of Finnish Woodworking Industries" and the "Federation of Finnish Industries") because they are based on plant and enterprise units, lack the driving power of the large economic organization with a mass membership behind them. These branch federations—and the same is true of the employers' associations—are unable in their dealings with the state to bring the kind of pressure to bear that mass organizations can bring. Only the latter can try to break the resistance of the political authorities by referring to the solidarity and potential readiness for battle of their numerous members who represent a considerable voting factor.

This effective means of pressure, on the other hand, does have a recognized place in the activities of the mass organizations on the labor-market and, more generally, in the competition for the distribution of the national income. To the federations of this category belong the real key organizations in the political-economic field, i.e., the three great central federations organized according to occupation—wage-earners, salary-earners and (independent) farmers. These are, respectively, the "Finnish Central Trades Union", the "Confederation of Salaried Employees and Civil Servants" and the "Central Union of Agricultural Producers". The latter union is concerned with everything related to agricultural income and is politically heavily involved, for farm income is subsidized by the state (by means of price regulation) and is also by law tied to changes of the wage and salary index.

Thus, it becomes evident that the fight for the distribution of national income and for an improvement of the standard of living is not solely the concern of interest organizations, because the state, as the biggest employer in the country, faces the federations of organized labor. Quite apart from this, the government, defending common interests, is deeply engaged in these conflicts and concerned about their outcome. Not only do the welfare objectives of governmental policy necessitate large transfers as well as considerable equalizations of income, they likewise call for measures ensuring full employment by state intervention. As soon as unemployment occurs on the free labor market, public works projects must be launched at normal rates of pay. Because of the responsibilities which the state has undertaken in this respect, changes in the employment situation do not have the same regulatory influence which they have in a self-adjusting economy. If the state has the necessary strength—or the necessary powers—to limit the claims of the organized interests on a level at which an increase in production or productivity can absorb the consequences, self-regulatory factors such as unemployment can be dispensed with. If this is not the case and if the government controls the Central Bank, an inflationary development will be inevitable. Until recently inflation has indeed ravaged in Finland to a greater extent than elsewhere in Europe except in France. For, independently of the particular weakness of political power in Finland, in a democracy the liberties of the citizen and the freedom of association necessarily limit the means which the state can use to interfere in the collectively-determined price formation on the labor market. Even if wages are regulated by the state (as was the case in Finland, to varying degrees, between 1941 and 1955), the state must always rely on an agreement with and between the large organizations which naturally have, in theory and in practice, the right to strike or to use other appropriate means of pressure. In these negotiations—depending on the greater or lesser political strength of the parties forming the government—the state always tends to be forced into the role of the weaker partner and to be compelled in some measure to foot the bill for the final agreements between the organizations—usually to the detriment of the currency. The state is in a weak position, for it must secure peace on the labor front and at the same time ensure a level of national production which will permit fulfillment of its economic, social, and financial commitments.

Having stated earlier that the political authorities always bear the responsibility for the measures which they have taken under pressure from the interest groups, we may perhaps be allowed to establish now the following simple working formula: the intensity of political activity by interest groups is determined on the one hand by the political strength and the constitutional powers of the public authorities and on the other by the extent of commitments undertaken by the state, and by the organizational possibilities for the development of power on the part of the interest groups themselves. As long as the first two factors outweigh the latter two, the exercise of pressure by organized interests can hardly become a serious political problem of a permanent nature.

In regard to Finland, it must be said that the first two factors neither outweigh the others nor even maintain the equilibrium. First, political leadership and the power of government are weakened by the relative small size of the six parties. Second, the powers of the state to intervene in the economy are restricted and hampered by certain rigorous constitutional provisions. Third, since nevertheless the state has very extensive obligations, it must depend for their fulfilment in the fields of economic policy and administration on the collaboration of the large interest groups. Fourth, these organizations have a virtual monopoly in their various fields of competence and are, therefore, often stronger than the political parties concerned.

Finland's present six-party system was formed, except for the Communist Party, as a consequence of the electoral reform of 1906 when Finland instituted its present one-chamber parliament with universal voting rights for both sexes and proportional representation. The percentage of votes cast for the different parties tends to be stable, and the fight for the floating vote is therefore a hard one. If a line is drawn between socialist and bourgeois parties—a line which no longer has the same significance as formerly—it will be seen that the Finnish parliament still contains a small non-socialist majority (103 out of a total of 200 seats).

The four so-called bourgeois parties are, in contrast to the two socialist parties, linguistically homogeneous. This means that there is a special Swedish party, the Swedish People's Party, which contains lesser groups corresponding to the other three, single-language (Finnish), bourgeois parties. The Swedish Party generally gets 80% of the Swedish vote. Since the Swedish-speaking population comprises 8.5% of the total population of Finland, this party has for the last twelve years held 13 to 15 seats (at present 13) in Parliament. The largest bourgeois party is the Agrarian Union, which since the war has obtained about a quarter of the total vote and at present holds 53–54 seats. Employment in Finnish agriculture is, relatively speaking, too large; due to the smallness of the farmers' plots (70% own less than 10 hectares of arable land), agricultural yields are low. While 41% of the population derives its living from agriculture and related occupations—in particular forestry— these occupations account for only about one sixth of the national product. In view of this situation, the Agrarian party strongly represents "social agrarian" interests, which in turn means a policy of governmental subsidies and a considerable degree of economic control. The Finnish Coalition Party is conservative and has, since the war, cultivated a cautious "liberalism" similar to that of the right wing parties in other Scandinavian countries. It has at present 24 seats in Parliament.

The Finnish People's Party advocates the interests of the less well-to-do middle class groups and the white-collar workers, and occupies a halfway position between a planned and a free economy. At the moment it has 13 seats in Parliament. The Social Democratic Party (bilingual) is thus far, electorally speaking, the largest in Finland. In general its aims are the same as those of its Scandinavian sister parties, though, because of the stiff competition for votes from the Communists, it tends more toward radicalism. Because of the Communists, however, the party has only just over a quarter of the electorate behind it (54 seats) and consequently lacks the parliamentary strength of the Social Democratic parties in other Scandinavian countries. Aside from its support among the wage-earners and small-salary earners in private and public service, the party has long had a following among the small and very small farmers. Outside of these five parties, which are, ideologically, based on the parliamentary democracy of the Finnish Constitution, stands the Communist Party. It was founded at the beginning of 1920, was declared illegal 10 years later, and was once more legalized after the war. Its parliamentary representatives are the so-called "People's Democrats", who have more than one fifth of the voters behind them and since 1951 have held 43 seats in Parliament.

The above will illustrate the peculiar difficulty of forming a government in Finland. The five democratic parties have, since 1948, refused to collaborate with the Communists in the government. In practice this has led to a situation in which the Finnish Conservatives have also been permanently in opposition, and in which "center" governments have been constituted on a majority or a minority basis. In a parliamentary system minority cabinets as a rule represents a less-desirable solution, which, however, is always preferred in Finland to dissolutions of Parliament by the President of the Republic and to "non-party" Cabinets composed of "specialists" or "officials". For the last 20 years there have been mostly majority governments. Since the war they were formed by the coalition between the Social Democrats and the Agrarians and, since 1951, with or without one or both People's Parties as a completing and stabilizing factor.

This governmental collaboration of the two largest parliamentary parties, which together have a simple majority, has given rise to continuous difficulties and unrealistic compromises which were caused mainly by the inevitable clash between the opposite wage and price policies of both partners. In regard to one group, that of the very small farmers (2–5 hectares of arable land), there has been a certain community of interests because this section of the population consists of small producers who are at the same time wage-earners, e.g., seasonal forestry workers, laborers, etc. When analysed, however, this community of views is really a competition for the votes and, therefore, a "partnership in rivalry" in which the People's Democrats take a most active part. In fact, they present a far more dangerous competition to the Agrarians than do the Social Democrats. In the impoverished agricultural and forestry municipalities of Northern and Eastern Finland the very efficiently organized Communists are really the only attractive political alternative for the agrarian voter. On the other hand, as has been said, there is much opposition between Social Democrats and Agrarians in all spheres where the interests of the industrial and the agricultural population diverge. Their governmental collaboration has collapsed again and again or has suffered severe crises every time the interest organizations connected with one or another of the parties, i.e., the Central Trades Union or the Union of Agricultural Producers, have exerted strong pressure, have interfered directly on the cabinet level, or presented ultimatums to the party leaderships and to the parliamentary groups in particular. This has several times been accompanied by the threat of a general strike by labor or a food distribution strike. At one time in March of 1956 both threats were carried out and strikes directed against each other actually took place, although a coalition composed principally of Social Democrats and Agrarians under a Social Democratic Prime Minister was in power at the time.

As has already been stressed, the economic commitments of the state are very considerable in present-day Finland. The government's powers of determining wages as a last-resort ceased since the beginning of 1956. This contributed to the outbreak of the general strike two months later. But in practice the power of the state cannot be entirely divorced from the outcome of the bargaining and from collective agreements between union and management since, for instance, other state regulations and commitments provide that excessive salary increases must be compensated by other economic measures introduced by the state. As to price controls, they still exist in certain fields and so does, at a diminishing rate, the regulation of foreign trade and currency payments. At least as burdensome as the administration of these regulations are the socio-political commitments of the state and the obligations it has assumed, under pressure of interest groups, regarding the improvement of the standard of living of certain categories of the population. It should be noted in passing that an inadequate resistance of the political authorities has at present, produced an acute crisis with an empty treasury and a national economy suffering from excessive costs and an inadequate supply of capital. All this is the result of the fact that the successful pressure of the economic interest groups has for years led the people of Finland to consume too much and to invest too little.

Finland's constitution was revised when she became an independent republic and a parliamentary democracy in the year 1919. Its provisions regarding the freedoms of the citizen are more precisely defined than, for instance, in Sweden—at least in regard to the economic mobility and the property rights of the individual. Hence, most measures by which the state seeks to intervene in this field require legislation which must be passed in the forms prescribed for "urgent" constitutional amendments and be accepted by a five-sixths majority in Parliament. Since the war this situation has in practice usually encouraged Parliament to pass general, temporary legislation for the purpose of granting special powers to the government. The result has been to grant certain general economic powers to the government, which is then entitled to issue decrees concerning relevant special questions. This system has lessened the inhibiting force of the constitutional provisions which under present-day circumstances are undoubtedly restrictive, but it has not diminished their importance for the protection of individuals and minorities.

Lately the three small parties in Parliament have considerably reduced the extraordinary powers of the cabinet. The whole system is obviously more difficult to manage than that prevailing in other Scandinavian countries where measures of economic regulation, although occurring less frequently, are passed as ordinary legislation and sometimes by mere government ordinance. Besides the power of veto in cases of constitutional amendment, which consist of one sixth of the votes cast, the regular parliamentary minorities (one third of all members) enjoy, even in ordinary legislative matters, a similar right of veto and can postpone the adoption of a bill until the next elections—a maximum of four years. Moreover, for the introduction of new or increased taxes levied for more than one year a two-thirds majority is necessary. In other words, a majority Cabinet, while directly controlling a simple majority in Parliament, may meet with great difficulties in carrying out its political intentions unless it can find support for them among at least a part of the opposition. It should also be noted that the State Central Bank, which falls under the administrative competence of Parliament, occupies a position of great independence from cabinet policies. Its directing board, if it wishes to oppose the government, can implement a monetary and credit policy apt to create further difficulties for the government in its negotiations with parties and interest groups. This is currently the case. The Bank of Finland is bringing pressure on the government in a direction opposed to trade union demands. Thereby, the Bank has become an extremely strong extra-parliamentary power factor. It should perhaps also be emphasized that the state has no effective power to intervene decisively—for instance by parliamentary action—in a major labor conflict. If the state mediation provided by law fails, the government is only entitled to forestall the outbreak of actual strife for a few weeks in sectors of unusual importance to community needs.

The foregoing brief sketch of the situation is intended to cast light upon the difficulties created by the structure of Finnish politics and by the limited constitutional powers of the public authorities in need of implementing a consistent and comprehensive economic policy. Politics in present-day Finland are in the main dominated by economic problems and conflicts of interests. Whatever the composition of the government and of the party coalition supporting it, the political leadership is *a priori* not well equipped to adequately gird itself for the task of imposing a policy on the organized economic interests. These difficulties are still more aggravated by the fact that the interest groups themselves have been able to develop considerable power and monopolistic strength.

In many countries organized interests develop along existing ideological, religious or territorial alignments. Where this is the case, rival organizations spring up which may diminish their ability to bring political pressure. However, such splits do not occur in Scandinavian countries; all groups are characterized by a very unified structure. In Finland the same type of pluralist society prevails so that it is difficult to find any field where interests, be they economic or not, remain unorganized. Nevertheless from the outset the language question has had an impact on the organizational structure at least of these ideological interests originating in popular movements. We could cite the youth movement, the sports movement, the popular education movement, the temperance movement, etc., for each of which there is not only a large Finnish, but a much smaller Swedish-language, federation. Both federations, however, always work together across the language frontier in a peak association or through other means. In the operation of the country's economy the language frontier is, understandably, far less important. As a matter of principle it is not emphasized at all in the trade unions. It exists however, mainly because of demographic facts, in the local unions. Elsewhere it is chiefly noticeable in the units based on local and regional interests as, for instance, in the agricultural societies which with the aid of state subsidies carry on educational and other related activities, in the producers' federations and farmers' cooperatives, in the retail trade, etc. Since the language question raises no burning political problem and since economic interests work most effectively through such extraparliamentary channels, the party leadership and the executive, common-peak organizations, or other effective forms of bilingual collaboration exist everywhere. For all interests concerned they actually achieve the desired concentration of economic strength. Especially in view of the smallness of the Swedish population, the rivalry of language groups is nowhere a debilitating factor.

Although the existence of Swedish-language regions and a Swedish-speaking minority has had little influence on the political power of interest groups, the situation is somewhat different on another frontier— that of class and party politics. The ideological and social differences between the "bourgeois" section of the population and between the large politically-undivided socialist camp were very sharp at the time of the First World War and brought about the Finnish Civil War. Such difference led to splits and to the development of separate federations, surviving until now in the realm of the sport organizations, in the small farmers' associations and in the unions of consumers' cooperatives where a non-socialist "neutral" and a socialist "progressive" union of consumers' coops exist. In terms of its potential scope the cooperative movement has had a very favorable field for expansion in Finland where capital is short. As a result, the movement is now relatively stronger than in Sweden, Norway or Denmark. Its present expansion, particularly in agricultural cooperatives, has led to a situation in which certain fields of cooperative action are beginning to come into conflict with each other, and there are occasional difficulties arising between the interests of the united producers' and consumers' cooperatives. It remains to be seen whether, and how, this will affect party politics. At present the common interests of the cooperatives have such an extraordinarily strong position *vis-à-vis* the three biggest parties (i.e., three-quarters of parliament) that they can count on effective support in both parliament and government. The same applies to the very small farmers and to the purely ideological interest, to sports and similar organizations.

Since World War II there have been some new political breaks in the front of the pressure groups. Nine years ago small farmers' associations became so politicized during the course of an electoral battle waged between the three biggest parties, that it was once more torn assunder. Since 1948 when the Social Democrats renounced their post-war political collaboration with the People's Democrats, there has existed a small farmers' federation dominated by the agrarians, a Communist federation, and a Social Democratic federation. These federations are regarded as party branches, although they receive state support for the agricultural educational projects carried on by them.

Another illustration of the disintegrating effect of party politics in post-war Finland is provided by the development of the Central Trade Union Federation. Details will be discussed subsequently. Here, it is sufficient to state, that since 1948–49 the Central Union has been under the leadership of the Social Democrats. This leadership was secured after a bitter internal struggle with the Communists. However, this Federation has been subject ever since to pressures from its communist members and member unions. This, in turn, has caused the organization to play a more radical and politically active role than has been healthy for itself and the Social Democratic Party. Both the party and the trade unions now have to pay for the too heavy trade union pressure of the last ten years. Both have suddenly been overtaken by a serious internal split produced by the disastrous situation of public finances and economic life. Thus, the leadership of the Central Union has now to fight within its own ranks a growing right-wing minority of Social Democrats who disapproved of the general strike in 1956 and who oppose the unrealistic economic policy of recent times. Some unions dominated by this opposition have already left the Central Union; some others seem likely to follow suit. What will be the outcome remains to be seen. It is possible that these same unions might form a new Federation of Trade Unions, thereby not only endangering the Social Democratic dominance of the present Central Union but also putting an end to the hitherto monopolistic Finnish trade union system.

Nevertheless, it must be said in conclusion that existing splits and differentiations between organizations as yet make little difference in the overall picture of Finnish interest organizations. The latter remain, on the whole, highly centralized. Their peak organizations rule undisputedly over their fields of concern, so that they emerge frequently, indeed perhaps inevitably, as dominating powers.

II. The Pressure Group Activities of the Economic Interest Organizations

Forms of Pressure

Pressure exercised by organized interests may either develop within the party machines and within the authorities responsible for political decisions or it may take the form of an influence exerted on these bodies from the outside by the interest organizations as such. Pressure from the outside is frequently commented upon in Finland and, when excessive, often criticized as "extraparliamentary force". Actually it is difficult to draw a clear line between internal and external pressures. Often, for instance, the government uses what is called the method of "remissers" (i.e., asks the organizations to give their views on legislative proposals affecting the interests of their membership, be they bills or decrees). The organizations are acting here as officially consulted experts, although this may result in serious pressure on the government. The same is true when they are represented on commissions set up for the preparation of bills, when they report to the committees of parliament, or when they are given extended hearings. The interest groups may be allowed to enter into other informal contacts with either an entire committee or with part of its membership.

Representation within the Parties

It has already been said that Finnish parties are very closely linked to different interest groups both through their voters and through their membership. Within the party organization an effort is made to give these interests adequate representation in the party organs. But this is not enough. The group in parliament is the focus of party activity. Therefore, it is essential for the organized interests behind and within the parties to see to it that as many representatives of the interest organization as possible are elected to parliament. Finland's peculiar proportional representation system facilitates such objectives. Thus, economic interest organizations which have a large membership tend to be very well represented in parliament. The author investigated this question in 1953. She considered as "special interest representatives" all those members of parliament who held important positions in the big organizations of the labor market or the economy, and/or claimed themselves to represent the interests concerned. The investigation showed that the cause of the cooperatives was directly supported by 85–90% of the deputies among the Agrarian group (especially producer's cooperatives and the "neutral" consumers' cooperatives) and among the Social Democrats and People's Democrats (mainly the "progressive" consumers' cooperatives); the Swedish Party advocates of the cooperatives constituted 35%, the Finnish Conservatives 17% of the deputies. The opponents of the consumers' cooperatives, the retailers who many years ago united against the now repealed tax alleviations for cooperatives, had supporters only in the three small bourgeois parties (a total of 17). The representatives of the industrial federations, the National Chamber of Commerce associations, the employers' federations, and other relevant entrepreneurs' organizations were in the main similarly limited to these small parties and to about two-fifths (20) of the deputies of these parties who, however, had many other commitments. A majority of these 20 members of parliament sat in the Finnish Conservative group; most of the remainder in the Swedish group.

Naturally, those organizations are of particular importance which have already been repeatedly characterized here as being pressure groups of high efficiency, i.e., the Central Trades Union, the Federation of Salaried Employees, and the Agricultural Producers' Federation, together with the various interests connected with them. Members of parliament directly representing the organized agricultural producers constituted ½ of the Agrarian groups, ⅓ of the Swedish party group and over ⅕ of the Finnish Conservatives. The Central Trades Union and its most important member associations unmistakably had the allegiance of ¼ of the Social Democratic deputies who were union officers and board or council members and could count on the somewhat vacillating support of more than another ¼ of the party who claimed to represent the trade union interests of the Central Union. That the Social Democratic Party, like the Agrarians, attaches great importance to party discipline is noteworthy in this connection. Among the Communist People's Democrats in parliament the situation was roughly the same as among the Social Democrats, though it must be taken into account that the Communist group invariably, unconditionally, and undividedly carries out the directives of the party leadership and so in actuality "represents" nothing save the will of that leadership. It must also be repeated that the Central Trades Union is subject to directives from a leadership which is Social Democratic in its majority and that there are a few Communist-dominated, dictatorially-led unions which stand by themselves, ever since they were excluded by the Central Union for unauthorized and consequently "illegal" strikes in 1949. Some of the Communist deputies were members of the governing bodies of these unions which nowadays have purely Communist membership. The Trade Union Federation has replaced them by unions amenable to its leadership. The Confederation of Salaried Employees was most solidly entrenched in the Finnish People's Party group (⅔) but represented also among the Swedish group (¼) and among the Finnish Conservatives (¼) who likewise embraced representatives of the nonaffiliated Union of University Graduates' Associations.

To sum up, it appears that, although the workers' and employees' organizations (including those of civil servants) have a surprisingly strong representation within the parliamentary party structure, the smallness of the party groups cancels out the relative strength of interest representation. (The two largest parties have only slightly over ¼ of the seats each.) This fact, together with the constitutional provisions to which we already referred, means that the big interest organizations must always be tempted to use the more effective means of external influence on parliament. Such influence is exercised mainly through different kinds of pressure on parliamentary committees and party groups. The groups make use of internal influence only additionally or in connection with less important questions. It is significant that the leader of the Central Trades Union gave up his seat in Parliament in 1954 in order to be free to further the Union's interests independently of party group discipline.

Pressures on the Government

To present their demands to and bring pressure on the cabinet has hitherto been the main field of interest group activity. It is likely that this will remain so, although the position of parliament tends to be stronger at present than it has been for years. This strengthening which has occurred was brought about by the recent decrease of the economic commitments of the state, by the governmental crises, and by the weakness of the minority-cabinets. However, it is necessary to keep in mind that the votes in parliament will frequently be based on government-introduced bills and proposals on which the interest organizations have already left their mark if the matters in question are of their concern.

The exercise of influence on the government may, and that on the bureaucracy must, seek other channels than the political parties. When regulating the economic life of the nation either politically or administratively, the government and its administrative departments are compelled to enter into constant contact with the big interest organizations whose direct collaboration is necessary. This collaboration is parliamentarily justified as long as at least a majority of parliament has confidence in the government leadership and supports its measures.

In Finland, as elsewhere, the interest organizations have installed themselves in the administration of economic, social, and fiscal affairs to a very considerable extent. Within the framework of the long-established commission structure the big industrial, commercial and agricultural federations were already collaborating actively with the state during and after the First World War in questions concerning tariffs, trade agreements, preparation of bills, subsidies and land development. This system is today more flourishing than ever. At present there function, in the realm of economic and social administration, a great many councils, boards, and commissions composed of officials from the appropriate administrative departments and agencies along with managers of the state enterprises and leading personalities of the relevant economic interest organizations; in general the civil servants are greatly outnumbered. These bodies do not only exercise preparatory, investigatory, and advisory functions but also frequently have powers of decision. Some of them also have judicial powers, such as the Labor Court in the field of collective agreements, and the Labor Council in questions concerning workers' protection. The pressure groups will always be careful to ensure that opposing interests are equally represented on the boards which are particularly well-developed and influential in the fields of commerce, navigation and industry, agriculture and forestry, communications and public works, welfare administration and labor (e.g., the powerful Wages and Prices Board, at present reconstituted as the Price Board), and financial administration (e.g., the Commission for Civil Servants' Salaries). The members of these bodies are in many cases appointed by the government, and usually by the appropriate ministry but the interest groups often have the right to propose their own representatives. The period of office may be limited or indefinite; commissions are as a rule set up on a definite time limit, their life expiring with the completion of their task. The boards and councils may be permanent or they may owe their existence to temporary economic powers of the government; then their life may be renewed when the legislation conferring these powers is extended by parliament. On the whole this method of interest representation within the administration works very satisfactorily, though forms and results vary a good deal.

The bureaucrats sometimes may show a certain affinity with the group representatives facing them. In politically explosive matters it may happen that the proposals of the competent board or commission are set aside and the appropriate ministry (or the entire government) handles the tricky problem by direct negotiation with one or more of the large organizations. This will usually happen when one or more of the big interests have been outvoted and therefore seek a solution acceptable to them by successfully exerting direct pressure. Undoubtedly, the very fact that such a situation can arise constitutes a flaw in the working of the bodies here described.

This flaw is particularly noticeable in the workings of the advisory economic councils which have been set up time and again since the war to assist the government in drawing up an economic program. The purpose in setting up these advisory councils was to encourage the large interest organizations to cooperate in deliberations and agreements on general economic questions; thereby the government hoped to obtain a broader basis for the implementation of its economic policy. It would be a great exaggeration to say that the economic councils have in general fulfilled the expectations placed in them. But this cannot solely be ascribed to the work of the councils themselves; the political factor is also responsible.

The first of the economic councils designed to give the organized interests more consideration than earlier and similar councils was set up during the war by an administrative decision of the government. This was done to strengthen the hand of the Finance Minister in the days of war economy and regulations. A bureau of the ministry was specially assigned to collaborate closely with the council. After the war this system was changed. In peace time the Finance Minister can not assume all responsibility for the economic policy of the government. The usual post-war type of coalition cabinets called for economic councils which were to advise the entire government on special questions. By the end of 1954 this system had developed to a point where the Economic Council is now appointed for two years by government ordinance; it has its own bureau which functions under the Minister of State within the chancellery of the cabinet. The Economic Council also has acquired the right to submit proposals to the government on its own initiative.

The essential organizational and functional weaknesses of the early economic councils have, however, subsisted beyond 1954. The Economic Council (1955–56) is under the direction of a non-partisan chairman and has 14 members (plus 14 alternates) who are, in part, representatives of the government (2 members) and certain departmental authorities

(1) and, in part, representatives of the government parties (3) but mainly of the major economic interest organizations (8). The purpose of this arrangement is to establish what is known as a political and economic "parity of interests" which follows the distribution of the non-communist parties in parliament and the approximate pattern of interest groups in the community. The 8 representatives of interest organizations consist of 3 trade union representatives and one representative each from the Employers' Central Union, the Finnish Industries' Federation, the Woodworking Industries, the Agricultural Producers and the Federation of Salaried Employees. Against the 3 trade union representatives there are, thus, 3 industrial employers' representatives. Following the lines of "political parity" of the 14 members 6 are Social Democrats, 3 are Agrarians, and 5 are "non-political" (bourgeois) members. The distribution of the 14 alternates, who sit as active members of the working committees of the Council, follows similar principles, although with a certain differentiation of interest representation which here includes commerce, agricultural employers, and the "progressive" cooperative federation.

It would be unfair to deny that the present Economic Council and its predecessors have made a number of positive proposals. The fault of the system lies partly in the fact that each project of the Council, as soon as it touches on important questions, is generally accompanied by reservations and proposed amendments from the outvoted interests which thereafter do not consider themselves bound by the Economic Council's proposals. That the members always follow the instructions of their organizations has a paralyzing effect. Part of the fault, however, lies with the government. Rent by internal conflicts, which cause an unsatisfactory working relationship in economic and political matters among the various ministers and ministries, it does not handle the proposals of the Economic Council with the requisite attention and firmness. It has been proposed to appoint only economic experts and interest group representatives to the Economic Council, and to exclude the party and government representatives, so that the government could deal with the Council's proposals without previously taking a stand, either on its own or along the lines of party politics, and without having shaped the proposals themselves. It has further been suggested that the Economic Council might be returned to the Ministry of Finance or abandoned altogether and replaced by a governmental delegation for purposes of negotiation and consultation with the major interest groups. At present the interest groups represented in the Council and the government itself set aside the Economic Council's proposals far too easily.

Party tensions within the government interfere with its workings and at times completely paralyze its activity. For these reasons it has not become a forum which forces the organized interests to engage in mutual collaboration and compromises nor has it mitigated their direct and many-sided pressures upon the government. On the contrary, their direct pressure upon the government has remained completely uninhibited.

If the government manages to remain unified within itself and in relation to the parliamentary groups and if it shows enough strength and initiative in the conduct of its policy, direct negotiations with individual interest organizations may be of great advantage to the government itself. Direct negotiations make for more elastic forms of contact with the pressure groups and give the government greater freedom of movement than when the interests first take up their positions and mutually raise the bidding on their respective claims. It is, however, necessary that in these negotiations the government has enough power to put across its own policy and that it resists serious pressure actively and in time. It has at times been able to do this (e.g., in 1951–52) and the result has been a noticeable quieting down of pressure group activities. But in general the government has not been strong enough to assert its leadership in negotiations with the interest groups. By engaging in general consultations, for instance within the Economic Council, and in some cases by concluding temporary truce agreements with the big federations, the government has, however, been able to get some relief from the necessity of defending itself simultaneously on several interest fronts.

In conclusion, we can definitely say that the scant resistance of parliamentary governments to the pressure of mass organizations has led to two serious phenomena. On the one hand the freedom of movement of the government has been steadily narrowed by interest groups and the state has been forced by them to undertake financial commitments in excess of its resources. On the other hand the pressures of the organizations on each other and on the state itself have created an entrenched system of economic claims which have obtained political sanction and have become identified with party interests. These now constitute a threat to the natural dynamics of economic growth and to the development of production. It cannot be denied that this is principally the result of the splintering of political parties and of the weakness of government. In their tactics the mass organizations have adapted themselves to this weakness. Their methods have been similar to those which the labor market organizations use against each other. They raise claims in the form of ultimatums which are accompanied by the threat or actual use of effective economic sanctions. The government has been forced to yield to them and to the dictates of the Central Trades Union. To a lesser extent, the claims of the Agricultural Producers have repeatedly influenced the cabinet far more than considerations for a democratically-formed and controlled party opinion. Simultaneously the same interest groups have sought to press party opinion into countersigning the decisions they wish to obtain. For this reason, the Central Trades Union in its days of strength had the ambition of controlling all major issues of economic policies. The Agricultural Producers have acted similarily. Both federations have brought pressure to bear when new cabinets were formed or old ones reformed. By presenting their own claims for inclusion in governmental programs, the Trade Union Federation interfered in the internal cabinet conflicts between the Agrarians and the Social Democrats; in 1954 they went so far as to threaten a general strike. When developing such pressures the two Federations have naturally derived great benefits from their strong representation in the parliamentary groups of their respective parties. But they usually obtain a hearing first as autonomous organizations and not as parts of political groups.

For some time past the Central Trades Union also has put forward a claim for a representation of its own in government outside of the group of Social Democratic ministers. Of late this claim has resulted in the entrance of representatives both of the Central Union and of the industrial employers into a minority cabinet. It was made clear that these ministers were not committed to any party nor could they be regarded as independent, since they were bound to act and speak for their organizations.

However, the significance of this development should not be overstressed. The acceptance of representatives of management and labor in the cabinet is, for the time being, due to the deadlock in party collaboration and to hard economic needs rather than to successful union pressure. The split in the Central Trades Union was already assuming very serious proportions when the cabinet was formed. Despite its composition this cabinet may mark the beginning of a decline in the corporatist trend of Finnish political life.

III. Some Remarks on the Internal Problems of Interest Groups

In addition to the factors mentioned before, the accentuation of pressure group activities in Finland is also due to serious internal weaknesses and tensions. The interest groups try to outweigh and overcome their conflicts by becoming more vociferous. Though politically the most active of the Finnish interest groups, the Central Trades Union does not stand alone in this regard. The Union of Agricultural Producers, the Federation of Salaried Employees and the Employers' and Industries' Federations all have to overcome considerable internal difficulties. Some of these difficulties are of a technical, organizational nature and have to do with the attitude of their member associations, but others result from the weakness and splits in the party system. These, in turn, affect both the group members and the leadership.

In a party system like the Finnish the interrelations between parties and interest groups must necessarily result in a disastrous vicious circle. The line of action adopted by a party gives way to the pressure of the interest groups. The lack of those inhibitions which in a system of stronger parties restrain the efforts of the groups, leads to an intensification of pressure and produces conflicts both within the party machines and among different parties. These conflicts then generate an inevitable reaction affecting the interest groups themselves. Political discord is transferred to them; their members become more radical and disagree among themselves, thereby creating internal tensions which transmit themselves to the leadership and intensify the political activity of the latter.

There are yet other complexities of political life which further aggravate disunity or intransigence within the groups. In the first place there are the often open efforts of the Communists who want to create parliamentary and economic difficulties within the Finnish democracy, so that the way is opened for the overthrow of the social and political system. The Central Trades Union offers to the Communists a welcome field for such activity. They endeavour to prevent the predominantly Social Democratic leadership of the Union from giving to economic demands a reasonably moderate form. Within the Agrarian Producers' Union it is hardly possible for the Communists to make their influence felt directly; they do, however, manage to exercise an indirect pressure. This is brought about by their activities on behalf of the very small farmers who, because of the organization's commitment to "social agrarianism", are politically of the greatest importance to the Agrarians. Consequently, the small farmers' influence increases and hampers the Producers' dealings with the government and the life of the Agrarian party in different and often complex ways.

The second most important political factor making for disturbances is the previously mentioned opposition between the economic interests of the "normal" coalition partners, i.e., the Social Democrats and the Agrarians. This opposition has been bridged by a perpetual dickering which results in unrealistic "deals" concluded at the expense of the state and of production. This situation, in which the undiluted labor and agricultural interests are relegated to the extreme wings of the Social Democrat-Agrarian combination, has led to schisms in both parties and has of late particularly threatened, and indeed damaged, internal cohesion of the Social Democratic Party. Those Social Democrats who are still defending the economic policies adopted under pressure from the Central Trades Union are now a minority in the party; that is to say, the power relationship in the party is the reverse of the one prevailing among the Social Democrats in the labor movement. The latter may now have to seek the support, or rather the neutrality, of the Communists in order to maintain their position. An early result of such weakness was a desire on the part of the union leaders to show a display of strength; they therefore authorized extensive wage demands. This has caused increased tensions on the labor market which has generally slackened in the face of hard economic realities and the prospects of large-scale unemployment. The nation-wide collective agreements concluded in recent months (without the assistance of the Central Union) bear witness to increased realism and readiness to compromise.

The weakness of the party system also affects the Federation of Salaried Employees. This organization is especially hampered by the third political problem, the division of the middle-class group into four parties, and by the unfavorable Agrarian attitude. The three small "bourgeois" parties which can be expected to support the Federation and its member associations often find themselves on different sides in parliament and together account for only ¼ of its seats. Because of this and because of the direct political action of the trade unions and the Agricultural Producers, the Federation has been driven to increase its pressures, and has become at times very effective. Its largest member union, the civil servants, depends on parliament for its salary demands. In 1947 it had recourse to a general civil servants' strike despite the fact that civil servants are legally secure against dismissal and have no actual right to strike. It is also true that the application of the strike weapon against the state is not in accordance with bourgeois party ideology. The contradiction between bourgeois individualism and its ideological values on the one hand and the solidarity in the struggle for an improved standard of living on the other is somewhat damaging for the activities of this union and also for the Central Federation.

In the white-collar-workers' organizations there exists a further split, predominantly conditioned by party politics. The Central Trades Union has certain unions for the numerous small officials, such as railway, postal, telegraph and customs employees which is structurally crowned by a common "cartel" for the purposes of negotiation. This situation aggravates the rivalry between the two central federations of workers and salary earners. By the same token it intensifies the political activity of both organizations and the efforts of the employees at centralization, especially because the Union of University Graduates, Akava, is not yet affiliated to it.

The difficulties which the major interest groups encounter when they seek to build up their organizations as effectively as possible are conditioned not alone by the action and reaction of politics and parties, but principally by the character and the reaction of their membership. In only one of the mass organizations, the Agricultural Producers, can the density and distribution of the membership be compared with parallel organizations, for instance, in Sweden. The proportion between organized and unorganized workers is less favorable to the unions than in the other Scandinavian countries. (Only 25% of all Finnish workers are union members.) To a lesser degree the same applies to the Salaried Employees' and to the Employers' Federations.

It is true that labor and management organized earlier in the other Scandinavian countries than in Finland where the central federations of trade unions and employers were not created until 1907. As a result the organizations were stabilized in those countries considerably earlier than in Finland. Strong communist pressure (the Communists dominated the trade unions in 1928–29) and small membership hampered the progress of organization. The employers consequently took advantage of the situation by favoring non-union workers and by refusing to enter into collective agreements. Only in 1940 did the Central Union of Employers recognize the Central Trades Union as an equal bargaining partner and as the representative of the whole of trade union interests. The two central federations concluded their first "general agreement" in 1944 and renewed it in 1946. This basic agreement provides for a system of nation-wide collective agreements between the member associations on both sides, based on a revised Collective Agreement Act; it relies on the Labor Court system set up at the same time (1946) on the Scandinavian model. In addition, there exists a Labor Council and the factory councils which are legally compulsory in all larger concerns.

This sudden, if timely, transformation of industrial relations was almost thrust upon the trade unions by the great changes in the internal and external political situation of Finland and at a time when the unions were not yet organizationally developed on a firm basis. The system of collective agreements and the active political attitude of the Central Trades Union coupled with the wage-fixing powers of the government and the need for averting strikes (so that reparations could be paid to Russia), led to a fourfold increase in membership between 1944 and 1947. This enormous expansion, however, brought the Social Democratic control of the trade unions once more into great danger—as had happened 20 years before—and the newly organized masses showed an extraordinary lack of organizational maturity and discipline.

With the defeat of the Communists in the 1948 elections and their disappearance from the government coalition, the Central Trades Union was given a chance for a much-needed internal spring cleaning and stabilization (1949). This led to the expulsion of three refractory Communist unions and turned the 1951 elections for the Congress—the highest decision-making organ of the Central Union—into a clear-cut Social Democratic victory. An effective centralization of the position and functions of the Central Union was carried through on the Swedish model. However, membership was about 20% below the 1947 level even before the general strike of 1956.

Finnish law does not recognize compulsory organization; it protects, first and foremost, the freedom of the individual to join an association. The law of association in Finland, based as it is on the constitutional provisions relating to this freedom, imposes the observance of democratic forms of organization and decision-making on all free associations of citizens. The by-laws must be in accordance with these provisions. Therefore, the interest organizations cannot compel recruitment and, formally speaking, there can be no question of union-shop or closed-shop methods. In practice certain groups are attempting to establish compulsory organization. This is particularly true for the Seamen's Union which has recently left the Central Trades Union. The Seamen are now collaborating with other rebellious unions and may well try to found a new central federation in competition with the Central Union.

It is natural for active trade unionists to exercise strong pressure at their places of work on non-union workers, trying to induce them to join the union. They also keep union members in line. Nevertheless, the membership of the labor market organization remains in flux and is never as large as might be expected. There exist in Finland a great many small entrepreneurs, shops, enterprises, etc., with but a few workers. These workers and employers usually stay away from their organization in order to save dues and to escape certain other obligations although they may respect existing collective agreements. This is, for various reasons, a great handicap for the organizations concerned. Aside from the fact that their finances suffer, a situation develops in which large numbers of employers and workers profit from the advantages obtained by the organizations without doing anything in return. This situation is demoralizing for the organized members and makes it more difficult for the leadership to maintain discipline. Membership may easily decline drastically if the same advantages can be obtained without paying membership dues.

In general the lack of organizational maturity of the Finnish worker who wants new advantages each year in return for his dues, has conditioned the political activity of the Central Trades Union. It is also interesting to note that the powers of the government to fix wages were detrimental to the recruitment efforts of the trade unions so that finally the unions no longer supported such powers. For the employers, the large number of small unorganized entrepreneurs means great insecurity in the matter of collectively agreed wages. (Wages have a tendency to slide upwards.) In a situation of full employment the unorganized employers find workers only if they exceed the agreed wage and they are able to do this because they do not carry the financial burden of other obligations agreed upon between the workers' and employers' Federations. Despite their numerous membership, the Agricultural Producers also have problems with their rank-and-file as do the salaried employees and civil servants' organizations. The latter have achieved a high density of membership while the employees' membership remains thin.

The problem of optimum membership is thus common to all major economic organizations and in this matter they do not oppose each other, since national agreements greatly profit from, indeed are based on, the presumption that there is comprehensive organization of all groups affected by them. The employers, for instance, are not likely to welcome a definitive breach in the labor unions, since this would seriously damage the system of agreements and create unrest at work. The political activity of the central federations and of their foremost branches similarly calls for concentrated and centralized authority. But centralization presents great technical difficulties for each organization —e.g., for the naturally very heterogeneous Federation of Salaried Employees—and these difficulties often counteract the effort for maximum recruitment. It is also true that for political reasons the Central Trades Union—in order to control the Communists within its ranks—had to be very careful in the recruitment of new members and in the building of new member associations. There is an ever-present danger that the

Communists will obtain a majority in union elections and subsequently in the election of officials of hitherto Social Democratic unions. In order to have more freedom of action in the unions, the Communists also oppose the centralization which the Central Union strives at.

The above considerations bring us to the problem of bureaucratization and to the interrelations between organizational democracy and between organization management and leadership. Formally speaking, all organizations have a "democratic" structure, i.e., the decision-making bodies of representatives and delegates are directly or indirectly elected by the members and appoint the executive boards. However, the activity of the "grass-roots" organizations and rank-and-file members is inadequate in every group. The manifold tasks of the interest groups are in the hands of a staff appointed or elected to office, i.e., employees who are dependent for their advancement within the organization on the leadership to which they are subservient. To a large extent the leadership controls the organizational machine in the mass organizations and the members through this organizational bureaucracy. This does not necessarily mean that those in power have nothing to fear. The less capable the members are of independent judgment, the more easily they can be swayed by demagogic methods. In the trade unions Communist agitation makes full use of this situation. The trade union locals and some organizations on higher levels can easily spring unwelcome surprises on the union leadership either in elections or in voting down concluded agreements. This can occur all the easier when the radical elements are present at poorly attended meetings and are thereby able to obtain an accidental majority. This applies, of course, *mutatis mutandis*, to all organizations and not only to the trade unions.

In general the leaders of the highly-centralized interest groups yield greater power than party leaders. Although they are elected according to the forms of organizational democracy and are responsible to the membership, they are not subject to the same controls as party leaders. The success of parties is always dependent on the way in which they deal with political questions and with problems of public concern. A party leadership that does not hold its own in this respect is not secure. On the other hand in an interest group leaders who fight hardest for the organization's gain are the most secure. No leadership is likely to totter on election day because it has advanced, and perhaps achieved, economic objectives which might be harmful to the community at large as long as this action has not harmed the interests of the organized members. Objectively speaking, this irresponsible attitude toward power on the part of group leadership constitutes a serious problem of central significance for the whole range of economic pressure activity in politics. There is a great rush for reaching the top of these organizations. A heavy competition for the leading positions and for the power which they carry often leads to internal leadership conflicts in the interest organizations, and thus to an increased political activity, since members' support is the most important objective. The present struggle within the Social Democratic party and the union ranks is probably less a conflict of principles than of personal controversies among leaders.

Apart from certain organizations that receive state support for educational and public tasks (e.g., the small farmers' associations and the agricultural societies), the Finnish interest groups draw their income from membership fees. It is quite usual for them to subsidize party activity and election campaigns with which they sympathize. This is true of all major economic interest groups. Special mention may, however, be made of the considerable financial support which the present leadership of the Central Trades Union grants to the minority within the Social Democratic party.

All large interest organizations are concerned with educational work. Perhaps paramount in this field are the organizations in industry and business, and the cooperative unions. Questions of public relations get considerable attention in all organizations, although this area is still somewhat neglected. All of the larger groups, especially those active in the field of economics, issue one or several periodicals of their own. The Central Trades Union as well as the Agricultural Producers own daily newspapers in which they publicize their position even where it diverges from the views propounded in the daily papers of the Social Democrats or the Agrarians respectively.

The Finnish press is not subject to one-sided control, although more or less linked to parties and interest groups. Critics of every shade of opinion can get a hearing. The radio is administered by parliament, and consequently by all the parties that compose it. It has been proposed to give the main organized interest a certain representation on the Radio Board.

This paper makes no pretense of discussing the deeper aspects involved in the problem of pressure group activities in Finland. In spite of the influence they exercise, the pressure groups have thus far not been subject to scientific study and there is almost no literature dealing with their power and activities or with the question of their place in the political structure of Finland. The frequent discussions in the press do not shed much light on the interest organizations. Ideological debates are rare and parties and organizations are more inclined to stick to dogmatic commonplaces—even when they are antiquated and ill-adapted to present-day circumstances—than to adopt a forward-looking ideology and contribute to the solution of basic problems. In regard to Finland's present dilemma, namely what to do about too great a power on the part of the pressure groups in the political field, some answer may lie in the formula given above. It is a matter of achieving a better balance between the factors of this formula, perhaps through a gradual decrease of the economic tasks shouldered by the state. In fact, at the present time these tasks have already been reduced considerably and an obvious moderation of pressures has set in.

SELECTED BIBLIOGRAPHY

G. von Bonsdorff, *Suomen poliittiset puolueet*, Helsinki, 1957.

R. Ilaskivi, H. Waris, R. Kuuskoski, *Yksilöjärjestöt-valtio. Suomalaisen kansanvallen kehitys*, Porvoo, 1956.

V. A. M. Karikoski, *Vapaamuotoinen järjestötoiminta. Suomalaisen kansanvallen kehitys*, Porvoo, 1956.

L. Krusius-Ahrenberg, *Kring intresserepresentationen i vår riksdag. Ekonomi och kultur*, Helsingfors, 1955.

——, "Synpunkter på intresseorganisationernas politiska frammarsch". *Vår syn III*, 1957.

T. Modeen, "Om gestalthingen av statsjänstemännens förhandlingsvillkor", *Vår syn III*, 1957.

C. Nelson (ed.), *Freedom and Welfare*, Copenhagen, 1953.

"Nordisk jordbruksforskning", *Finlands häfte*, 1949–50, No. 2.

R. Oittinen, *Työväenkysymys ja työväenliike Suomessa*, Helsinki, 1953.

A. Salonen, *Tutkimus taloudellisesta kilpailusta (Diss.)*, Helsinki, 1955.

G. Stjernschantz, "Den ekonomiska politiken under intresseorganisationernas och partiernas tryck", *Ekonomiska samfundets Tidskrift*, 1955, No. 1.

H. Waris, *Suomalaisen yhteiskunnan rakenne*, Helsinki, 1948.

POLITICAL PRESSURES
BY INTEREST GROUPS
IN FRANCE*

GEORGE E. LAVAU

I. INTRODUCTION

French political science is beginning to be passionately interested in "pressure groups" or "interest groups." The research, generally conducted by very young investigators whose works have as yet not been completed or published, is still very fragmentary and is conducted along lines that are very often still groping for appropriate methods. However, such scholarly investigations are urgent and necessary because, for some years past, public opinion has been "stirred up," far too passionately, by the misdeeds of these groups.

Democratic tradition in France has fused the political technique of representative and parliamentary democracy with public ethics. This tradition is forcefully expressed by J. J. Rousseau: "Therefore, it is essential, if the general will is to be able to express itself, that there should be no partial society within the State and that each citizen should think only his own thoughts." Although the concrete historical effort of multiple categories of Frenchmen has consisted for centuries in demanding from the State the liberty to form groups and to constitute in actual fact "partial societies," this has remained for French democratic tradition within the category of the *Sein*; it has not reached the level of political theory, the *Sollen* (which in the opinion of the public constitutes the only noble part of politics). Hence, there is widespread consensus to condemn interest groups morally, or more exactly, to condemn their unwarranted interference in politics.

It is precisely because for the past fifty years or so the action of pressure of interest groups on the organs of political power has cast a shadow on the technique of representative and parliamentary government, that the existence and strategy of the groups have provoked a moralizing reaction. More than anything else they are a cause of opprobrium.

The opprobrium also stems from the fact that public opinion has been

* Translated from the French.

especially polarized and excited about certain pressure groups whose goals are—or seem to be—immoral. For the general public pressure groups are above all a "maffia" of disreputable hotel keepers, alcohol merchants, supporters of colonial expansion, swindlers or "merchants of death." In this respect, it is interesting to note that the word "lobby" was used in the French press for the first time to our knowledge to expose to public opinion the political maneuvers of certain French interest groups in North Africa (the North African lobby). By virtue of this prejudice (which is above all a moral one) public opinion does not consider an association or a group whose activity is considered praiseworthy as a pressure group.[1]

Thus, a moral or political judgment on the legitimacy of the interest at stake is consciously or unconsciously incorporated with the very notion of pressure groups. To us such an attitude seems radically anti-scientific; the political scientist must not exclude any group whatsoever from his research.

Too often public opinion also imagines that the only groups deserving attention are those whose political action consists in secret, and consequently unavowed, maneuvers (bribes given to parliamentarians or officials; electoral or financial pressure, etc.). This way of thinking conceals the amplitude and diversity of the means used by pressure groups as well as the depth of the problem. Now, this problem is most certainly that of the relationship between the State and its organs on the one hand and the non-political groups on the other.

We wish to state from the outset that the existence of groups of all kinds seeking to supplement their economic, educational, and other activities by political action and even by pressure on the political system and on the administration is a natural thing which is not scandalous *a priori*. Indeed we cannot see why workers, farmers, doctors, the opponents of clericalism, and the advocates of non-violence would form groups if it were not to defend, conquer, or extend their statute, their rights or their privileges, both in regard to other antagonistic groups and to the public authorities. We may consider this regrettable in itself,

---

[1] This hostile ideological and moral climate surrounding pressure groups in France reacts in its turn upon their behaviour. Whatever be the effrontery of some of them (and it is sometimes rather stupendous) they go to a lot of trouble to convince public opinion that they are working in the interests of all, to make a pretense of being the honest defenders not of a particular interest but of French genius as a whole. The trade journal of the manufacturers of carbonated drinks calls itself without any false modesty "Carbonated France," that of the home distillers "The Distiller of France." Camouflage is customary; so, the trade journal of tavern- and barkeepers takes cover under the inoffensive title of "The Lemonade Dealer of Paris."

we may blame excesses, but unless we imagine (or seek to create) a society without particular groups standing between society and the individual, we must admit that it is the nature of groups (and of all of them) to turn into pressure groups. Seen from this vantage point, there is no difference between oil companies and trade unions, between ideological and non-ideological groups.

Why then are political scientists suddenly so curious about such an ordinary fact? This question amounts to asking ourselves what fundamental problems are involved in the political action of non-political groups. As long as that question remains unanswered we shall not only have difficulty in distinguishing between our political judgments and preferences and between our scientific analysis, but we shall also approach the study of pressure groups without knowing exactly what results we hope our research to yield.

Now, if I try to discover what there is in the action of pressure groups that poses a problem to political science in France (and doubtless, at least in part, in other countries) the following points need attention:

There is a dichotomy between our concept of political power as a power ordained to defend the common good and the attempt of groups to make this power serve their own interests, even if only momentarily and partially. By its very nature a group does not feel responsible for the common good. Political power may permit that, within a limited sphere—the limits being set by itself—the groups fulfill a mission and submit their possibly contradictory claims to arbitration by the state with due respect for the rules of public order laid down by the state. But political power can not permit the groups threatening its own mission, which is, by nature, universal.

Now, if it so happens that the power of the groups is increasing and that political power is not in a position to hold the line against them, then the pressure of these groups threatens the very mission of government.

There is a contradiction between the ever-more effective action of the interest groups and the democratic fiction according to which elected assemblies assume a twofold function: that of representing conflicting interests and of sublimating them, and that of defining in their decisions a general will (if not in each particular concrete decision, at least in the continuity and the aggregate of legislative work).

We then can observe that the groups (or some of them) are not satisfied with this kind of representation, which in their eyes does not really establish an equilibrium, and that they refuse to wait for the peaceful arbitration by the political power. They seek to subjugate the latter all the more so as the government has considerable means at its disposal (legislative, regulatory, financial, and administrative power).

The very principle of democratic government, and more particularly of the parliamentary system, facilitates and even provokes to a certain degree the "colonization" of Parliament and Government by pressure groups inasmuch as it organizes the confrontation, competition, and control by the elected representatives and the compromise between groups. It could only be otherwise (and that is precisely one of the assumptions of the democratic doctrine) if either there were no political parties but only isolated elected members acting purely upon the commands of their conscience, or if political parties were organizations, radically different from other groups and totally impervious to the particular preoccupations of whatever group (or of several of them).

There also arises another problem. In France the administration, long considered as the very place where the general interest was being formulated and preserved, and whose independence and indifference to pressure were considered as an antidote of the democratic and parliamentary form of government, no longer seems to be safe from the activity of pressure groups. Not that there is suspicion of collusion, but there is nevertheless realization of the fact that the bureaucracy alone cannot build the dam that is needed.

Moreover, the syndicalism, which is characteristic of the mentality of numerous civil servants, and the increasingly "corporatist" spirit of some administrations and ministries (for instance Agriculture, Trade and Industry, National Education, the Postal Service) are as many worms in the fruit.

Such being the problem, the possible avenues for a scholarly study of political pressure by groups other than political parties might be the following:

1. To measure the exact degree of the political activity of these groups. To define political activity, to study the forms of such activity and of the means used, to classify the groups according to the activity displayed and the means used. In a word, to know exactly what we are talking about and to verify whether the pressure of the groups is really as intense and as excessive as is generally believed.

2. To seek out the factors which, either in the nature or the structure of the groups themselves or in the nature and behaviour of political parties or in the functioning of institutions, encourage, balance, or limit the political activity of pressure groups.

3. To study in which directions pressure is exercised and which results are obtained. Such a balance-sheet is necessary to obtain a true picture

of pressure group activities as well as an exact appreciation of the degree to which they are distorting the political process.

4. To study new techniques or, more unpretentiously, mere measures of protection which would appear capable of either limiting the undue use of influence by the groups in regard to political power or of subordinating their activity to the demands of the general interest.

II. Measurement and Descriptive Study of the Political Activity of Groups

1. Why do non-political groups have a political activity?

In the first place because no political party, even if it were exclusively and totally the party of one class or of one occupation, can reflect the complexity and diversity of interests which are often mutually contradictory. Even a peasant party could not, especially in a country where agriculture is as varied as in France, devote itself exclusively to the defense of one category of farmers without dissatisfying at a certain moment another category. If this party were to obtain an advantage for wheat growers, corn growers in turn will demand another advantage (which might hardly be compatible with the preceding one), etc. Therefore, each group tends to organize itself, to win acceptance for the solution which suits it best and to see, if possible, any compromise and any halfway measure excluded. It might well be that it is miscalculating the effects, but that is another story.

In the second place, groups are to a certain degree condemned to act on public authorities as a result of the increasing intervention of the latter in the economic field. This is a fact on which we shall not insist,[1] but confine ourselves to the remark that this intervention by the state is actually very often—and more and more frequently—solicited by the groups themselves: thus, they maintain the phenomenon which motivates their action.

Besides, how could they avoid appealing to the public authorities? The economic policy of a highly centralized state is using means far too powerful, too varied, and too detailed for an interest group not to seek to use them to its own advantage. The State distributes credit and subsidies, fixes wages and prices—directly or indirectly—increases or reduces taxes, enters into contracts, buys crops, grants import licenses, decides

---

[1] See on this point J. Meynaud, "Contribution à l'analyse des groupes d'intérêts dans la vie politique française", *Revue de l'Institut Sociologique*, *(Solvay)*. (1956), pp. 225, ff.

on "shock" imports, regulates a part of consumption, etc. How could such a power be neglected?

2. *Against whom and against what is the pressure of groups directed?*

A complete list would be interminable. Let us confine ourselves to a few very general indications.

Properly speaking interest groups (i.e., non-ideological groups) act in the first place against the tax power of the public authorities, which includes also the so-called parafiscal measures. This activity has even given rise to specialized movements such as the League of Taxpayers or the *Bloc des Patentés*. In a general way we may assert that this is the chief reason for the existence of a considerable number of interest groups.

Dirigisme (i.e., the broad intervention of the State in the national economy), in order of importance, is the second target of the interest groups. All of them solicit help and protection against the demands of certain administrations, against foreign competitors, or against rival groups, but all of them also vehemently denounce the intervention of the State when it threatens their own freedom, their privileges, their relatively favorable tax position, or the right to fix prices or salaries.

All this is well known, but what is generally forgotten or overlooked is that often an essential part of the activity of interest groups (and even of those groups that are non-economic and non-professional in character) is directed against other rival groups: beet growers against makers of alcohol, road haulage against rail transport, home distillers against commercial distillers, retailers against chain stores and co-operatives, "former inmates of Nazi labor camps" against "former political prisoners," defenders of the public schools against defenders of the parochial schools, etc. *Le Betteravier Français*, the organ of the General Confederation of Beet Growers, boasts of representing "a huge organization whose aim is to defend the beet-growers' interests day in and day out to the best of its ability, *vis-à-vis* industry as well as *vis-à-vis* the public authorities."[1] The action directed against the public authorities is in itself very often an indirect action against rival groups.

3. *Which groups make use of political action?*

All of them, without any exception. But there are innumerable degrees of intensity.

There is no difference as to the nature of such action. This would

[1] *Le Betteravier Français*, February, 1956.

hardly deserve substantiation if there were not some controversial situations, such as the case of the trade unions. It is a universally defended thesis in France that the political activity of trade unions is radically different from that of other interest groups. Indeed, far from pursuing aims limited to strictly professional and immediate interests, the unions are considered to have "conceived the ambition of rebuilding the *cité* on entirely new economic, political, and moral foundations." (See for instance, F. Perroux, *Syndicalisme et Capitalisme*. The same idea is expressed by Georges Burdeau in his *Traité de Science Politique*.) This assertion is only valid for certain trade unions in France, Spain, and Italy. As far as the French trade union movement is concerned, it seems to me to apply only to the CGT from its creation to 1919, and to the CGTU from 1923 to 1936. Today it only remains true of the CGT because of the semi-colonization of the central administrative apparatus of this organization by the French Communist Party; hence, it is an outside factor and not the syndicalist nature of the CGT which prevents it from acting like any other pressure group (and even that is not entirely correct).

The other trade unions display a political activity which may occasionally be different from that of other groups as to form, but never as to its essential nature. It is true that in the last quarter of the nineteenth century the French trade union movement had dreamed of supplanting political parties without entering into relations with them. But nowadays trade unions have given up this dream. Henceforth they have the choice between binding themselves to and conforming to the political action of a party which adopts their revolutionary aim or of acting, with a few more or less marked differences, like any other pressure group.

Another controversial situation arises in regard to groups which are the satellites of a political party. Their case will be examined later.

The intensity of pressure varies according to the moment and to the nature of the group under consideration, but it is always considerable. Let us examine, for instance, the pressure brought to bear by groups at the time of an election campaign (in this case that of December, 1955). At that time pressure appeared, especially, in a flood of letters and questionnaires sent to each candidate. These letters asked the candidate to make precise promises (to be duly signed by the candidate in person) to support or to fight, if he was elected, bills or amendments concerning questions which generally had a very limited importance. The different groups boasted of the throngs of voters they represented and more or less threatened to order their members not to vote for candidates who failed to give the desired pledges.

Who sent these letters? The most varied groups. However, it should be noted that certain powerful organizations, such as the C.N.P.F. (Council of French Employers), did not take part in this election campaign, at least not in the way described here. It is rather remarkable, too, that the C.G.T. did not send any letters to candidates either. On the other hand, a great number of letters came from groups of the "weak" or the "small," such as the artisans, pensioners, former prisoners of war, paralyzed, ill, or disabled people. The majority, however, on the one hand came from groups of small shopkeepers and on the other hand from unions of civil servants and, above all, of teachers.

If all groups engage at one time or another in political pressure, there are nevertheless, degrees in the intensity and continuity of this action which distinguish one group from another. Most groups resort to political action only occasionally, when it is necessary and, especially, when a threatened privilege must be defended. The degree of intensity varies according to multiple factors (group aims, social composition, economic policy of the government, etc.).

At the other end of the scale we may find certain groups whose, if not exclusive, at any rate main, function consists in acting upon the public authorities. Such is apparently the case of two rival ideological groups: "The Teachers' League" and more clearly perhaps, "The League for the Defense of the Freedom of Teaching" (the former an anti-clerical; the latter a Catholic group). Jean Meynaud (*op. cit.*) has also mentioned the "Association to Finish the North Canal" whose object it is to obtain from the public authorities (and from them alone) a decision (and credits) in favor of certain interests.

Among this same category we might, to a certain degree, classify certain groups, as for instance, The Economic Front of Defense against Taxes or the Association for Free Enterprise. The main activity of these organizations (but not their only one) consists in lobbying; they are systematically reserving seats on their boards to members of parliament entrusted with promoting in the assemblies a current of active sympathy for the politics recommended by the organizations. Such associations bear a resemblance to the *"groupes parlementaires d'études"* which, as a rule, although they are exclusively composed of parliamentarians, are in fact instigated, animated, and directed by interest groups outside parliament and which act as pressure groups.

Some groups are condemned frequently because due to the membership that they represent they have an intense political activity. We may mention as an example: The Federation of the Press, Association of the Regional Press, and Association of French Mayors.

Doubtless, we must reserve a place apart for certain groups whose chief, though in general unavowed, aim it is to ensure the election of deputies or of representatives in local assemblies who can be counted upon to defend the interests of a definite group or, more often, of a federation of groups. It happens that a group which is rather powerful financially may establish an organization which is a mere facade for an electoral fund furnished by the interest group. Such was the role under the Third Republic of *L'Union des Intérêts Economiques* and such may be the role today of the committee *de la rue de Penthièvre* which seems to be nothing more than a fund constituted by certain employers' organizations. It is true that we cannot say anything more precise with any certainty and that we cannot prove that the responsibility of the entire C.N.P.F. is involved in the activities of this committee.[1]

The maximum degree of political activity can be observed when groups which were originally non-political change into political parties or establish political parties.[2] It is also reached by an exactly opposite process—when an economic or ideological organization falls under the sway of a political party or is created by the party to serve as a "sound-box."[3]

In a general way, if we leave aside the special situations we have just considered, we seem to find that the political activity of the groups becomes appreciably more intense as we draw away from local organizations towards central formations; in the same way, it appears to be greater for aggregates of groups than for highly specialized groups; but this general rule needs certain modifications and certainly no longer holds true as soon as a highly specialized group faces a definite threat.

4. *What are the forms of political action?*

We shall limit ourselves here to a few very general indications and to an attempt at classification.

[1] For more details, see Henry W. Ehrmann, *Organized Business in France*, 1957, pp. 224, ff.

[2] Under the Third Republic the War Veterans' Association, the *"Croix de Feu"* first broadened into a political league; then, legally dissolved at the end of 1936, it subsisted in fact and was doubled by a political party (the P.S.F.). In 1955–56 the professional organization called the U.D.C.A. gradually turned into the *"Mouvement Poujade"* to which then a parliamentary group (*Union et Fraternité Francaise*) was added.

[3] The case of the "parallel" organizations of the Communist Party is the best known and most clear-cut. But it exists, too, in a less definite form in other corners of the political chessboard.

Electoral Action

It is rather clear that certain groups very generously finance certain candidates. Mere common sense indicates the truth of this statement; even a superficial observation of the parties and of the huge campaign expenses demonstrate it in an impressive way. But the caution of the different groups concerned is so great that, at least to our knowledge, no scientifically-established proof of these facts can be validly given.

We have hardly any greater possibilities of investigation concerning the preparation of elections by pressure groups. Do the interested groups intervene in the establishment of party lists; do they take part in drawing up platforms; do they furnish elements of information to the parties before the opening of the campaign? It is difficult to give an answer and even when we possess elements of information, it seems that our conclusions must differentiate carefully.

Let us put aside the case of the many organizations that gravitate around the Communist Party. There, it seems that an active collaboration (though rather unequal due to the fact that the active fighting wing of these organizations is generally composed of Party members) takes place for the long-range preparation of elections. The case is obviously very special. But, in a more general way, we may say that only the groups intimately connected with a party really prepare elections. The others get on the move only at the opening of the electoral campaign; precisely because they have prepared nothing, they are compelled to suddenly flood candidates with letters and to besiege them with remonstrations.

That is the essential part of the electoral activity of pressure groups. We have tried above to give an idea of its intensity. We would like to use the same example to indicate the techniques applied.

Almost all the letters sent to candidates by interest groups during the 1956 campaign requested an exact and specified answer. Almost all of them included a questionnaire to be sent back to the organization within a very short time so as to inform their members, or to publish in their specialized papers (or eventually in the great newspapers) the candidates' answers along with the electoral advice of the organizations. The answer demanded was "yes" or "no" and the candidate was always required to sign his promises.

The promises that are requested generally concern (and this is the most important point) very precise and limited questions; it is almost always a matter of voting or not voting for bills in abeyance in parliament. If it is a bill which dissatisfies the organization concerned, the latter sometimes submits a counter-project or amendments drawn up by it and requests candidates to promise their support and vote. Sometimes a certain group asks a candidate to promise, in case he is elected, to become a member of the *"groupe parlementaire d'études"* corresponding to the pressure group's own activities.

The printed form used by the "Confederation of Small and Medium-sized Enterprises" is worth quoting:

"I the undersigned ... declare that I agree unreservedly with the program attached hereto and solemnly promise, if I am elected, to act with a view of carrying it into effect and for this purpose, to work in close touch with the Confederation."

Most of these letters are alarmingly stupid. Yet, some of them may be useful to candidates because they define certain problems clearly and objectively and may really enlighten them about certain technical questions. But just how much effect do they have?

Their chief aim is to give the alarm to the parties and the eventual successful candidates at a time when they are naturally particularly receptive to all complaints; from this point of view the result sought after is certainly obtained. But what remains afterwards? The solemn engagement signed by the eventually successful candidate must doubtless embarrass him if he does not fulfill it later on, since certain groups during the election campaigns publicize certain "betrayals" of the incumbents. This is certainly not a pressure to be overlooked. But a deputy seldom wholly betrays his promises, just as he seldom wholly respects them. Moreover, the organizations themselves do not seem to attach too sacred an importance to these promises (if they demand them it is apparently much more to convince their members that they are represented by gallant champions). Moreover, the situation at the time of the next elections will be much too confused for a real "show down"; in fact, it was this semi-complicity between the elected candidates with certain interest groups and their tacit agreement to let bygones be bygones which has caused the exasperation of the "little men" and gave birth to the U.D.C.A. and the *Mouvement Poujade*.

On another plane this electoral pressure may have a more serious consequence. This avalanche of frantic demands, limited to very narrow matters, diverts the candidates' and parties' attention from bringing general problems before the voters. Deafened by the clamor of pressure groups and fearing their hostility, they are tempted to think that the electorate as a whole is similar to these groups specialized in the use of intimidation. Hence, they avoid dealing with large problems and hesitate to show the sacrifices which every valid solution demands.

The Continuous Action of Influence

Far more profitable than electoral activities is undoubtedly the permanent influence that interest groups must bring on the public authorities to maintain a favorable climate. This is the type of activity in which well-organized groups reign supreme. They are discreet about their methods and dispose of powerful financial means as well as a carefully distributed network of personal connections in political circles and the press.

Such a group must be permanently concerned with the search for allies in parliamentary circles (and if possible in several parties); it must maintain among them a fruitful rivalry and dispose of quasi-permanent employees (very likely remunerated in an indirect way by one of the members of the central organization) but it must also, and at least at certain times this becomes even more important, obtain the backing of occasional allies. These allies must be brought together in the *groupes parlementaires d'études* (about which we have unfortunately no exact details). The latter will maintain a desirable climate in the assemblies, keep in touch with the organizations concerned, propose bills and amendments, act within the permanent committees, and eventually delegate one of their members to the cabinet, etc.

The influence will also be exercised by means of conventions and formal banquets to which ministers, members of parliament, and even highly-placed civil servants will be invited. When the elected representatives meet there influential men and generally the press, they can hardly ward off such influence.

Also, activities concerned with mutual information belong to this type of influence "mongering."

A pressure group must not only use its influence with the papers to have a favorable press, but also directly with the elected representatives; members of parliament and successful local candidates are generously submerged with printed matter, often very well written and presented with a certain objectivity. It is designed to make the needs and demands of the interest groups known. Others, the so-called "struggle" organizations, resort to more brutal techniques—more or less threatening circular letters, delegations, pamphlets, etc.

Information, persuasion, and influence must also be brought to bear upon the administration. This is naturally more difficult, since the latter is more aloof than political circles. A perfidious technique consists in hiring for a pressure group a former civil servant of those administrative services upon which the group wants to use its influence. More often it is above all a question of getting information from the administration, of knowing its plans, and in turn of furnishing it information. Finally, the ideal of a pressure group is to influence the administration concerned rather discreetly (and this will be easier if, for many years, the minister has been a "friend") in order to convince it to espouse, at least partially, the cause of those under its jurisdiction. In case of success the following situation is established: the ministry will then act within the framework of the over-all administrative apparatus as a pressure group (of a special kind, of course, and in a very restricted way) with respect to other specialized administrations and above all with respect to the Ministry of Finance which, as it has no particular groups under its jurisdiction, is assaulted by all.

Episodic Offensive or Defensive Operations

Though "episodic," the offensive and defensive actions in question are nevertheless very frequent. Each debate on the budget (and in one form or another they are very numerous in France) gives rise to such operations. But budgetary debates, of course, are not the only occasions when these pressures are brought to legislative debates. The examination of bills by committees, the preparation of regulations and administrative orders in the Ministries, the work of the Economic Council, etc. may give rise to—and often does—the intervention of pressure groups.

The categories of techniques used are very different: letters to members of parliament; delegations sent to the minister concerned or delegations by the local sections of the group to successful candidates in the department; interventions with the members of the ministerial cabinet, in certain cases direct pressure with ministers or with the executive of parties; suggested bills, amendments, or counter-projects; and finally parallel to all this, direct action directed against hostile political forces, appeals to public opinion by means of lectures, statements to the press, distribution of booklets, leaflets and pamphlets. As a last resort there remains (when the type of organization allows it) the threat of a strike and the effective recourse to strikes, the threat of suspending the payment of taxes, of putting off the delivery of crops or of reducing production, of suspending all operations by postal money orders to inconvenience the Treasury, of closing down enterprises hoping that this threat will lead trade unions to back up the claims of employers and that the Government will be less indifferent to their intervention, etc.

The tactics of a definite group often vary, depending on whether the government, or more often the minister concerned, is considered a "friend" or a "foe." But how can a "friend" be defined? A friend is a minister who has already given proof of his goodwill or comprehension towards the group in question, or, better still, the one who "belongs" or who, thanks to his connections and interests, knows the millieu of the group or who may even be elected in a *département* where the group concerned represents real electoral power; of course, a "friend" is also a minister whom the group counts among its traditional allies, who has upheld its claims before, who has belonged to a corresponding *groupe d'étude* in parliament and who has also faithfully attended its public meetings. In the presence of a cabinet whose premier is a "friend" or in which the organization concerned has a minister who is a "friend" (preferably in charge of that ministry in which the group is particularly interested), the usual strategy of the organization will be flexible and vigilant; it will be above all preventive. At first, it will consist, if possible, in introducing into the minister's personal cabinet a confidential agent. If this is not possible, the group will try to detect among the minister's closest collaborators the man to whom he listens most, in order to furnish this man with the necessary documentation and to submit their complaints and requests to him; it will try to neutralize if need be the inevitable influence that the administrative services have on the minister and his associates. An attempt will be made to get the minister and the government to expedite the vote of a private member bill, or of a public bill if it is considered favorable to the objectives of the group. In this case the group will not even hesitate to advise the minister to abandon legislative procedure because it is too slow and subject to surprises and to resort to an appropriate administrative regulation. If on the other hand the government is an "enemy" or hostile to them, the groups will in general prefer recourse to the legislature, which will leave them the weapon of amendments and the possibility of a "rear-guard" battle in the Council of the Republic. The groups will see to it that ministerial circulars and instructions for application are less rigid than legislative texts if it has not been possible to obtain a law that thoroughly satisfies the interest group. The pressure on a "friendly" government is always discreet and noiseless; it very willingly dispenses with publicity except in the internal bulletins of certain organizations that need to prove to their possibly disgruntled members that they are efficiently defended and in the periodicals of those ideological groups which are allied to a political party and wish to prove the great merits of the party representatives.

Faced with an "enemy" or "questionable" government or minister, the strategy is generally very different. Most often it will consist, at the time the government is formed and during the first weeks of its existence, in asserting very loudly the group's fears and suspicions so as to stir up public opinion beforehand. All this moreover will not prevent groups from trying, as in the preceding case, to find some allies within the ministry; they may even go further and try to oppose one minister to another. Also, here they will harass the minister and his collaborators with requests for an audience, with arguments in defense of their cause, with protests and the like; but instead of being discreet about all this, they will, on the contrary, see to it that their interventions be given the maximum publicity by communicating them to the press by other methods. This is the technique of arousing public opinion; in a perfectly conscious and calculated way these organizations use the frantic language of the exasperated and the underprivileged. At such moments the large organizations of employers and the general staffs of confederations let the groups of "little men" come to the foreground, since public opinion finds their activity less questionable and since they can use more easily a dramatic force. It is also the time for ephemeral or more or less spontaneously formed groups that will engage in spectacular demonstrations.[1]

This action on public opinion also depends on the help of the press; regional dailies, above all, almost never refuse to insert statements and reports just as long as they are not frankly political in character.

The maneuvers by a dissatisfied organization may sometimes be advantageously carried on by another apparently less interested organization if the latter has more political weight.

III. The Factors which Explain, Promote or Hinder the Political Activity of Pressure Groups

Organization and Structure of Groups

The boisterous character of pressure group activity does not necessarily indicate the degree of its real efficacy. The latter depends mostly on factors peculiar to the group. But exactly what are the ideal conditions for political efficacy?

To answer this question in a pertinent way it would be necessary

---

[1] An excellent example of the whole range of defensive and offensive maneuvers used by a combative pressure group is furnished by the struggles conducted by the *Union Nationale des Débitants de Boisson* against the regulations of November and December 1954 issued by Mendès-France's government, a struggle which after a year-long battle led to the complete dismantling of the government's anti-alcoholic measures. A young author, Jean-Marie Cotterel, in a work now being prepared, (and which will doubtless be published in the *Cahiers de la Fondation Nationale des Sciences Politiques*) has very minutely analyzed the ups and downs of this battle.

to have engaged in many anatomical and physiological studies, not only of representative trade associations and trade unions but also of certain professional branches. It is on this level of study that economists and sociologists might contribute in an inestimably interesting way to the study of pressure groups. Already some research done under the direction of Jean Meynaud (especially studies about the automobile industry) furnishes us some invaluable information. But indispensable studies about certain sectors, for instance, about the milling trade, building, pharmaceutics, banking, firms specialized in overseas trade, etc., are still lacking.

For lack of such studies we are reduced to making a few fragmentary and very hypothetical remarks:

1

The financial power of a pressure group is not a direct factor determining political efficacy, with the exception of those cases, probably exceptional, where a pressure group tries to outright bribe certain politicians.

On the other hand, financial power is a powerful means of indirect action. It alone enables the groups to publish attractive periodicals, which are well written and generously distributed to members of parliament and other influential circles. It alone enables a pressure group to enlist the active sympathy and backing of the large newspapers and, even more so, of the economic and financial press—and thus to influence the public and consequently the electorate. It alone enables a pressure group to maintain "permanent" employees and research departments which closely follow governmental plans to draw up plans of their own, to furnish reports and documentation and collaboration to the ministries, to perfect its network of public relations, and to organize its propaganda.

It is quite natural to ask where the resources of pressure groups come from. This question does not exactly come within the scope of our study; yet it is incidental to the very topic that preoccupies us; for if we succeeded in determining the origin of its funds, we should also, to a certain degree, succeed in knowing who holds influence and power inside a pressure group. We may also presume that all research along this line would encounter great difficulties.

In the present state of our knowledge, it does not even seem possible to give any approximate indications about the financial means of a given group. Only one thing seems certain; taking into account the fact that the expenses sustained are probably enormous, there are very few trade associations (to mention only them) that can meet them with membership dues alone.

2

Of course, the number of members and the discipline of the organization are also important factors of political efficacy.

Unfortunately, it is not only in the labor unions that it is difficult, if not impossible, to obtain sincere and exact data about the number of members. The same is true of almost all organizations.

If we leave aside the labor unions, we may mention among the groups with the largest number of members: the *Syndicat National des Bouilleurs de Cru* (2,500,000 in 1955); the *Ligue de l'Enseignement* (about 3 million in 1957); the *Fédération Nationale des Syndicats d'Exploitants Agricoles* (claimed to have 700,000 members in 1956).

For very obvious electoral reasons the great number of supporters makes the members of parliament and the political parties listen to the complaints of mass organization. The administration itself, even if the minister—a politician—does not bring pressure to bear on it, cannot remain completely indifferent to the argument of numbers.

Yet the weight of this factor is rather relative. In the first place, it depends on the aggressiveness of the staff and the leadership of the group, on the degree of organization and of discipline prevailing within the organization. There are countless groups which make up for small numbers of supporters by faultless organization and a high discipline of their members.

The weight of numbers may also be neutralized by the political determination of the members of an organization. The Movement for Peace, at one time, had more than one million supporters, but its real political strength has always remained fairly slight because it was obvious that a huge majority of its supporters were composed of Communist voters who moreover were firmly decided to remain Communists. Numbers become a respected political force only if the political indecision (real or supposed) of the membership allows parties or deputies to hope for the votes of at least a fraction of the group's members. The more the class represented by the organization diverges in its political leanings, the larger the audience of the organization will be. If such a politically diversified class usually divides its preferences between two neighboring but rival parties, which are equally likely to belong to cabinets, then a pressure group—well directed by men who are well conversant with political subtleties—may have some happy days; its leaders will simply have to frown to see ministers, deputies, and party leaders "raise the stakes."

Yet, once again, this is not always true. The "model" presented here will really develop only if the organization can be sure that its members obey strictly its directives as to how to vote. This may be the case, for instance, for the General Confederation of Beetgrowers because a beet grower depends for his livelihood on his farm, which is often chiefly devoted to the growing of beets, and also because he depends on the privileged regime granted by the government to the cultivation of this crop. The situation would not be the same for the amateur fisherman who generally becomes a member of his local association for convenience's sake but who would not expect to gain much from the national group and who would very probably not follow its voting instructions if the group were to issue any. On the political level, the angler is not "conditioned" by his favorite sport, whereas the beet grower may be so conditioned by the legislation concerned with the privileges of the beetgrowers.

3

A pressure group must be vouched for by the "small fry" and by the "pure" ones:

No French politician, even if he were known for being allied to big business or finance, can allow himself to intervene publicly in favor of the "big." That is why the C.N.P.F. is so discreet. Thus pressure groups must take shelter behind "the small and innocent" to make politicians and the public listen to them.

The "humble" members, who are always the most numerous, and whose economic and professional difficulties are the greatest, serve as a justification for the pressure group which aligns the demands of the whole category represented by it on the needs of those that are most unfairly treated. However, the latter are seldom the real leaders because their financial contributions are small and because they have scarcely the time or the means to devote themselves to the life of the organization.

This phenomenon is so well known that it is unnecessary to insist. Nevertheless, it is worth emphasizing that it seems to be particularly marked in agricultural organizations.

A group that is really composed only of small people or that apparently organizes the simon-pure (i.e., those that are so considered by public opinion) has obviously an excellent chance of attracting the attention of politicians at least under the following conditions: if it represents a sufficiently large body of people or if it is supposed to have an appreciable electoral influence; if it is well directed and dynamic; and if it represents a milieu where the party or the politician that are being solicited have a real chance of finding supporters (family associations are heard by the M.R.P. or by the conservative parties; teachers' unions have the ear of the S.F.I.O.).

4

The vertical concentration of several closely related organizations is also, in certain cases, a means of putting action into low gear and of concentrating the political power of pressure groups.

In a federal or confederal association of interest groups it happens very often that in fact one of the member organizations occupies a dominant position; its leaders are also the leaders of the peak-association; it lends its premises and administrative staff, and it contributes the largest share of the dues. So dominant a position enables the organization to maneuver the confederation. It will lead the latter to assume the defense of its members' particular interests every time that it seems inopportune to the member organization (especially with regard to public opinion) to act in its own name. For instance, the distillers of beet-root alcohol will have the most difficult lobbying done in their behalf by a confederal organization which groups, besides them, wine-growers, cider-makers, home-distillers, etc. In these confederal organizations the central administrative apparatus exercises often considerable power, mainly because it controls the technical and administrative staff and the finances of the organization. But its power is also due to other factors. Since it is its function to arbitrate or mediate possible conflicts between different member organizations, this role confers upon it, in the eyes of the administration and the politicians, a considerable dignity. Frequently, the leaders of such peak-confederations are influential and indispensable men who have a seat and play a prominent part in the Chambers of Commerce or of Agriculture, in the Economic Council, in the Council of the Modernization and Equipment Plan, and in various consultative technical committees which are composed of group representative and civil servants (sometimes also of members of parliament) and which may enjoy broad administrative powers.

5

Finally the political efficacy of a pressure group depends to a very great extent on whether or not there exists opposite it another well-organized, forceful rival group.

The example of the victorious battle waged in 1954–55 by the *débitants de boisson*, the bar and tavern keepers, proved this. Indeed we cannot emphasize too much that next to their fight against taxes the essential part of interest groups' activity is directed against other rival groups.

This might explain the influence of certain organizations like those of war veterans (when they are not politically divided) whose claims do not directly run counter to any organized interest since they are addressed above all to the Ministry of Pensions and since war veterans do not arouse the same sort of envy, among the non-wage earners, as do civil servants.

Relations between Pressure Groups and Parties

Is the political effectiveness of a pressure group enhanced by the existence of closely-knit bonds with one or several political parties? If so, up to what point?

Here too we shall limit ourselves to a few very general hypotheses.

In the first place, the objectives of non-ideological pressure groups which seek alliances with or the benevolent neutrality of parliamentary committees or ministers do not call for too close or too constant bonds with an entire political party. More exactly they have everything to fear from a well-organized party that exercises effective control over members of parliaments and over its leaders. For, in such a party, decisions are made and policies are adopted publicly under the control of the central and local organizations of the party. This hinders maneuvers and more or less secret agreements and it hardly allows successful candidates to become as individuals too closely associated with the destinies of a definite interest group. Should that happen, nevertheless, the elected representative who has been won over to the cause of an interest group will have to reckon with the party; he will not be able to freely propose bills and amendments desired by the pressure group. He will not even be free to vote as he pleases; in the parliamentary committees to which he will be delegated by his party he will move under the watchful eye of his party. This is why pressure groups prefer to work through members of parliament belonging to "supple" party organizations, such as the Radical Party, the Independents, the U.R.A.S., or the U.D.S.R.

The activities of pressure groups are greatly enhanced by the mixture of social classes that make up the clientele of the parties, by the great number of French parties, and by the fact that many social groups which are homogeneous on the professional and economic plane have very different political attitudes. While this statement may seem obscure, it can be proven quite easily. Moreover, the following propositions will throw light upon it.

If two or three parties contend for the clientele of a group of whatever nature and if that clientele constitutes an appreciable fraction of the traditional following of the parties, the political role of the pressure group may be considerable.

A few examples will illustrate that point: the offensive which the League for the Defense of the Freedom of Teaching organized on the morrow of the elections of June 17, 1951 in favor of the "Barangé Law" was successful and caused a breach between the M.R.P. and the S.F.I.O. that had previously formed an alliance because the Catholic clientele was disputed by the M.R.P., the R.P.F., and the Independents; the anticlerical groups and the organizations of the leading profession draw their strength from the fact that they play on the competition between three parties (Radicals, Socialists, and Communists).

The strength of the various agricultural organizations stems from the political wavering of the farmers in general and from the fact that their political leanings vary according to regions, types of farming, family traditions, etc. Nevertheless, we must introduce some modifications of what has been said. Our proposition holds mostly true for the transitional period when a party, hitherto ensured (because of old traditions) of the votes of a certain clientele, sees this "privilege" and monopoly threatened by the growth of a new party or when part of the following of an interest group moves over to another party. When, on the contrary, immobility prevails, when positions are firm and when, for instance, the farmers steadfastly divide their votes between two parties, e.g., according to regions or religious beliefs, then the political power of agricultural organizations will be less great. Whereas they will doubtlessly be able to maintain a *status quo*, they will not have the strength to obtain new advantages because the parties, content with their usually reliable electorate, will not be inordinately concerned.

If an interest group becomes the satellite of a party, this is profitable only for the party. Inversely, if a political party becomes too exclusively the voice of an interest group (even if the latter is wide open to all) this slows down the growth of the party's following outside the milieu represented by this group.

In France, in any case, most interest organizations are mostly concerned with preserving their "a-politism" though it would be more exact to speak of their "non-politization."[1]

---

[1] The home distillers, for instance, declare "For the triumph of our demands, my fellow distillers, let us continue our action in complete independence from political parties.... If a political party fights against us, let us avoid adopting a definite position regarding it before we have tried to convince it. Let us appeal to the home

Inversely, political parties, and even more so, individual politicians insist on stressing the fact that their political positions do not make them indifferent to the preoccupations of any pressure group.

The ideological character of most French political parties is on the contrary a hindrance for pressure groups that are ideological in character. It prevents them from acting on several parties at the same time, all the more so as apart from the satellite organizations of the Communist Party and a few organizations of the Extreme Right, these groups are generally lacking in vitality and above all in great financial means.

Yet, groups like *La Ligue Française de l'Enseignement* or, at least under the Third Republic, *Le Grand Orient de France* (Free Masons) possess a far-reaching network of public relations and considerable financial means, because they play on the keyboards of at least two or three parties of which at least one always belongs to the governmental majority if not to the cabinet itself.

On the contrary, a group of war veterans with a definite leaning toward either the Right or the Left loses, due to this politization, the benefit of the very wide-spread sympathy which normally a group of war veterans would enjoy in all political parties, since all of them have war veterans among their following; such a group is destined to become very rapidly the satellite of a party or to be transformed into a party or a political league.

Whatever traditional affinities a given group may have with a political party, its allegiance will never be staunch enough not to attempt influencing another party which is temporarily in office. Indeed, in our political system the Government has so many weapons at its disposal that no interest group can afford, as political parties do, the luxury of "an opposition cure."

The opportunism of cabinets usually strengthens the hand of pressure groups. But every rose has its thorns. Indeed the parties harbor no illusions about the gratitude or loyalty of pressure groups; they are well aware that, for them, holding a key position in a governmental majority or, better still, occupying certain minorities constitutes the most efficient means of satisfying the demands of interest groups. That is why they may listen absent-mindedly to the complaints and threats of these groups, as long as they are not in power; they know very well

---

distillers that are active members of this party; let us ask them to use their influence with their leaders to persuade them that our cause is the cause of justice and liberty, the cause of people of small means who are the victims of the coalition of powerful financial interests and stupid prejudices." A. Lyautey, *Le Bouilleur de France*, April–May, 1956.

that the latter will no longer have a serious grudge against them as soon as they have returned to power and that it will then be much easier to win over the groups, at least momentarily, by granting them some favors.

Legal Recognition of Organizations

We are convinced that this is a very important but little known factor of the political effectiveness of pressure groups.

We do not have in mind here the constitutional "representation" of interests in the Economic Council which can be justified even according to the principles of the representative regime. Besides the Council has the merit of being known; there is a lot of publicity about it; moreover a balance is established by the presence in its midst of innumerable categories of groups with divergent interests.

What we want to stress here is rather the growth of what has been very rightly called "professional power," i.e. the development around the administration of countless committees, councils, commissions, interprofessional groups, and boards whose functions are generally advisory, which are attached to one or several ministers and whose attributions consist, in the preliminary study, the preparation and sometimes the final drawing up of governmental and administrative regulations concerning a branch of economic activities or a group of related activities.[1]

Under the chairmanship of a "parachuted" high civil servant and sometimes of the minister himself, less often of a member of parliament who is the president or vice-president of a committee in the National Assembly, these organisms invite the collaboration of representatives of the profession concerned,[2] sometimes of deputies,[3] sometimes, too, of personalities chosen for their scientific competence.

The development of these bodies presents a new and threatening phenomenon: interest groups become administrators, take over administrative functions, and assume (not as such but within these organisms and in close cooperation with the civil servants belonging to them) certain prerogatives of the State. The Executive of the C.G.B., who is also a member of the Superior Council of Alcohols, did not hesitate to declare during a meeting of the Council: "We have all taken a more or

[1] See André Heilbronner, "Le pouvoir professionel," *Et. et. Doc. Conseil d'Etat,* 1952.

[2] Theoretically designated by ministerial decree but in fact co-opted by the most representative organizations.

[3] The "Superior Council of Alcohols" presided over by M. Guyon, a Socialist Deputy, has seven members of parliament among its fifty-three members.

less active part, and rather more active as far as I am concerned, in *drafting the regulation of August 9, 1953. . . .*" (and this in spite of the fact that "legally" the Council has only an advisory capacity.)

When a government, such as that of Mendès-France in 1954 in the domain of alcohol, tries to reduce the power of these organisms to more moderate proportions, there is an outcry of indignation.[1] Agricultural organizations in particular are apt to consider that they alone are qualified to protect and organize agricultural markets provided that the State places its resources at their disposal.

This participation of interest groups in quasi-administrative organisms gives them considerable moral prestige with public opinion and even with the administration. It "authenticates" them, as it were. In addition it gives the group invaluable means of accomplishing their objectives although they will take great care not to admit this publicly and will even pretend not to have obtained satisfaction.

The groups derive still another though more subtle advantage from such a participation. When they are faced with governments whose intentions seem hostile to them, the groups noisily refuse to sit on these committees any longer. This brings forth a twofold advantage: on the one hand, the groups thus stir up public opinion and give the alarm to their "friends" in the houses of parliament. On the other, they impede the functioning of organisms to which the law has given far-reaching attributions and which, very often, should be consulted by the new government to study the new measures which it proposes. Thereafter, the only thing left for the administration to do is to take these measures alone which will sometime result, we must admit, in a blunder and which will in turn enable the groups to denounce loudly the procedure of decree-laws, nevertheless praised as long as a "friendly" government was in office. Then the groups can parade as the victims of the misuse

---

[1] In a note to his group in which he criticizes the measures by which the Mendès-France Government had reorganized the Interprofessional National Group of Beetgrowers, Dr. Gal of the Confederation of Beetgrowers wrote: "This new group holds no delegation of public power . . . (it) examines questions . . . informs public authorities about the elements of the market, expresses its opinion, proposes solutions . . . (but) in all cases the decision depends on the public authorities. No proposal may be transmitted to the authorities unless it has obtained a majority of ¾ of the members . . . ." After a comparison of the new with the old organization which gave the group much greater powers, the author concluded: "This text was conceived by an administration most jealous of its prerogatives. It used the procedure of decree-laws which enabled it to keep aloof from the organized interests. It refused the delegation of powers to the group. Yet will it insure the administration of agricultural markets? One of the most valid requests of agriculture vanishes in the procedure of the decree-laws . . . The Administration has won the first round."

of power by a government unfettered by controls. Of course, these maneuvers do not always succeed and they are sometimes double-edged. But a well organized group which has at its disposal an active lobby and the backing of the press, may find these maneuvers useful if it is faced with a harassed government, that has only a slim majority and is undermined from within by controversies between the different ministers.

Political Customs, Methods and Techniques

The role played by this last factor has already been shown in much of what has been said previously.

First hypothesis: It seems that because of a lack of political analysis and courage almost all members of parliament and all parties considerably over-estimate the political weight of pressure groups. Such a myth is lazily handed down from generation to generation within the parties and political circles like a legacy of political wisdom drawn from the experience of the old. One forgets, because they are not sensational, the numerous cases when pressure groups have failed.

Another feature of political morals: party comradeship. When the representative of a party in parliament is admittedly the spokesman of a pressure group, and there are perhaps less than sixty in this category, the party will doubtlessly avoid pushing this man to the forefront but it will also avoid breaking its ties with him. If such a deputy "controls" a big federation which ensures an appreciable share of the party finances, his bills and amendments might even get the party's votes. He will influence the ministers belonging to his party even if they hold him in low esteem.

But it is useless to insist further on the topic of political morals; it could fill a volume.

IV. The Role of the Government

The heterogeneous character of French governments is, of course, a factor that facilitates the pressure of interest groups inasmuch as the latter are in a position to exploit the rivalries of ministers and of their parties. All this is well known.

When for reasons of political balance the same sector has been divided among several ministers with different political affiliations (e.g. a Radical has been placed at the Ministry of Finance, an Independent at that of Commerce and Industry, a "social" M.R.P. at that of Industrial Production) then the situation is almost ideal for a skillful pressure group. If it knows how to maneuver and to moderate its demands somewhat, it may well succeed in winning one of the ministers as an ally in the very councils of government.

We may wonder whether the fact that a minister, and above all the Premier, is also administratively responsible to a party, does not make him more vulnerable to the pressure of interest groups than a minister without administrative responsibility in the party; indeed the former must be more attentive than others to the party's electoral interests and may have a less developed "governmental spirit." However this is simply an hypothesis.

The ever increasing importance which members of a minister's personal cabinet have for the minister and even for the whole government also seems to offer pressure groups many facilities for infiltration and influence. These "messengers" and collaborators of ministers replace the minister in many circumstances, conduct in his name negotiations with their colleagues in other ministries and with the representatives of interest groups; they frequently make promises which the minister, snowed under with work, cannot control. For the representatives of groups, they are the valid interlocutor; they may happen to be well informed about the questions that are put before them; generally their "boss," the minister, listens to them; much more confidential information can be obtained from them rather than from the head of an administrative service for they are well informed and want people to know it.

As, furthermore, they have absolutely no responsibility as all they risk is to be eventually fired, they may be precious allies for the groups. This is all the more true as decisions may actually be made directly by them, since many of them are very competent, and since the minister may feel free to short-circuit the administrative service concerned.

On the other hand, certain cases are known where a minister's personal cabinet is less submerged by the solicitations of groups than a long established administration which has undergone group pressure for many a year.

V. THE ROLE OF PARLIAMENT

It is beyond argument that pressure groups find considerable facilities in the fact that the finances of political parties are not the object of any sort of publicity whatsoever. Undoubtedly, even publicity and control would never completely eliminate occult and unavowable sources, but the mere existence of such controls and of sanctions against parties and "donors" would already appreciably limit the abuse and restrain the pressure groups.

The presence in parliament of the famous *"groupes d'études"* (formerly "defense groups"), created by pressure groups to do their lobbying, is probably a considerable asset to the groups. Very precise research in this field would be necessary, but the researchers would doubtlessly run into a rather general conspiracy of silence. Occasionally one could be lucky enough to take advantage of the rivalry between two "groupes d'études"; but that would not necessarily yield trustworthy results and furthermore there probably exist "non-agression pacts" between them.

The standing committees in parliament have very often been accused of favoring the action of pressure groups.

It is true that their great number, their specialized character, the great permanence of their staffs which are small enough to make individual contact with each one of them possible, their power to substitute the text of a bill as adopted by them for the initial version and to compel the Assembly to debate the committee's version are all factors that promote group action. In addition, their very great authority in debates, their almost complete discretion to decide that a text will be adopted without a debate, their almost limitless power to postpone the transmission of a bill to the plenary Assembly work in the same direction.

Yet all this favors pressure groups only insofar as the latter have succeeded in securing trustworthy allies on these committees. How do they succeed in doing so?

The committees of the National Assembly have only 44 members which undoubtedly limits the avenues of approach; nevertheless, a pressure group, except in some quite exceptional cases, can never count on the absolute devotion of a majority, i.e. of 22 or 23 members of a committee. As a matter of fact that is not necessary since not all committee members are active. Indeed, assiduousness is not the chief quality of them.

Finally, the action of pressure groups on committees is greatly favored by the non-publicity of their work. Like certain animals of the night, pressure groups fear the light of day.

VI. TECHNIQUES OF DECISION-MAKING

Legislative procedure has unquestionable advantages for pressure groups, above all when the majority is not *a priori* hostile to the groups. Only legislative procedure gives the alarm to warn pressure groups in time about threats hanging over them, it alone enables them to mobilize their allies, to intervene with committees, to wage the battle of amendments, etc.

All that is made possible and becomes effective only because of certain principles of our constitutional law on the one hand, and because of the working methods of our parliaments, especially of the National Assembly on the other.

The principle of parliamentary sovereignty results in the following: even when a law has turned over to administrative regulations those matters which previously had been the domain of parliament, such a redrawing of the lines between law and regulation does not bind parliament. The latter may very well take back its prerogatives over a domain which it had abandoned some months earlier, possibly during a session with not more than 40 deputies present. When the rules concerning a trade, such as that of the bar- and innkeepers, are entirely determined by laws and thereby, reserved forever to the legislature, unless parliament relinquishes explicitly its power, the pressure group concerned is safe from any major surprise action by the administration. Having nothing to fear from that direction, its lobbyists can concentrate all their efforts on parliament and especially on about twelve members of the Assembly's standing Committee on Drinks. This situation may change only when the Government uses emergency powers which enable it to act by decree and thus to take the groups unaware.

The methods of legislative work also bear a large share of responsibility. The very far-reaching right of every deputy to move bills and amendments allows pressure groups to exercise, through some of the members of the Assembly an actual right of indirect legislative initiative. Some deputies have no scruples about depositing, in their own name, bills and amendments which are simply and entirely borrowed from drafts drawn up by interest groups.

The procedure of administrative regulations unquestionably offers fewer opportunities for pressure groups to act. The minister himself, who is not very conversant with technical questions, has little time to deal with them, and if the members of his departmental staff, hold out against the pressures coming from interest groups, the minister generally lets the administrative services prepare the decisions. Most of the time, he defends his own services firmly against his colleagues in the cabinet. Now, the administration, on the whole, is rather impervious to the solicitations of interest groups unless it defends its clientele, i.e. people under its administration against the Minister of Finance or a minister directing a rival sector.[1]

---

[1] Another problem not directly connected with our investigation arises when certain very particularistic administrations, because they think that either their privileges or the interests which come under their purview, are threatened, come close to using certain methods of pressure groups with regard to other ministers and the parliament.

For some years past we have, for instance, seen the Army parade rather openly its recognized spokesmen in parliament. Not only the Army, but also other administrations such as the *Quai d'Orsay* intervene during the formation of governments to promote such and such a candidate for "its" ministry and try to push aside others. To bring more light in this matter, it would be necessary to write the political history of certain ministries or of certain *grands corps* of the administration.

But in the first place the administration is sometimes rather shy or at least respectful of the separation between the administrative and the political domain. In a situation where it comes up against a vigorous intervention of pressure groups and especially if the groups threaten to resort to extreme measures, labor or tax strikes, road-blocks, and the like, it may be inclined to have politics take over and leave the responsibility for all necessary decisions to the minister.

Besides, the guarantees which the procedure of administrative ordinances offer as a rule, dwindle rather considerably when the regulations and decrees are in fact no longer made by the administrative services alone and not even after a mere conference with representative organizations, but originate more and more frequently in those technical committees and councils where civil servants and group representatives sit together. Here it may often happen that civil servants are compelled to take as the basis of discussion a text which has been prepared by the interest groups. Moreover, it has become a widespread practice never to issue any regulations without soliciting first the opinion of the trade unions or trade associations. While in a few cases this method has led to desirable results, it generally gives many groups too many opportunities to make prevail demagogic and irrational claims.

The recourse to emergency powers granting the government the right to issue decree-laws or regulations of the same type offers the advantage that the scope and the strength of decisions taken in this way are generally considerable. Hence, pressure groups do not appreciate this procedure very much, at least not when it is used by a government in which they have few friends.

Yet this weapon of government wishing to govern is losing its edge more and more. In the first place, it has quite often happened since 1950 that the law granting emergency powers has insisted on the approval of all decrees by a parliamentary committee, usually the Finance Committee of the National Assembly. This alone gives pressure groups another chance—a limited chance, it is true, if the committee does not actually take part in drawing up the regulations. The procedure of the *loi-cadre* which lets Parliament discuss and amend regulations within a certain time limit, may offer the same type of possibilities.

Moreover, the optimum use of emergency powers would suppose that harmony reigns within the Government. Now, pressure groups soon understand that when the Government possesses emergency powers, the maximum strategic effort must be brought to bear on the ministers and no longer on parliament and its committees. But to be successful is undoubtedly more difficult since the minister is apt to become the advocate of his services and to acquire more or less consciously the "governmental spirit." It remains, however, possible to play on the rivalries between the different cabinet ministers and on the opposition of the parties forming the governmental team; it is also possible to try, preventively, when the cabinet is being formed, to push a "friend" into the suitable ministry or to neutralize a "questionable" minister by favoring a "friendly" under-secretary. In any case, we can see that the procedure of emergency powers obliges pressure groups to use an infinitely more complicated and difficult strategy which is beyond the means of a small organization or an organization whose only strength are the number of its members and verbal violence. All the latter can do then is to resort to the violent and spectacular methods that have been mentioned.

In any case, if it shows tenacity, a pressure group is not definitely disabled by emergency powers: the sovereignty of parliament allows it to undo what the government has done by decree, by virtue of a formal authorization of the same parliament.

VII. General Trends and the Results of Pressure Activities

The "Tone"

There exist certainly some very effective pressure groups in France which we never hear of except in a rather mythical way (the "money wall" for instance), because they are discreet and act behind the scenes. No scholarly study of their behavior or endeavors can be pursued very far. Hence we are compelled to investigate those that act openly or almost so.

As far as the latter are concerned, the most striking feature is the growing exasperation of their behavior during the last few years.

The difficulties of France, the rancour left by the war, the bitterness caused by the indecision of the political teams that have succeeded one another in power and the more and more apparent defects of our political system have made political struggles very bitter. People quickly accuse one another of the worst offenses, they customarily resort to exaggerations.

The result is a frenzy which soon reaches its climax in the declarations and positions of the different interest groups and even of the most harmless ones. All confidence in discussion and in the impartiality of the state seems lost. Everyone seems to think that only a demonstration of strength will attract attention to his claims and to his point of view. For fear of being outdistanced by others or of being placed before an accomplished fact, the groups demand and threaten before the danger is imminent. They demand not only to be consulted but also to take part in decision making, they claim the right not to accept it if it does not give them at least 90 per cent satisfaction; for safety's sake they carry their claims to 110 per cent.

Trends

French employers and business organizations have often been accused of always exerting their political pressure in a very strictly protectionist and conservative way (in the economic meaning of the word). Of course, many examples could be furnished to back up this thesis.

Nevertheless our personal impression is that this attitude is undergoing a transformation at the present time. Undoubtedly as a result of a greater degree of economic education we see fewer prejudices about the mechanism of the economic intervention of the State, a lessening, albeit a cautious one, of the passionate distrust of all official activities in the field of economic forecasting. If the permanent staffs of trade associations and of other corporative organizations still find it necessary to justify their functions by vehement and systematic protests at the least alarm, we may observe, on the other hand, a more rational and subtle behavior among industrialists and even among less "engaged" farmers. More and more we see that they are anxious to get first as much exact information as possible (and preferably from other sources than those of their own organizations) and not to refuse contacts with certain administrative services. The distrust of new techniques and methods, as well as of such terms as reconversion and modernization, remains great but has become less systematic.

A convincing enough token of this change of attitude was the recent behavior of interest groups with regard to plans for the European Common Market.[1] Doubtlessly the mechanism of a liberal economy established by the Common Market, the hopes entertained by some businessmen that indirectly the new institutions, by fixing costs at an average European level, could result in a slight reduction of the French social charges, might have created a favorable predisposition. However, all this does not compensate for the considerable risk that French industry

[1] The author of this paper is personally hostile to the plan for the Common Market in its present form.

and even some agricultural producers will run on the Common Market. Although these risks have been weighed with apprehension in most circles, it is nevertheless remarkable that they have been evaluated objectively, sometimes after rather searching study, and on the whole have been accepted.

From May to June 1957 (our analysis is limited to this period) a great number of interest groups pronounced themselves in favor of the Common Market.[1] Those that were opposed were far less numerous.[2]

The Results of Political Pressures

It stands to reason that not all pressure groups are all-powerful. But do some of them succeed in imposing, in most if not all cases, their will on the public powers? Or, to put it more generally, does the total amount of the innumerable pressures of all groups (powerful and weak) succeed over a long period, in neutralizing or "domesticating" political power? Who governs?

Any definite answer, in one direction or the other, must be more or less conditioned by the political and ideological convictions of the person who gives it. One thing seems certain to me, namely that at the present time we do not possess sufficient objective data in France for an objective and balanced answer to the questions raised.

Most certainly there is no lack of cases in which a sufficiently direct relation between the political action of the interest group and the authoritative decision by the state yielding to such pressures can be established. The previously discussed struggle of the alcohol lobby against the anti-alcoholic measures of the Mendès-France government is a good illustration.[3] One may mention other cases selected at random:

—the pressures and obstructionist maneuvers of quantities of interest groups (medical circles, agricultural and employers' organizations, mu-

[1] For instance, the National Trade Association of Wool Industries, the National Council of Commerce, the Confederation of Wholesalers, the National Committee of the Middle Classes, The Congress of Consumers' and Agricultural Cooperatives and of Credit Unions. A more reserved position was taken by the Congress of the Hatters' Trade, the General Confederation of Small and Medium-sized Enterprises, the Association of great French Harbours. Of course, this does not mean that after expressing a favorable opinion, these interest groups will not use strong pressure on the government to obtain serious protection before the effective opening of the Common Market. Nevertheless all this represents quite a distinct change in behavior.

[2] For instance the National Associations of the Cotton Industry, and of the Engineering Industries.

[3] For an analysis of this situation see also Bernard E. Brown, "Alcohol and Politics in France," *The American Political Science Review*, vol. LI (1947) pp. 976-994.

tual benefit societies) succeeded in blocking for many a month the administrative ordinances enacting the law of April 5, 1928 on Social Security. The same forces wrested from parliament the law of April 30, 1928 granting farmers special treatment.

—in 1945 the C.F.T.C., (Catholic Trade Unions), the family associations and the mutual benefit societies exercised strong pressure on the M.R.P. and the moderate parties, in order to ensure against the advice of the Ministry of Labor and the C.G.T., the autonomy of the Funds for Family Allowances. In 1946, on the other hand, the C.G.T. obtained the principle of the administrations of the Funds by the workers and the nominations of the administrations by the most representative labor unions; in 1957 a front composed of employers' organizations, independent workers and the middle classes succeeded in blocking the enforcement of a law extending old age benefits to all non-wage-earners; also in 1957 the medical and pharmaceutical associations held in check reform proposals which the Minister of Labor wanted to enact in the field of Social Security.

—in the course of 1955 the strong pressure of the Poujade Movement on political parties led the government of Edgar Faure to abandon certain attempts at stricter enforcement of the tax laws.

—in 1951 the pressure of the *"Secrétariat d'Etudes pour la Liberté de l'Enseignement"* brought to bear especially against the M.R.P., led to the vote of the Barangé law, and delayed the formation of a government for six weeks after the elections.

—in 1954 the unflagging pressure campaign certainly contributed to the rejection by the National Assembly of the Treaty on the European Defense Community.

—from 1928 to 1939 the continuous efforts of the Confederation of Beetgrowers succeeded in exempting the price of beets from the slump in world prices, through effective tariff protection (1929), through a renewal of quotas (1934) and finally through an "alcohol statute" which ensured producers that the State would purchase their produce for the distilling of alcohol well above world prices (1935).

—after the formation of the Bourgès-Maunoury Government, the Association of Presidents of the Chambers of Commerce, by a letter to the Chairman of the Finance Committee in the National Assembly obtained a change in the proposed tax reform.

Examples of this kind (and we have given but a very small selection) are of course impressive. Nevertheless a few remarks must be added to show their exact scope:

a) Relatively speaking it is much more difficult to keep an exact account of the failures of pressure groups. But they exist.

b) We should notice that the most notorious successes obtained by interest groups are defensive in character. They frequently succeed in blocking measures; they are perhaps less fortunate when they try to achieve new advantages. But this, of course, does not attenuate the harmfulness of the pressure.

c) the efficacy of pressure groups seems to be greater in a period of economic depression or financial crisis when the governments themselves hesitate about the measures to take. Besides the groups always take advantage of a predisposition existing within parties or within certain ministerial or administrative cliques; they seldom succeed in altering completely the policies of a whole party or even of a government.

In conclusion we offer three additional observations:

(1) The degree of independence asserted by the political power with regard to the injunctions and pressure of interest groups poses both a theoretical and a practical problem. The theoretical problem presents itself as follows: do the constitutional texts empower the representative organisms to express the general will and is the present mode of representation adequate? If the problem is not insoluble, it is most certainly too vast to be treated here. The technical problem is the following: what means can guarantee as far as possible the autonomous decision of the instruments of political power, or, what techniques may enable the legislator, the government and the administration to deliberate and to reach decisions secure from pressures which are all strictly particularistic?

These problems give rise to all but unlimited reflections. In the case of France, we would like to suggest two remedies on the administrative level.

In the first place there is serious danger in the proliferation of technical committees and councils which take an increasingly large share in the functions of the administration and often usurp them. These organizations literally decompose the very function of the power of the state insofar as they impregnate them with a particularistic spirit. The objection will be raised that this collaboration of "professionals" in the administration of things (but also, finally in the government of men) is indispensable because it will offset the lack of experience of civil servants. The argument does not seem absolutely valid to us. In fact, the argument raises the problem of the training of civil servants, especially by the university. It is true that, as a result of a formation which is far too theoretical, the majority of civil servants are too often at a loss when they are faced with concrete questions; they do not know much about running an enterprise, or the functioning of a market, have never set foot in a trade union office or a dairy cooperative, etc. The entire educational system, beginning with the primary schools, must be reorganized; the whole method of recruiting our civil servants, especially for the central administration must be reconsidered. The problem here considered also brings up the question of technical decentralization. In our opinion there is an advantage in maintaining an administration that makes its decisions alone, provided that its training is adequate. But the administration ought to make relatively few decisions, leaving a rather large autonomy to the organized interests which however must act within the framework of general directives.

In the second place, the so-called advisory boards and councils must be criticized for comprising only specialists belonging to the same field or trade, since this crystallizes and hardens their particularism. On the contrary, organisms uniting representatives of several fields and representing different interests ought to be encouraged and increased in number. Perhaps it would be just as well to prevent that the various organizations are automatically represented on these organisms by members of their permanent staff, for the latter are by their very calling "officials of protestation." It must be admitted that technically the problem is difficult to solve.

(2) The power of pressure groups, their influence on political circles, and the very incoherence of their claims would be considerably lessened if the political and economic education of the public were better developed. If that is a commonplace, it is nevertheless a serious problem.

(3) A problem of capital importance involves those categories of people whose interests are not defended at all or are badly defended, by the existent network of interest organizations. The typical case in France at present is that of people who are poorly, insufficiently, or too expensively housed. If no pressure group whatsoever existed, their voice would be heard by the political power. But plagued as it is by the claims, threats, and pressures of the best equipped interests groups, political power is reduced to estimating the legitimacy and urgency of interests according to the importance of the organizations speaking in their name. Especially for the sake of the unorganized interests, the real, even if only partial, independence of political power from the pressures of organized interests, must be obtained and safeguarded.

BIBLIOGRAPHICAL NOTE

Bernard E. Brown, "Pressure Politics in France", *Journal of Politics*, vol. XVIII (1956), pp. 702–19.

Bernard E. Brown, "Alcohol and Politics in France," *American Political Science Review*, vol. LI (1957), pp. 976–94.

Henry W. Ehrmann, "The French Trade Association and the Ratification of the Schuman Plan," *World Politics*, vol. VI (1954), pp. 453–81.

Henry W. Ehrmann, *Organized Business in France*, Princeton 1957.

Georges E. Lavau, "Note sur un 'pressure group' français: La Confédération Générale des Petites et Moyennes Entreprises," *Revue Française de Science Politique*, vol. V (1955), pp. 370–83.

Henri Mendras, "Les Organisations agricoles et la politique," *id.*, vol. V (1955), pp. 736–60.

Jean Meynaud, "Contribution a l'analyse des groupes d'intérêt dans la vie politique française," *Revue de l'Institut de Sociologie (Solvay)*, (1956), pp. 225–56.

Jean Meynaud, "L'intervention des groupes d'intérêt dans la politique économique," *Revue économique et sociale*, vol. XIV (1956), pp. 256–77.

Jean Meynaud, "Essai d'analyse de l'influence des groupes d'intérêt," *Revue Economique* (1957), pp. 177–220.

Jean Meynaud, "Les groupes d'intérêt et l'Administration en France," *Revue Française de Science Politique*, vol. VII (1957), pp. 573–593.

Jean Meynaud, *Les groupes de pression en France*, Paris, 1958.

René Rémond, "Les anciens combattants et la politique," *Revue Française de Science Politique*, vol. V (1955), pp. 267–90.

Jean-Michel Royer, "Quelques groupes de pression vus a travers leur presse," in Association Française de Science Politique, *Les Elections du 2 Janvier 1956*, Paris 1957, pp. 142–64.

Philip Williams, *Politics in Post-War France*, London, 1954, pp. 327–41.

Gordon Wright, "Agrarian Syndicalism in postwar France," *American Political Science Review*, vol. LVII (1953), pp. 402–16.

Various Authors, "Pouvoir Politique et Pouvoir Economique" *Esprit* vol. XXI (1953), pp. 817–976.

SOME REMARKS ON INTEREST GROUPS IN THE GERMAN FEDERAL REPUBLIC*

WOLFGANG HIRSCH-WEBER

I. IDENTIFICATION OF INTEREST GROUPS

This paper will list a few of the interest groups which may be considered to exercise most influence in Western Germany. No attempt at rigid classification will be made, since the author believes that for such an attempt the time is not ripe. More should be known about the aims, the membership, the structure, and the activities of the groups before a systematic classification can be undertaken. At present, it should be sufficient to group the organizations loosely.

The question immediately arises, which groups are to be called "interest groups." The author will not attempt to define the term, because he thinks that common discussions at the Round Table will be better suited to produce a comprehensive definition than his own limited research. Instead, he will use the word as it is commonly done and will include in his list those organizations that are by wide agreement termed interest groups. The agreement, of course, is not complete. It can be argued, for instance, that the trade unions are a social movement, and, as such, are of a different order than manufacturers' associations, or that the Churches have aims which are not of this world, and which escape classification as "interests." This may be true. But one cannot deny that, besides their ideological or religious goals, these groups have specific interests, which can be furthered or curtailed by the state, by other groups or by individuals. Inasmuch as they pursue their interests through channels which are basically the same, namely those of the given state and the given society, the activities of these groups can be reduced to a common denominator. True, some of the groups listed below may not only be interested groups, but they are also interest groups.

* The writing of this report was greatly facilitated by the help the author received from his colleagues at the Institut für politische Wissenschaft, Dr. Günter Remmling, Dr. Heinz Rothenburg and Klaus Schütz. Very valuable were the comments and the advice of Dr. Renate Mayntz.

For investigations of a different scope than that given to this paper it might not be sufficient to view them as interest groups, but for the present purposes such an abstraction is viable.

Trade Unions and Employers' Associations

It may be useful to start with a description of the organizations which represent the conflicting interests of labor and employers. On the labor side, the most impressive organization is the *Deutscher Gewerkschaftsbund* (DGB), a federation of associations. This federation consists of 16 national "industrial" unions with about 6.1 million members—this and the following figures refer to September 30, 1955—while the number of gainfully employed in the Federal Republic amounts to about 18.3 million. Each union tries to organize a whole industry, branch or service, including all salaried persons: workers, employees, and public servants. The unions are federated in the DGB not only on the national, but also on regional and local levels. While they maintain complete independence in their wage-policies (despite some recent efforts of co-ordination), it is the task of the DGB to represent "common interests in all matters, especially those of economic, social and cultural policies." This does not mean, however, that political activities are restricted exclusively to the DGB. Industrial unions can become politically active in questions of their special concern.

Since Rosa Luxemburg and Robert Michels it is assumed that German unions are highly bureaucratized and controlled by an oligarchical leadership wielding almost unlimited power. Unless we have scientific insight into the organizational structure of the unions, and know more about members' participation in trade union activities, Michels' hypothesis cannot be proven or disproven. On the basis of superficial knowledge, one might be safe in saying that, while Michels overstated his case, the union-leaders have great authority indeed and enjoy long tenure of office. The power vested in the higher leadership is not concentrated exclusively in the executive committee of the DGB; the regional "bosses" and the heads of the industrial unions participate in it. In this context it may be mentioned that, while this paper is being written, the headquarters of the Social Democratic Party (SPD) seem to make an attempt to get seats in parliament for at least the chairmen of the biggest industrial unions. The president and the two vice-presidents of the DGB refused to be candidates!

The power of the union leaders is not unlimited. Two checks seem to be specially strong: overlapping membership and the views of the workers (and of their wives) on the need for wage increases and the advisability or non-advisability of strikes. To explain overlapping member-ship, it is necessary to refer to the unions' history. Up to 1933 there existed in Germany Socialist, Christian (mainly Catholic), and Liberal trade unions, the socialists attracting about 80% or more of organized labor. The different organizations were not always on the best terms, but they presented often a common front, and shortly before the nazis took power, the political and economic situation encouraged efforts to amalgamate the Socialist, Christian and Liberal unions. It was too late. In May, 1933, the unions were prohibited, many of their leaders persecuted. It was mainly due to their common experiences under nazi rule, that after the war, unionists of all convictions joined efforts in building the DGB. Among the members, as well as among the leaders of this organization, the socialists outnumber by far the Christian group and the numerically unimportant Liberals. (Communists are barred from union office.) Since politically interested union members are more prone to engage in organizational work than the politically aloof, union officials are usually recruited from the former group. And as the So-cialists have a majority in almost all of the constituent bodies, they could easily outvote the Christians and the Liberals for nearly all posi-tions of higher officialdom. In fact, the presidents of the industrial un-ions are with minor exceptions exclusively Social Democrats. However, in order to maintain unity the unions have to give due representation in their executive bodies to the Christian members. Also in their poli-cies, they do not want to ignore the confessional and political loyalities of the minority, and try to remain neutral between the Christian-Demo-cratic-Union (CDU) and the SPD. On the other hand, the DGB can-not disregard the views of its militant socialist members. In the past, there have arisen a few conflicts between the DGB leadership and Chris-tian trade unionists (notably in 1953, when the federation published an election-manifesto which the CDU considered to favor the SPD). Unity, however, could be maintained, and only a very small minority of Christian unionists, led by a CDU-deputy, stood in constant opposi-tion, and in 1956 finally left the organization to found the *Christliche Gewerkschaftsbewegung Deutschlands*. They were supported by the International of the Christians Unions and by part of the higher Catho-lic clergy, but could not get Protestant approval. How many members this organization has, cannot be established with certainty. There seem to be very few.

The DGB wishes to represent the interests of workers and employees alike, and has succeeded in organizing about 640.000 white-collar work-ers. More than 420.000 employees, however, are associated in the *Deut-*

sche Angestelltengewerkschaft (DAG). This split in the union movement is due to a view, fairly widespread among white-collar-workers,
that they have particular interests which should find organized expression. As the industrial unions refused to have special associations of
employees within the DGB, the DAG was set up as an independent
union. The two organizations are separated not so much by their programs (both advocate socialization of basic industries, co-determination,
"social justice" etc.) nor by major policies, but by organizational rivalries, which have sometimes led to bitter fights. Before 1933, the Socialist white-collar union had to compete with strong associations of
other political convictions, and attracted only about 25 to 30% of organized salaried persons. Accordingly, among the DAG members, the
Social Democrats cannot claim as strong a support as in the DGB.
Among the civil servants, however, this party holds a majority also in
the DAG.

Far more fundamental than the differences between the DAG and the
DGB are those between the latter and the *Deutscher Beamtenbund*
(DBB). In the German Federal Republic a very high percentage of public employees have tenure, are *"Beamte"* (full fledged civil servants).
Both the DGB and the DBB, and to a very small degree the DAG, try
to win them as members. The DGB has room for *"Beamte"* only within
its industrial unions, while the DBB is purely a civil servants association.
In the former there are about 420,000, in the latter almost 520,000 civil
servants, wherewith nearly all *"Beamte"* are organized. The interests
represented by the DGB and the DBB seem to differ, due to social and in
some degree due to economic differences in the membership. In the DBB,
members of the upper echelons of the civil service are more numerous
than in the DGB. The DGB, on the other hand, is strong among workers
of the railroads, post office, etc., many of whom have tenure, thus being
"Beamte." The economic interests of these groups are common as long
as a general raise in salaries is demanded, but there are tendencies,
voiced by the DBB, to widen, or at least conserve, existing wage differen-
tials. Nevertheless, the basic disagreements between the DBB and the
DGB are not economic, but of other nature. In publicly owned industries, railroads, etc., intense animosities between workers with or without tenure, and the higher ranks of civil servants are frequent. These
animosities cannot but leave a mark on the two associations which recruit their members, as a rule, from different ranks of the public service.
Furthermore, there exist, perhaps not independently of what has just
been said, ideological differences. While the DGB is friendly towards
the Social Democracy, there are few Socialists on the executives of the

is on the whole conservative. Besides, there are or-
ries and jealousies also between these two associations.
g enough to warrant separate associations embodying
ic, but differing political and social interests.
ployers' side, there exists in private industry one all-embrac-
ion, the *Bundesvereinigung der Deutschen Arbeitgeberver-*
e BDA is a federation of federations, organized on the na-
d on regional levels, its members being federations of employ-
ociations in all branches of the economy: industry and mining,
, agriculture, commerce, banking, insurance, and other trades. The
A tries to coordinate the wage policies of the thirty-five constituent
derations, and pursues common interests in social policies which
transcend particular economic branches and territories. It emphasizes
the need for solidarity of employers from all branches of the economy
in defending private property, the entrepreneur's initiative and his
right to unhampered decision-making. This solidarity, the BDA says,
should be national and international, and should guide the members
also in political matters.

Very little is known about the way in which decisions are arrived at in
the employers' associations. Big business seems to be quite influential in
the federation, and apparently a relatively small number of industrialists hold a rather considerable number of positions in the associations.
But there is no information about how highly the different branches of
the economy are organized, how heavily they weigh in the federation,
and how actively the members intervene in the decision-making process.
In the BDA, disruptive influences springing from overlapping membership are not apparent. Some economic interests might sharply conflict
within a branch, or between the different branches of the economy, but
this will not necessarily disrupt an organization based on the common
interest of employers, at least not if the overwhelming majority of them
profess basically similar social philosophies. This they do. Thus, the
employers oppose a single organization to a not so highly organized, and
not completely united labor front.

Business, Artisans, and Agriculture

Business is densely organized in the Federal Republic, and of its
many groups, the most impressive, and probably the most powerful, is
the *Bundesverband der Deutschen Industrie* (BDI). The BDI comprises
38 industrial associations, themselves federations. While in the BDA
property owners belonging to all branches of the economy, are organized
as employers, the BDI accepts only industrialists who, as employers, are

simultaneously members of the BDA. (It is understood that the terms "owners" and "industrialists" apply to individuals as well as to corporations.) The BDI represents the common interests of manufacturers and is the official spokesman of industry as a whole in public relations as well as in its relations with the legislature and the executive.

The decision-making process in the BDI has yet to be studied. As regards bureaucratization there is no doubt that staffs are numerous, indeed: The BDI comprises about 700 single associations (the corresponding figure for the BDA is 800), each with their own executives, experts, secretaries, etc. It would be wrong, however, to deduct from their number that all the power rests with the paid staff members. The members of the highest decision-making bodies are themselves industrialists, patrimonial owners or managers, but preponderantly executives of big corporations. It is not clear how far the BDI's policies are determined by them or by the organization's staff.

One of the presidents of the *Reichsverband der Deutschen Industrie*, the Weimar forerunner of the BDI, once said that perhaps the most difficult problem in a peak association is the balancing of conflicting interests. Undoubtedly, also in our time interests of different industrial branches may be contradictory, and the larger the interest groups are, the more this is felt. However, there also exist the uniform interests of industry as distinct from the rest of the economy, and the basic interest of capital-owners; both of those factors help to unite the manufacturers' associations. This unity is bolstered by common social philosophies, which give to the policies of both BDI and BDA a definite slant.

The cohesion within the BDI which is brought about by common interests and fundamental ideologies is not destroyed by the members' loyalty to different political parties. Several parties are friendly towards capital and attractive to property owners. (Of course, some businessmen are affiliated with the SPD, but their number is small.) It is not known if conflicts between the "bourgeois" parties are leading to controversies within the BDI. But as to the parties themselves, the sources of their finances, to be discussed subsequently, obviously do not permit them to ignore the opinions of the BDI.

Together with the BDA, with the organizations of banking, commerce, insurance, shipping, etc., with the union of chambers of industry and commerce, and with the central association of artisans, the BDI forms the *Gemeinschaftsausschuss der deutschen gewerblichen Wirtschaft*. It should be noticed that this all-embracing organization of business interests is a coalition of federations whose members are federations themselves. Thus, we get a picture of numerous specialized business groups, forming federation which unite in central organizations and, finally form a general coalition. The contacts between the specialized groups are, however, not restricted to their meeting in central organizations. Just as individual firms can be members of many interest groups—different trade associations, employers' organizations, a chamber of commerce, etc.—so the interest groups can, and frequently do, join several federations.

The above mentioned central association of artisans is a kind of national guild of handicraft. Its avowed object is to reach a uniform policy and to represent common interests before the Government. The association has formed, together with the central organizations of the owners of houses and of real estate, of the retail trade, with the federation of civil servants, and with the agrarian organizations, the *Deutsche Mittelstandblock*.

Probably, the most highly organized sector of Western German economy is agriculture. Almost all farmers are members of associations which united in a central coalition, render very important services. As in the Weimar Republic, the cohesion of agricultural associations is not destroyed by conflicting interests. The "green front," not seldom aggressively engaged in politics, has a remarkable unity of purpose. In the political sphere, there is little danger from conflicting party loyalties. More than 50 per cent of the farmers vote CDU (Christian-Democrats). In farmers' associations there is, however, discontent with certain aspects of the CDU's agrarian policy. This moved some officials of farmers' groups to ask members to vote for other bourgeois parties. As a matter of fact, in some rural regions these parties, such as the FDP (Free Democrats) and the DP (German Party) are deeply rooted. The CDU is working closely together with the DP, but since recently is in conflict with the FDP. Only among agricultural labor has the SPD rural following of any consequence.

Expellees, Disabled Veterans, etc.

Nazi-rule, the war and its aftermath have had varying conseqences for different parts of the population. There are the persecuted of the nazi-regime, the millions of persons driven out of Germany's Eastern provinces or those who fled the Soviet zone of occupation, disabled veterans, war orphans and widows, former active nazis and expellees who lost their civil service jobs, etc. All these persons can put forward claims—for restitution or redistribution of property, for pensions, etc.—and many associations have sprung up to organize these interests. By the nature of their claims, the main addressee of these groups is the government. Effects of overlapping membership can be observed in several associations, but not in all.

The Churches

A very powerful interest group in the Federal Republic is the Catholic Church. Its points of access within the governmental process are the parties as well as the legislature and the executive. To secure a parliament and an administration favorable to its positions, the Church calls on the Catholic citizen, most intensely in rural districts, to vote "Christian" (i.e. CDU). The Catholic interests are furthered not only by the Church proper, but also through a great number of subsidiary associations. The Protestant Churches do not intervene in party politics. Quite a number of protestants are, of course, actively engaged in politics, but the Churches as such do not take a position for or against political parties.

Civic Groups

The number of civic associations is small, and their membership is not significant. Only a thorough analysis of Western German society could explain this phenomenon satisfactorily. Several possible reasons, howere, may be suggested:

(1) The tradition of the authoritarian state. Only during the 14 years of the Weimar Republic, and in the last 10 years, have Germans lived under conditions favorable to the individual citizen's political initiative. This is a short time to learn the ways of civic activities.

(2) Frustration or distrust. The fate of nazism has left many of those frustrated who believed in its ideology, and has caused a general distrust against the emotions often associated with civic activities. On the other hand, the "restorative" course of German politics after 1947 has disappointed those who, after the disaster, had hoped for fundamental social changes.

Perhaps the most important reason for the absence of strong civic groups, is the existence of ideologically oriented political parties. If parties voice civic interests, advocate for instance democratic or liberal government, there is no incentive for forming other associations with the same aims. As we have seen labor, business and other groups are permeated by social philosophies and have ideological aims. This too makes civil groups seem superfluous.

Group Financing and Anti-Lobbying Legislation

Detailed studies on the financing of groups are lacking. It can be assumed that in most cases they are financed mainly by members' dues.

This is true of the trade unions, which, however, probably draw some income from their properties and investments. The BDA raises dues in proportion to the wages and salaries paid by the members. One or the other public interest group, as well as expellee-organizations, etc., obtain government subsidies.

The Basic law of the Federal Republic provides that party finances be made public. Since the implementing laws are not yet passed no such publicity obtains as yet. A commission of university professors was called together by the Minister of the Interior to advise on the drafting of these laws. The commission also discussed the advisability of legislation concerning lobbying activities, though it did not pronounce itself officially on this matter.*

II. Interest Groups and Public Opinion

The esteem in which public opinion in Western Germany holds different interest groups has never been analyzed thoroughly. The author can only report impressions. Besides, since there is not one public opinion, but a number of divergent opinions any appraisal is made more complicated.

Several scholars, some political circles, the press and a wider public, view in general interest groups with disfavor. But whether the majority of the population holds a clear and discerning opinion on "interest groups" is more than dubious. One reason for the bad reputation of interest groups touches on mythology: a belief in the state as a separate, independent, superhuman entity whose intercourse with the individual should be free from interference by "outside" agencies such as interest groups. But one does not need profess this credo to be legitimately concerned about the practices and about the growing number and power of interest groups. The population of the Federal Republic has reached general consensus on relatively few matters, its present political system is young and not very deeply rooted. In such a situation, there is danger that associations defending special interests may challenge successfully the preponderance of institutions like parties, parliament and the administration which should represent and defend the widest general interests. Thus, out of influence could grow control of the governmental process by one group or by a coalition of interest groups. A development in this direction might be checked by strengthening the roots of democratic government, and by making the parties less financially dependent on interest groups. While it is to be doubted whether lobbying really

* The bibliography to this report contains the commission's suggestions on party finance, and an essay by Professor Stammer, based on his work on the commission.

can be driven into the open, a check on the power of oligarchies in interest groups could be established by vitalizing the democratic processes within the groups themselves. In the last resort, democracy requires that there be democrats. It should be clear that the governmental process in its present form is doomed if the strongest interest groups are not aware of a minimum of civic responsibilities.

Some people would say that all interest groups are evil, but that trade unions are more evil than others. Other people, of course,—but they are fewer—would find fault only with business groups. This was not always so. Immediately after the war the unions were—besides the Churches—the only German institutions with any authority, and had occasionally to take over governmental functions. Instead of putting forward claims, they calmed the hungry workers. Since at that time progressive tendencies were widespread in the society, the unions were held in high esteem. All this has changed. With the increase of restorative tendencies the unions power and prestige diminished. But there were also other reasons for this development. The unions, especially when putting pressure on parliament, made psychological mistakes. Besides, there was a skillful, and sometimes malicious anti-union campaign exploiting a "natural" fear of the DGB as a wealthy organization of 6,000,000 members which could paralyze economic life. One cannot dismiss completely the possibility that the unions may disrupt the governmental process by exaggerated pressure on parliament or the executive, but they will hardly do so intentionally. The DGB considers itself to be the strongest guardian of democracy, and has declared that it would defend the Federal Republic, if need be, against Nazi or Communist subversion, as the unions did in the Weimar Republic with a general strike against the reactionary Kapp-upheaval. (A remarkable example of an interest group defending civic interests!)

For members and their colleagues the DGB published, in 1955, 69 weekly and monthly newspapers and magazines with a total circulation of more than 8 (possibly up to 13) million. However, the unions have no dailies or weeklies with which to reach a public wider than the trade unionists and their colleagues. For this they are dependent on the reporting of the general press, which they supply with a Press and Information-Service. This, of course, is not sufficient for maintaining satisfactory public relations, especially as the unions cannot count on favorable reporting in all daily newspapers. However, they have a possibility to secure unbiased news-broadcasts, the radio stations in the Federal Republic being public institutions. Their boards include members of the state legislatures and governments, representatives of the

Churches and the universities, the trade unions and employers, writers' and composers' associations, etc.

The unions have extended educational interests. The DGB and its affiliated unions own a number of schools and academies in which members are trained for varieties of elective offices accessible to trade unions, and for administrative posts within the unions themselves. Besides, they are interested in vocational training and in adult education. Several union leaders are members of educational and university boards and of academic foundations.

Employers', businessmen and artisans' associations have quite a different standing in the community than the unions. First of all, they are rarely forced to work in the open, but can operate behind the scenes. Thus, people are far less conscious of their very existence than of that of the unions. But even if wider circles were informed about them, they would be more popular than labor because they seem more respectable and because their members have a higher social status. The values they hold—private property, authority, etc.—are those of the majority. Especially when they speak about the defense of the middle classes, they can be sure of broad sympathy. Always in calm times, things are easier for the defenders of the established order than for those who want changes. But even if all this were not true, the prestige of organized business in public opinion would be bolstered by the good contacts it has with the press through ownership and advertising. Last but not least, the leaders of these associations, experienced as they are in marketing, are much more conscious of the value of and are skillful in public relations work than union officials. The business organizations publish a regular press service, and can count on the general, though not always unconditional, sympathy of several daily papers.

Other associations whose existence and whose influence are not widely publicized, are those of agriculture. This anonymity has not precluded their effectiveness. Their pressure has succeeded in securing a high degree of agrarian protectionism within an economy priding itself on being laissez-faire. One should not suppose that these groups themselves desire to remain in the dark. Farmers feeling somewhat antagonistic towards industry and the city, are proud of their role in society, and adhere, naturally, to ideologies which exalt them. Contrarywise, it is doubtful whether romantic peasant ideologies would nowadays, after certain recent experiences, be as well received in the city as twenty or thirty years ago.

As to the churches, Nazi persecution heightened their prestige and strengthened their position in post-war Germany. They are treated with utmost care by everybody, and even the SPD reacts weakly, if at all, against attacks by the Catholic clergy. Some Protestants and liberal Catholics feel apprehensive about Catholic policies which could be termed assertive, but any outspoken criticism is rare. Both churches are represented in the boards of the broadcasting systems, of movie-self-censorship, and other cultural institutions. They are highly interested and influential in education and in the training of teachers. Confessional schools, desired by the Catholic Church, are politically highly controversial with the CDU in favor, the SPD and FDP opposed.

III. Interest Groups and Political Parties

Interest groups and parties interact intensely. For the purposes of this report, it should be sufficient to outline the relationship between the two big parties—CDU and SPD—and several interest groups, and to mention only in passing the small parties—the FDP, the DP, and the GB/BHE (All-German Block Association of the Homeless and Disenfranchised).

The structure of the CDU is extremely complicated. To describe it in a few sentences, one has to simplify dangerously. The remarkable regional differences, for instance, in the party's structure, and the relative influence of interest groups within it, cannot be discussed here. The CDU shelters many and divergent interests. It aspires to unite Christians of both denominations, has a labor wing, and maintains close contact with industry, big business and middle class groups. To give these sometimes conflicting interests a representation within the party, special committees are set up. The majority of their members belong to associations or identify informally with certain interests groups: the "Social Committee" consists mainly of Christian trade unionists, in the "Economic Committee" are to be found distinguished industrialists, bankers and businessmen, in the "Refugee Committee" officials of expellee-organizations. Here, we are not confronted with pressure the interests groups bring to bear on a party, but with activities of interest groups within it. The CDU takes thus a role which classical theory had reserved for the state, namely that of integrating diverging interests. Of course, the interest groups within the party are not equally successful in determining the party's policies, and it has not always been easy to settle conflicts between them, but up to now cohesion has been maintained. Whether this will always be the case is yet to be seen. Nevertheless, it should not be overlooked that the party's cohesion is maintained not only by the dominating figure of its leader, and by the successful integration of economic interests, but also by common ideologies and political views. The bargaining between interest groups is probably facilitated by the fact that the CDU is not a party based predominantly on membership. It has about 200,000 members, three times less than the SPD, though it rallies considerably more voters. Moreover, the overwhelming majority of the members are not very active in determining the party's policies. Their basic views, however, must be respected. Decisions originate with the regional and national executive committees, into which the interest groups reach, and with the party leader.

The small number of members and their reluctance to pay high dues make the CDU dependent on outside financing, and it receives indeed generous contributions. (With the help of several deputies from other parties, the CDU had a law passed which allows tax deductions for contributions to parties!) The money, generally, is not given by single wealthy persons, but by sponsors' organizations set up by business associations which in turn levy their members. The banding together in the common front of sponsors' organizations naturally strengthens the position of the donating business groups in their dealing with the recipients. The help the CDU obtains at election time—generally wholesale, but occasionally also pinpointed—is not only financial. There are special associations making propaganda for the coalition parties in newspaper advertisements, etc. Besides, there are the exhortations from the pulpit to vote for a "Christian" party, and the insinuations of several associations to vote for "a party sympathetic to the group's aims." Both the Catholic Church and many associations publish a great variety of papers and magazines devoted to the information of their members. (The Catholic Church and its subsidiary associations publish altogether 254 periodicals with a circulation of 10.5 million). Some of these publications openly support the CDU.

The SPD is close to certain groups within the Protestant clergy and among its voters and deputies the Protestants outnumber the Catholics. Overlapping membership can be observed between the SPD and associations of expellees, disabled veterans, etc. In addition, there are several organizations affiliated with the party, like Consumers' Co-operatives, Socialist Youth, etc. But none of these groups is nearly as important for the SPD as the trade unions, though conflicts within the party resulting from the struggle between the DGB and the DAG, the white-collar organization, are not missing. Before the federal elections in 1953, the DGB issued a manifesto which was widely understood as favoring the SPD. In 1957, it exhorted its members to vote for candidates friendly to labor, irrespective of their party membership.

Because of the doubtful esteem in which public opinion holds the unions, their outspoken support may not be a blessing. The DGB does not contribute money to parties, but it probably gives in many instances non-financial assistance—clerical help, canvassers, etc.—to candidates who are union members or officials. This indirect help benefits the SPD, a party which, like the BHE, is financed mainly by membership dues.

The FDP has connections with business, middle-class, and agricultural organizations. It has set up its own fund-raising organizations and receives funds from sponsors' associations. When it broke with the CDU, with which it had formed government coalitions, the FDP faced some hard sledding since the sponsors' associations do not like middle-class parties to fight each other instead of fighting socialism. Support was stopped, and if it flows again now, it does not flow amply. More generous help was offered for the 1957 election campaign, if the FDP were to promise before the elections not to join an anti-CDU coalition cabinet. The FDP refused to bind itself. In this respect, the DP is much better off for it is a staunch ally of the CDU. The GB/BHE's members are in their great majority expellees' and refugees' organizations. As the expellees and refugees are by no means concentrated solely in the GB/BHE, this party does not receive financial help from their associations. Both the SPD and CDU are careful to nominate a number of expellees as candidates for parliament.

IV. INTEREST GROUPS AND THE LEGISLATIVE PROCESS

Nomination processes vary from party to party. As the wishes of the constituencies must never be completely disregarded, however influential bureaucracies may be, interest group representatives can seldom be imposed as candidates against the will of party members. Accordingly, the many members and officials of interest groups in the Bundestag, the federal parliament, should not be considered as "outside" elements.

When the Bundestag met in 1953 for its second session, 54 out of 260 CDU deputies were trade union members, 7 of them paid officials. Among the industrialists, merchants, bankers, artisans, etc., who belong to the CDU group in parliament, 21 hold leading positions in interest groups, either in honorary capacity, or, in a smaller number, as members of the associations' paid staff. Though not a few of them are distinguished in their professions or associations, the owners or managers of the biggest firms, and the top men in the BDI and BDA, are hardly to be found in parliament. A different and very impressive picture is presented by agriculture. Twenty-three honorary or paid officials of agrarian interest groups belong to the parliamentary CDU. One of them is the national president of the *Deutsche Bauernverband,* 9 others are regional chairmen or members of the national executive of their central organizations.

Among the 162 deputies elected on the Social Democratic ticket, 131 were members of a union (which does not necessarily mean that they had been workers or white-collar employees by profession). Nine of them belong to the DAG, the others to the DGB. Though it could not be established exactly how many SPD deputies were paid union officials at the time of their election or at an earlier date, there can be no doubt that their number is considerable. Ten members of the parliamentary SPD are top union leaders. Interest groups other than unions have very few Social Democratic representatives in the Bundestag.

Of the FDP members of Parliament, almost one half are honorary or paid officials of industrial, commercial, middle-class, agrarian, and similar associations. Several DP members belong to middle-class and agrarian groups, most GB/BHE deputies to expellee and refugee organizations.

Parliamentary committees are important, and the kind of work they engage in makes them particularly significant for the observer of interest groups. In several committees, deputies belonging to specific interest groups are concentrated. As the parties are not monolithic, it can happen that the majority of a party disagrees with the decision of its members in a certain committee. Compromises reached in the Labor Committee, for instance, in which union representatives are numerous, were on some occasions disregarded in plenary session. Moreover, the different composition of committees can affect their accessibility to specific interest groups, and their work on a bill. Within the CDU the milieu from which committee members are drawn may vary somewhat from one committee to another. As a consequence, a bill which is discussed for instance in the Economics, as well as in the Labor Committee, may receive a very different treatment in the two committees. In this context, it should be noted that party discipline is not absolute. The labor wing of the CDU voted several times with the SPD, and other interest groups in parliament—for example the lawyers—show likewise occasionally a cohesion which transcends party lines.

The activities of interest groups are not restricted to the influence of their members in the Bundestag. When they are concerned with bills under consideration, both the associations which have members in parliament and those which do not, approach committees and the plenum. They state their opinions, give technical information, and advise on the drafting of bills. If they are keenly interested, and strong enough to do so, they use pressure to achieve their ends. This pressure can be pointed at single members, at parties, or at coalitions of parties in parliament. As the electoral system gravitates toward proportional representation, the individual deputy can resist pressure better than he would under straight plurality representation. Parties are not very vulnerable to the demands of poor interest groups with a small clientele. But it may be difficult or impossible to resist a wealthy association, whose financial support is essential, an agricultural organization which influences the votes of its numerous membership, or a big trade union able to call a strike. With the exception of a few remarkable instances, very little is known about lobbying in Bonn. An indication for its vigor may be found in the fact that a very distinguished industrialist and deputy, chairman of the Committee on Finance and Taxation, refused to be a candate for the Bundestag again, partly because of his disgust with the growing influence of pressure groups.

The second chamber in the Federal Republic consists of delegates of the Länder governments. As this chamber is of secondary importance, it is not approached by the groups as intensely as the Bundestag. Nevertheless, it can happen that a group finds the political constellation to be more favorable to its aims in certain Länder than on the federal level. Then it may try to influence federal legislation through the governments of those Länder. At this point it should be emphasized that, while this report deals only with national phenomena, pressure can be observed as well in regional and local politics.

There is no Economic Council in the Federal Republic. But trade unions and other interest groups advocate its creation.

V. INTEREST GROUPS AND THE EXECUTIVE

Again, the rapporteur deplores his lack of knowledge which is particularly marked in respect to the excutive. It cannot be established whether the executive is approached by interest groups more often than parliament. Some light, however, is thrown on the subject by the yearly reports of the BDI. They list the association's "most important memoranda" of the year. The overwhelming majority of the petitions were addressed to members of the cabinet, almost none to the Bundestag. (Several memoranda were directed to international bodies, whose contacts with national interest groups it may be interesting to study.) Of course, it is possible that day-to-day contacts between interest groups and members of the Bundestag are as frequent as between the former and the administration. But from the mere fact that the administrative apparatus is so much more extensive than parliament, and that the administration of a law over a long period involves so many more decisions than its enactment, one is tempted to conclude that interest groups approach the administration more frequently than the legislature.

In the Federal Republic the cabinet is dominant over parliament. In addressing cabinet members, interest groups see in them not always the heads of the administration, but also party leaders able to control or influence their friends in parliament, and possibly, susceptible to insinuations regarding the interests of their parties. It seems that several times groups had this in mind when they approached the Chancellor in matters of deep concern to them.

When drafting bills (where their "know-how" often gives them an advantage over parliament), as well as when administering them, members of the bureaucracy frequently ask interest groups for technical advice or an explanation of the groups' point of view. Where there are conflicting interests, much depends on a group's superior ability to state its case. The trade unions, for example, are sometimes found unable to provide the same quality of technical information which the employers' associations supply. Naturally, the groups are not always content with getting results through advising, but resort to pressure. One can assume that parties are more susceptible to pressure than civil servants, and that therefore pressure is preferably applied by approaching the political heads of the administration or those public officials who are party men.

Several groups are not limited to the influence they wield from the outside, but reach into the administration itself. The CDU government is carefully observing and regulating the proportion of Protestants and Catholics in the civil service. Especially in the educational system the churches themselves seem to have men of their trust. There are several Ministries—Economy, Agriculture, Labor, Expellees—in which a number of officials and in the last three also the Ministers themselves are members of interested associations. Above all, the agricultural groups hold the opinion that the Minister should have their confidence and defend their interests, as a kind of pressure "group" within the administration. Those groups which have influence on parties reach into the executive also indirectly through the party men serving in the bureaucracy.

The often voiced criticism against this state of affairs is wrong as far as it suggests that civil servants can be, or ever were, "neutral." Under the monarchy, the higher echelons of the service were recruited almost exclusively from the nobility and the upper strata of the bourgeosie. Even now, after the Weimar Republic had facilitated access, and after the nazis had put into the service quite a number of their men, it cannot be said that all social classes are represented equally on the higher levels of the bureaucracy. Undoubtedly there is ideological and social affinity between many bureaucrats and certain interest groups. The opening of the service to party men, and to the representatives of interest groups, is in a sense a democratization of the bureaucracy. Nevertheless, the often forgotten fact that bureaucrats always have social ties does not invalidate the argument that they should be aware of their civic responsibility and of their duties as servants of the general public. It seems that such notions are still widerspread in the service, and that—here some authors would disagree—in cases of real importance the bureaucracy is still strong enough to "hold the line" if it wishes to do so. (The question whether the administration in a unitary government may not be able to withstand pressure better than that in a federal system remains to be studied.)

In Germany, there is an old and strong tradition in favor of "social self-government" of institutions in which labor and employers are equally represented. The most important of these bodies are the Labor Courts, the employment and the social security agencies. The Labor Courts, which decide on all individual and collective disputes growing out of labor law, are administratively placed under the control of the Minister of Labor. With the exception of the Supreme Labor Court, they consist each of three judges. In the lower courts, the presiding judge should, and in the higher courts he must, be a learned jurist. The other two judges are representatives of labor and employers, nominated by their respective associations. Only in the Federal Labor Court the jurists—3 as against 1 representative each of labor and employers—are in majority on the bench. The office for Employment and Unemployment Insurance, which has, besides the duties suggested by its name, responsibility for relief and vocational advice, is set up on local, regional and federal levels, and administered by labor, employers and representatives of public institutions. In all other branches of Social Security—as is well known, Germany has a vast and highly developed system of social services—the Insurance Agencies are administered exclusively by labor and employers' representatives.

VI. The Need for a Conceptual Framework

As was said at the beginning, the term "interest group" is not defined in this paper, and neither is there a definition of such concepts as "access," "approach," "pressure." No doubt, to acquire theoretical depth, exact definitions would be indispensable. But how should one go about defining precisely, when little is known about the subject? Until more is about interest groups and their ways, it is difficult to establish a terminology which may be meaningful for political theory. On the other hand, one cannot deny that as soon as we are engaged in research, we will always be committed to some kind of theory, to some more or less interrelated views on the political system. But this pre-research theory, quite often of a speculative nature, indicates to us little more than the direction in which it may be useful to look, it cannot let us perceive the results. Fortunately, our subject is receiving increasing attention in several countries, and national studies—at least when they describe phenomena in countries with similar political systems—may be compared and used for theoretical conclusions. Thus, the discussion at an international round table conference may help to sharpen our concepts. Still more, it may give insights which could provide more theoretical perspective to research. But even once we are able to theorize more about our subject than hitherto, we should be aware that a theory of interest groups will remain a kind of middle-range theory, and as such of necessity incomplete, as long as we do not interrelate it with theories on parties, parliament, and other institutions. The quest for a conceptual framework which fits the interest groups and their role in the governmental process, is in the end the quest for a theory embracing the political system as a whole.

Bibliographical Note

Although the origin of some of the interest groups here discussed dates from the second half of the last century and in spite of the fact that their activities were noticed even then, their systematic study is still in its beginning. What is lacking most are empirical case studies of single groups or of situations where group action has become significant. For these reasons it was impossible to submit here a balanced report. Trade unions, for example, have been treated somewhat out of proportion to their importance, because relatively much is known about them. The relative weight of the facts that are known cannot easily be evaluated; what is unknown may be more important than what is reported upon. Hence I had often to resort to impressions and superficial knowledge. Nevertheless I found a number of publications helpful, some of which are listed here.

Abendroth, Wolfgang, "Die deutschen Gewerkschaften." *Kleine Schriften zur politischen Bildung*, No. 5/6, Heidelberg 1954.

Almond, Gabriel, "The Political Attitudes of German Business," *World Politics*, Vol. VIII, (1956) pp. 157–186.

Breitling, Rupert, "Gesellschaftsstruktur und Organisationswirklichkeit der Verbände," *Die Neue Gesellschaft*, II, 3, May/June 1955.

Breitling, Rupert, *Die Verbände in der Bundesrepublik*, Meisenheim, 1955.

Deus, Franz, ed., *Gewerkschaften und Parlament. Viertes Europäisches Gespräch in der Schule der IG. Bergbau, Haltern*. Hrsgg. im Auftrag des Deutschen Gewerkschaftsbundes. Düsseldorf 1956.

Cassau, Theodor, *Die Gewerschaftsbewegung. Ihre Soziologie und ihr Kampf*. Halberstadt 1925.

Eisermann, Gottfried, "Parlament, Parteien und Verbände," *Kölner Zeitschrift für Soziologie und Sozial-psychologie*, V, 1952/1953.

Eschenburg, Theodor, *Herrschaft der Verbände?* Stuttgart 1955.

Heidenheimer, Arnold J., "German Party Finance: The CDU," The *American Political Science Review*, Vol. LI, 1957, pp. 369–85.

Hirsch-Weber, Wolfgang; Schuetz, Klaus *et al.*, *Wähler und Gewählte. Eine Untersuchung der Bundestagswahlen 1953*. Schriften des Instituts für politische Wissenschaft, Vol. 7. Stuttgart und Düsseldorf, 1957.

Hirsch-Weber, Wolfgang, ed., *Gewerkschaften im Staat. Drittes Europäisches Gespräch in der Engelsburg Recklinghausen*. Hrsgg. im Auftrage des Deutschen Gewerkschaftsbundes. Düsseldorf 1955.

Kaiser, Joseph H., *Die Repräsentation organisierter Interessen*, Berlin 1956.

Krüger, Herbert, "Die Stellung der Interessenverbände in der Verfassungswirklichkeit,": *Neue Juristische Wochenschrift*, IX/34, August 1956, pp. 1217 ff.

Lange, Max Gustav, *et al.*, *Parteien in der Bundesrepublik: Studien zur Bundestagswahl 1953*. Schriften des Instituts für politische Wissenschaft, vol. 6. Stuttgart und Düsseldorf, 1955.

Naphtali, Fritz, ed. *Wirtschaftsdemokratie. Ihr Wesen, Weg und Ziel*. Hrsgg. im Auftrag des Allgemeinen Deutschen Gewerkschaftsbundes. Berlin 1928.

Pritzkoleit, Kurt, *Die neuen Herren. Die Mächtigen in Staat und Wirtschaft*, Wien-München-Basel 1955.

Remmling, Günter, "Die Interessenverbände in der westlichen Welt. Zur Frage der gesetzlichen Regelung des Verbändeeinflusses in einzelnen Ländern," *Zeitschrift fur Politik*, vol. IV (1957) pp. 169/86.

Scheuner, Ulrich; Weber, Werner *et al.*, *Der Staat und die Verbände. Gespräch veranstaltet vom Bundesverband der Deutschen Industrie in Köln am 27. März 1957*. Göttingen, Heidelberg 1957.

Schulz, Gerhard, "Die Organisationsstruktur der CDU," *Zeitschrift für Politik*, vol. III (1956) pp. 147 ff.

Schuster, Hans, "Die heimlichen Parteien. Uber die politische Rolle der parlamentarischen Demokratie," *Politische Bildung*, No. 41, 1953.

Stammer, Otto, "Interessenverbänder und Parteien," *Kölner Zeitschrift für Soziologie und Sozialpsychologie*, vol. IX (1957).

Strickrodt, Georg, "Gruppeninteressen und Staatsgewalt," *Neue Politische Literatur*, II, 5.

Sternberger, Dolf, "Der Staat der Gegenwart und die wirtschaftlichen und ausserwirtschaftlichen Interessengruppen. Rundtafelgespräch zum 11. Deutschen Soziologentag in Weinheim 1952," *Kölner Zeitschrift für Soziologie und Sozialpsychologie*, vol. V, 1952/53, pp. 204–219.

Teichmann, Ulrich, *Die Politik der Agrarpreisstützung. Marktbeeinflussung als Teil des Agrarinterventionismus in Deutschland*, Düsseldorf 1956.

Triesch, Günter, *Die Macht der Funktionäre. Macht und Verantwortung der Gewerkschaften*, Düsseldorf 1956.

Tuchfeldt, Egon, "Wirtschaftspolitik und Verbände," *Hamburger Jahrbuch für Wirtschafts- und Gesellschaftspolitik*, Vol. I, 1956, pp. 72 ff.

Weber, Werner, *Spannungen und Kräfte im westdeutschen Verfassungssystem*, Stuttgart, 1951

Weber, Werner, *Legitime Interessenvertretung in der modernen Gesellschaft. Vier Referate einer Tagung vom 20.–23. Januar 1956*, Loccum 1956.

Weber, Werner, *Rechtliche Ordnung des Parteiwesens. Probleme eines Parteiengesetzes*. Bericht der vom Bundesminister des Innern eingesetzten Parteienrechtskommission, Berlin 1957.

Weber, Werner, *Der Weg zum industriellen Spitzenverband*, Darmstadt 1956.

In addition, I was able to draw on an as yet unpublished investigation of a member of the Institut für politische Wissenschaft, Martin Virchow, on interest group representatives in the Bundestag, and on my own doctoral thesis on Trade Unions in Politics (publication forthcoming).

About the work currently being done a few indications follow, which do not claim to be exhaustive.

Under the guidance of Professor Wolfgang Abendroth, two doctoral theses on interest groups have been finished: one by Fritz Opel on the metal-workers'-union between 1913 and 1918, and one by Hans Schumann on the destruction of the German unions and the creation of the Nazi "Labor Front." They are soon to be published in the series of the Marburg Institut für politische Wissenschaften. In progress are studies on associations of expellees, disabled veterans and war orphans, and on Protestant Youth Organizations in the Third Reich. Abendroth himself is investigating the associations of persons persecuted by the Nazi regime.

The Heidelberg group under the direction of Profesor Dolf Sternberger is constantly observing pressure groups and their activities. Rupert Breitling will publish a study on the membership of deputies in associations, and Peter Moit, in an historical investigation of the Reichstag, is taking into account the members' affiliation in interest groups.

At the Institut für politische Wissenschaft, Berlin, several investigations are in progress. In a book on the first years of the Nazi regime, soon to be published, Karl Dietrich Bracher, Gerhard Schulz und Wolfgang Sauer are analyzing the interactions between the rulers and interest groups. Gerhard Schulz is working on the "Osthilfe," the famous help of the Reich to its Eastern provinces, in which interest groups played an extremely important part. Klaus Schutz, in collaboration with Mr. Kitzinger of Nuffield College, is observing the nomination process in the elections of September, 1957, and the part played therein by interest groups. Finally, Professor Stammer, the author, Günter Remmling and associates are engaged in a study on the influence of trade unions and other interest groups on legislation.

INTEREST GROUPS AND THE POLITICAL PROCESS IN GREAT BRITAIN

S. E. FINER

I. TERMINOLOGY

The most popular terms in this field seems to be either "pressure groups" or, "interest groups". It is obvious, however, that many interest groups (e.g. an Anglers' Association) do not use "pressure" or do so intermittently. It is equally obvious that many organizations using "pressure" do not represent any economic or social 'interest' (in the Eighteenth Century sense), but represent an attitude (e.g., The Peace Pledge Union (pacifism)).

The organizations which seek to influence government are of both these types. For "all groups or associations which seek to influence public policy in their own chosen direction, while declining to accept direct responsibility for ruling the country"—I propose to use the term "the Lobby."

The Lobby embraces two types of organizations viz. (a) Interest groups, proper. (b) Promotional (or propaganda) groups. By their very nature interest groups are primarily concerned with the welfare of their own members. (e.g. a trade union, a trade association). They only make contact with public bodies where the interest of the members demands this. "Lobby" describes these interest groups solely in so far as they seek to influence public policy.

Promotional groups exist primarily to advance a cause. The term "Lobby" applies therefore to the bulk of their activities all the time.

Some interest groups, e.g. the National Union of Teachers are also "promotional" groups: The N.U.T. not only campaigns for better conditions for its members, but has a genuine faith in Education. Some organizations, e.g. the *Roads Campaign Council*, are promotional groups set up and financed by a number of interest groups. Both interest groups and promotional groups may at times use "pressure." It ought to be recognized, however, that very often they merely state a case to the responsible authority, and neither intend nor threaten sanctions if that case is turned down. I do not regard the mere putting of a case as the exercise of pressure. I shall mean by "pressure," the application, or threatened application, of a sanction should a demand be refused.

II. General Characteristics of the Lobby in Britain

The number of organizations seeking to influence public policy in one way or another is very large. It is impossible to count up the number of professional organizations. An idea of the number of charitable and social-service organizations could be gleaned from *"The Charities Annual Year-book and Digest."* No attempt whatsoever can be made at estimating the number of purely promotional bodies, large numbers of which come into existence and die out every year. The only fields in which firm numbers can be ascertained are those of trade associations or trade unions.

The number of *manufacturers'* trade associations is estimated at 1200; this compares with only an estimated 800 in the U.S.A. The number of trade associations of all kinds, including wholesalers and retailers and regional bodies, is estimated at 2500.[1] This compares with a figure of 2500 in the U.S. for *all* business associations, including professional groups which are excluded from the British figure. In addition, in the U.K. one must add 270 employers' wage-negotiating bodies, which have 1600 regional or local branches, often largely antonomous.

The number of Trade Unions at 1953 was 687 of which 17 unions had two-thirds of the total membership.[2]

The density of representation by these interest groups is also extremely high. This will become apparent below when particular organizations are described and cited.

Since the First World War, there has been a three-fold trend among industrial and professional bodies, viz:

(1.) Larger total numbers embraced in organizations of one kind or another. Thus the number of Trade Unionists has risen from 2½ million (in 1910) to 9½ million (in 1953). The number of members of the Federation of British Industries has risen from a few individual firms and fifty associations in 1916 (when it was founded), to 7533 firms and 283 trade associations (in 1956).

[1] For the names, and in some cases also the description, of trade associations, see P.E.P., *Industrial Trade Associations*, London 1957. For retail associations see Hyman Levy, *Retail Trade Associations*, London 1956.

[2] There is a very large literature on trade unions. See especially P.E.P., *British Trade Unionism*, London 1955; and B. C. Roberts, *Trade Union Government and Administration*, London 1956.

(2.) The expansion of the number of specialist organizations; coupled with the federation and amalgamation of such bodies. Thus there are fewer Trade Unions today than fifty years ago, when there were some 1400.

(3.) There are more manufacturing trade associations today (1200) than in 1919 when there were 500; but since then they have federated in F.B.I. (founded 1916) or N.U.M. (founded 1915). There are indisputably larger numbers of professional and technical associations today, corresponding to the rise of new professional and technical classes; but so far, no tendency to federation has shown itself.

III. THE MORE IMPORTANT ASSOCIATIONS, CLASSIFIED BY ECONOMIC OR SOCIAL FIELD

Industry and Commerce

Membership of some organization or other is said, authoritatively, to be "all but universal" for manufacturing enterprises.

Figures for manufacturing, and also for all commercial associations have been given above—some 2500.

In a special category stands the powerful National Farmers' Union. Its membership was only 20,000 in 1913. Today it is 208,000, some 90% of the total farmers in England and Wales.

In another special category stands the Institute of Directors. This antique body (founded in 1903) was of no consequence until its reorganization in 1948. It increased its membership to 4,500 in 1951: to 10,000 in 1954: and today has 26,000 members. The term "Director" is somewhat elastic in the U.K. (which is the principal reason for members joining the Institute and getting its *"cachet")* but the number of names in the *"Directory of Directors"* is about 30,000. On this basis the Institute has about 80% density of representation. Its chief work is to lobby for improved conditions for directors—e.g., in the fields of superannuation law, surtax law, income tax allowances, etc.

There remain the great "Peak" Associations. There is the British Employers' Confederation, federating all the 270 individual employers' negotiating bodies. Its duties are to provide for consultation between its constituents: to collect, collate and circulate information to them; to act on general matters; but it is forbidden by its constitution to interfere with the functions of any of its members, or to act inconsistently with their full autonomy. It negotiates with some 70% of the employed population.

The Federation of British Industries has a dual membership of individual firms and trade associations. So has the *National Union of Manufacturers.* The former tends to attract the larger firms; the N.U.M. claims to speak for the small and middlesized ones. Both cater for manufacturers only, though the National Farmers' Union has recently joined the F.B.I. Membership stands at: F.B.I. 7533 firms, 283 trade associations (1956); N.U.M. 5500 firms, 71 trade associations (1955). The F.B.I. claims that, by individual or affiliate membership, it represents some 50,000 firms. This is the equivalent of $6/7$ths of all manufacturing firms which employ over 11 workers apiece. Many firms are members of both organizations.[3]

Many of these firms, together with all the chief "service" firms (insurance, banking, shipping, etc.) are members of one of the 100 (local) *Chambers of Commerce,* which are entirely autonomous, but are (genuinely) confederated in the Association of British Chambers of Commerce. This very influential body claims to represent 60,000 firms. Of these, 30,000 are manufacturers.[4]

There are several hundred organizations *calling* themselves "Chambers of Commerce" or "Chambers of Trade" which are not affiliated to the A.B.C.C. The reason is that their title is a misnomer. They are really Chambers of TRADE i.e. local organizations of *retailers.* (The true Chamber of Commerce only admits the wholesalers). The Chambers of Trade throughout the country are federated under the *National Chamber of Trade.* Other "peak" organizations of retailers are the *Retail Drapers' Association* and the *Drapers' Chamber of Trade.*

The F.B.I., N.U.M. and A.B.C.C. frequently co-operate on matters of joint concern. There is a close liason between the A.B.C.C. and the National Chamber of Trade.

The distinction between the A.B.C.C. on the one side and the F.B.I. and N.U.M. on the other is the distinction between a territorial and a functional federation. There is *no* rational reason for two bodies, F.B.I. and N.U.M., to divide the field between them, and there is considerable rivalry between their respective partisans. The B.E.C. handles labour problems and the other three organizations do not touch these at all, delegating them entirely to the B.E.C. There are some common frontiers, however, e.g. training, which may lead sometimes to a certain amount of friction.

[3] For the Federation of British Industries, see S. E. Finer, "The Federation of British Industries," *Political Studies,* vol. IV (1956), pp. 61/84.
[4] See A. R. Knowles (the Secretary General of the Association), *The Organization and Function of British Chambers of Commerce,* London.

Labour

There are about 20 million people, including women and juveniles in the labour force, (excluding the Armed Services and the professions). There are 9½ million trade unionists. Thus about half of the eligible labour force is unionized.

Of the 9½ million, only one million are not affiliated to the Trade Union Congress. Only two Unions not so affiliated have more than 100,000 workers apiece. (N.A.L.G.O. and the N.U.T.)

The 8½ million unionists affiliated to the T.U.C. belong to 183 Unions, some of which are themselves federations. The "Big Six" account for half of the affiliated membership. They are:

Transport and General Workers' Union:	1,260,000
National Union of General & Municipal Workers:	809,000
Amalgamated Engineering Union:	800,000
National Union of Mineworkers:	640,000
National Union of Railwaymen:	400,000
Union of Shop, Distributive & Allied Workers:	345,000
(figures relate to 1952).	

The T.U.C. (founded 1869) is a Congress. It cannot bind its constituents except perhaps, morally. It has developed a tolerable H.Q. staff of specialists, who, working with the committees of the General Council, draw up policy reports for Congress and act upon mandates received from Congress. It does *not* negotiate wages—this is a matter for individual Unions. It is, in fact, the employee's counterpart to the F.B.I.—the "general staff of labour."

The Co-operative Movement: This is an exceedingly powerful lobby, though less so perhaps than its gross membership would have one believe. It is also exceedingly puzzling.

In 1953 there were 988 retail co-operative distributive societies, with a total membership of 11.2 millions; their trade being 12% of our total national retail trade. There are also 44 productive societies and 4 wholesale societies.

All such bodies may affiliate to the *Co-operative Union*, the "peak" organization of the movement. (Formed 1869: and holds the Annual Co-operative Congress). 96.42% of all Societies were affiliated to it, at the end of 1953.

There is also a Co-operative PARTY, formed in 1917. Only 647 of the thousand-odd co-operative societies were affiliated to it. (Annual affiliation fee = halfpenny for each member of affiliating retail societies; and agreed lump sums for affiliated national societies). In 1954, its affiliated membership was 9.6 million, or 85.8% of the total membership. This party is associated with the Labour Party by an agreement of 1946, replacing the original (Cheltenham) agreement of 1927. This governs selection of candidates. Co-op candidates take the Labour Whip in Parliament.[5]

Professional Associations

Every profession has its own specialized association. Among the politically most important are the *National Association of Local and Government Officers* representing the clerical and administrative grades in local government and in *some* of the nationalized industries. Its membership numbers 185,000. Next, the B.M.A. (British Medical Association) represents the bulk of the medical profession. There is one small union of doctors affiliated to the T.U.C. (about 4500 members), but the B.M.A. represents 85% of the profession.[6] Thirdly, there is the National Union of Teachers. With over 200,000 members this, too, represents some 80% of its clientele. There is a separate quadri-partite Union of teachers "in secondary schools" with about 35,000 members. There are some technical associations too, e.g. The Association of Teachers in Technical Schools, but these are eligible for N.U.T. membership. Two bodies, however, are "proscribed"—membership in them is incompatible with membership of the N.U.T. These are the National Association of Schoolmasters and the National Association of Women Teachers. Both are secessionist bodies—differing (from their respective standpoints) over the Union's attitude on equal pay for women.[7]

Civic Associations

1. There is a host of charitable and philanthropic societies. One of the most important peak organizations in the field is the National Council of Social Service which federates local councils of Social Service (which in their turn, federate at local level as many local bodies as will join them), and also federates national associations e.g. The Red Cross, The National Society for Prevention of Cruelty to Children, etc.

[5] See J. Bailey, *The Co-operative Movement*, London 1956.

[6] For the British Medical Association, see E. M. Little, *History of the B.M.A. 1832–1932*, London 1932. See also the Symposium *Fifty Years of Medicine*, London 1950, at pp. 300–10; and H. Eckstein, "The Politics of the British Medical Association," *Political Quarterly*, vol. 26 (1955), pp. 345–59.

[7] An admirable study of the history of the teaching profession is A. Tropp, *The Teachers*, London 1957. For the professions generally see A. M. Carr Saunders and P. A. Wilson, *The Professions*, Oxford 1933; and R. Lewis and A. Maude, *Professional People*, London 1952.

The nature of voluntary philanthropy makes it impossible to talk of density of representation. It is made up of volunteers. It has no mass membership.

2. There is a number of important quasi-constitutional bodies e.g. the Magistrates' Association. Politically, the most important by far are the five organizations representing respectively the types of local government authority, viz: Association of Municipal Corporations, County Councils Association, Urban District Councils Association, Rural District Councils Association, and Parish Councils Association.

All but the last have very nearly 100% membership. To a large extent they are almost joint-participants with the Ministries in most matters affecting structure and duties of local authorities.

3. There is also a vast, fluid and uncountable mass of societies for promoting this or preventing that. The Proportional Representation Society, The Campaign for the Limitation of Secret Police Powers; The Howard League for Penal Reform; Federal Union; World Government. Some of these, for example the Howard League, are important and very respected. Some, like the Equal Pay Campaign Committee are propaganda councils set up by a number of interest groups.[8] Some, e.g. the now moribund Middle Class Alliance and the People's League for the Defence of Freedom, aspire to a mass membership—which they cannot get, such being the hold of the established political parties.

Special Social Sectional Associations

Among these may be noted the Automobile Association and Royal Automobile Club with some two million members—two-fifths of the private car and motorcycle population. These have a joint standing committee for questions of common concern. The British Legion (847,000 members in 1954) is the sole association representing ex Servicemen, very well established and reputable.[9] There is also the National Federation of Old Age Pensioners Association with 1,600 branches and a membership of 400,000. All four are of some importance politically but there are hundreds of others, such as Anglers' Association, the National Cyclists' Union, the Pedestrians' Association.

[8] See Allan Potter, "The Equal Pay Campaign Committee," *Political Studies*, vol. V (1957), pp. 49–65.

[9] See Graham Wootton, *The Official History of the British Legion*, London, 1956. See also the excellent studies by Professor J. H. Millet, "British Interest Group Tactics—a Case-Study," *Political Science Quarterly*, vol. 72 (1957), pp. 71–82; and "The Role of an Interest Group Leader in the House of Commons," *Western Political Quarterly*, vol. VIII (1956), pp. 915–26.

Religious and Evangelical Associations

E.g. the Churches themselves; evangelical bodies like Christian Union, the Society for the Propagation of the Gospel in Foreign Parts, the Lords' Day Observance Society and so forth. These are numerous and often highly influential.

Recreational, Cultural, and Educational Associations

Some are interest groups: e.g. British Equity is the actors' trade union, affiliated to the T.U.C. Others are professional: e.g. The Royal Institute of British Architects. Others are promotional: the Society for the Preservation of Rural England. The Universities form a respected and powerful group.

IV. INTERNAL ORGANIZATION AND PROCESSES

The Flexibility of the Lobby

"Unity" gives external strength but calls for internal compromises; sectional specialization gives clear-cut policy, but at the expense of bargaining power.

The British Lobby has found numerous and highly successful ways of having the best of both worlds. It should not be regarded as a set of separate sectional associations, mutually exclusive, and operating side by side, but should be regarded as a highly complicated network of interconnecting associations.

(1) The specialized basic associations unite in *different* peak associations for *different* purposes. The Society of Motor Manufacturers and Traders, for instance, is a constituent member both of the F.B.I. and the A.B.C.C. In addition, however, like some 110 other national organizations of trade and manufacturers, it is a member of the British Road Federation. This body exists to promote the interests of those concerned in the construction or the use of roads, to promote improvements in the law relating to roads and to promote the construction of roads. The S.M.M.T. is also, however, a member of the Traders' Co-ordinating Committee of Transport. Together with 102 other associations this body co-ordinates traders' bargaining with all transport providers, as to rates and conditions of transport. The S.M.M.T. is also a member of the Roads Campaign Council, a propaganda body set up by a number of road-interest-organizations to make propaganda by film and public meeting for the immediate provision of better roads.

(2) In so far as most of these peak organizations are quite voluntaristic—no sanction attaching to following a different line from the ma-

jority one, or even to quitting the peak organizations altogether—minority groups often strike off on their own account. For instance, when the nationalization of road passenger transport was feared, in 1946, the peak organization of the industry, (The Public Transport Association), resolved to express no opinions until the Government published its proposals. This did not prevent a powerful group of the more militant companies from conducting militant anti-nationalization propaganda through their organ, the *British Omnibus Companies Public Relations Committee*. Similarly, when the Restrictive Practices Bill came up, in 1956, some fifteen trade associations of manufacturers wholesalers and retailers, who indulged in re-sale price maintenance, temporarily detached themselves from the main peak organizations to set up the *"Fair Prices Defence Committee"*. (The Committee claimed to represent 35,000 firms).

(3) Finally, "peak" allies with "peak" for common purposes. The A.B.C.C., F.B.I., N.U.M. set up a joint committee on the Restrictive Practices Bill, to draft agreed amendments and to use its supporters in Parliament to get these passed. The three bodies likewise set up a joint working party on the Customs Duties Bill of 1956. They have just published a joint report on the Free Trade Area. The British Employers Confederation often makes a fourth partner with the three.

Likewise, when the Transport Bill was before Parliament in 1946–7, a *Central Committee of Transport Users* was set up to press for amendments. It consisted of the A. B. C. C., N. U. M. and F.B.I.; the Traders Transport Association; the Traders' Co-ordinating Committee of Transport; the Mansion House Association; and the British Road Federation.

This ease in combination for special purposes and in certain cases, coupled with *ad hoc* division for special purposes, helps to mitigate conflicts over policy inside organizations.

Internal Cleavages and Modes of Handling These

Some organizations do however contain such clearly divergent interests that special arrangements are made to mitigate possible cleavages of opinion.

(1) One method has been to "unscramble" the interests, create a separate organization for each, and re-unite these in a loose federal relationship. Up to 1945 there were five organizations catering for road hauliers. In each one the haulier found himself cheek by jowl with other motor operators, some of whom were primarily concerned with passenger services, while others represented the private haulage-fleets

of large industrial firms. In the eyes of the professional haulier, these firms had no business to be carrying their own goods—they were taking bread from the professional hauliers' mouths. In 1945 all the existing organizations were scrapped and were reformed into one for professional hauliers only, one for the commercial users' only, and one for bus-operators only: viz *The Road Haulage Association,* the *Traders Road Transport Association,* and *Passenger Vehicle Operators Association.* All these were federated under the *National Road Transport Federation* to which they nominated members.

(2) Another device has been to combine a territorial network with a functional one. Thus the Transport and General Workers' Union is made up both of Regions and National trade groups—both uniting at the peak in its Biennial Conferences.

The F.B.I. Grand Council is likewise composed of three types of representative: those of the individual firms who vote in industrial panels; those of the trade associations; and a number nominated to represent the Federation's Regional Councils.

The *Road Haulage Association* is organized on a territorial basis, of Regions and Districts; but it is also divided at the national level, into specialized "Panels" representing each aspect of the industry.

(3) *"Weighting":* There are also various devices to give due weight to the association's varied interests,[10] e.g.

(a) According to size of firm, (or branch, in case of a Trade Union). e.g. *National Paint Federation* where only half the council comes from the small firms who have, in fact, a *numerical* majority in the organization.

(b) According to geographical location. *The Boot and Shoe Manufacturers Federated Association* weights its Regions according to the number of member-firms contained therein.

(c) According to techniques: *The British Iron and Steel Federation* has 60 Council Members. Twenty-one represent the British Steel Producers' Conference, seven the Light Rolled Steel Conference; six other Conferences have three to four representatives; and two have two apiece.

The Locus of Decision Making

Paper constitutions are notoriously no guide to the true centres of decision-making. Since almost none of the British interest-groups have been studied with a view to ascertaining the *de facto* distribution of

---

[10] The logic underlying such organization and a catalogue of the diverse factors making for centrifugalism and centripetalism are to be found in P.E.P., *op. cit.,* (fn. 1).

power within them, it might seem pointless to discuss this matter any further. One or two *impressions* on this matter might prove helpful, if only as working hypotheses. They are offered in this spirit.

It seems to me that the locus of decision making has singularly little to do with the paper constitution in most instances, despite all the "fancy franchises" mentioned above. It appears to depend on factors like the following:

(1.) *Is the organization a negotiating one? Alternatively do its policies bind the members?* In such bodies, the leadership will usually be in for a rough time and we usually find more rank and file participation than in other types. In the last year, for instance, the Executive Committees of the National Union of Teachers, the National Farmers' Union and the British Medical Association have been all but repudiated by their members, in rowdy Conference meetings.

This situation also occurs in some of the promotional type of association. It is the *raison d'être* of such associations, not only to plug a line, but to *have* one to plug. The discussion of the correct line is central to the members' participation and in the nature of the case—e.g. matters of temperance, blood-sports, women's rights—it tends to produce uncompromising attitudes which are philosophically irreducible. Hence member-participation tends to be high.

Per Contra, member participation in policy tends to be very low where the association is largely for the domestic convenience and protection of its members. Members join the motoring organizations (the R.A.C. and A.A.) for instance, simply to get emergency service, help with routes, or legal aid. They are not interested in road-politics. On the whole the A.A. and R.A.C. are not highly involved in them either, but when they are (as in the case of parking meters or the use of radar speed-traps), the committees of the R.A.C. and A.A. tend to act without the formal sanction of any but an infinitesimal minority of their members. The *National Federation of Property Owners* has a territorial organization—it federates local branches; but it is a protective rather than a policy initiating body, and members pay their dues to it in the expectation that the federation will take all necessary steps to scrutinize public and private bills for them, and contest these where necessary: which it does. The *Licensed Victuallers Defence League* which federates 388 local organizations is of similar type. In the branches most of its activities appear to be social. Legal and Parliamentary work is left to its national headquarters.

One sometimes finds both active participation co-existing with good temper and deference to constituted authorities. This seems to occur

127

in bodies whose aim it is to work out policy of an *advisory* nature. Despite occasional tumults, most of the T.U.C.'s work is of this kind. Although it is an exaggeration to say that the T.U.C. General Council's committees make the policy, that the General Council is a sounding board and the Congress a more noisy sounding board, it is not a gross exaggeration. Similarly, and more so, with bodies like the F.B.I. or N.U.M. or A.B.C.C. "More so" in such cases because (1) if there is a sharp division of opinion amongst members these organizations wisely record the common measure of agreement and leave it at that, and (2) members need not follow the policy (this is also true of the T.U.C.) and (3) they can always quit, (legally but not morally practicable in the T.U.C.).

(2.) *What is the social composition of the body?* Members have different ways of behaving according to their social background. The Road Haulage Association is largley composed of the so-called "small men" who, when attacked, display an almost poujadiste attitude. This has consistently been in evidence since the threat to their industry developed in 1945. The "big men" tend to be much less vociferous and more self-controlled—probably because they feel more secure.

The behaviour of the medical and teaching professions provide the queerest puzzle. Both seem capable of great hysteria. I am inclined to belieye that this is because their social status which, in the provinces especially, was very high indeed, is now seriously threatened. *Not* because they are earning less, but because the manual workers are earning much more than hitherto and spending it in conspicuous ways.

Limits of Majority Rule

There are some "voluntary" associations which in fact it is hard to quit. A price-ring is one such; a trade union, with a closed shop outlook is another.

On the whole, however, one can quit. In some bodies, e.g. the F.B.I., this very fact keeps the organization together: the knowledge that firms may leave leads to compromises.

Certain associations—notably those that must negotiate for the whole profession or industry—are in a dilemma. Unity provides the only hope of successful negotiation, but there may be serious cleavages of interest inside the organization.

Some examples illustrate this. In 1943, when the road-haulier associations were uniting to form the new Road Haulage Association, as described above, a rank and file movement developed against the leadership. This was accused of representing the "big men" against the small, and of favouring a rapprochement with the railways which could only damage "the small man". Both accusations were in fact true—for there was a serious cleavage, both economic and social, between "small men" and "big men" in the industry. The small haulier finally broke away to form the *Hauliers' Mutual Federation* and a great contest developed for the capture of the bulk of the rank and file. In the end the established leadership won, and the H.M.F. slowly dissolved away.

The N.U.T. however has largely held together. Its two chief internal cleavages were due to (a) the snobbery of grammar school teachers during the pre-1914 period and enduring to recent times and (b) the quarrel between men and women over equal pay. The first led to the formation of associations to cater for grammar school teachers. These still exist. The second cleavage caused two splinter groups to fly off from the N.U.T. The first was an Association of Women Teachers. This was formed in 1909, during the suffragette agitation. The second was the National Association of Schoolmasters which broke away in 1922 (after an initial break in 1919) because the N.U.T. appeared to be moving towards the principle of equal pay for women. Now that equal pay has been conceded, both splinter organizations will probably dwindle away.

The other cleavage in the teaching profession—between the N.U.T. and the "Secondary School Associations"—reflects a situation sometimes met in Trade Unions. There it takes the form of a cleavage between skilled and unskilled. Thus there are three railways Unions and not one. The largest is the N.U.R., with a great majority of the unskilled and semi-skilled. It carries on a bitter feud with A.S.L.E.F. (drivers and firemen) and a less bitter one with the T.S.S.A. (salaried staff), accusing them of destroying the unity of the profession. The other two Unions, however, decline to be absorbed.

The Trade Union Congress also faces strains of a similar kind. At the moment (September 1957), the smaller Unions get left behind in the competitive struggle for wages. These Unions favour the T.U.C. exercising a centralized wages control over the whole movement. Some of the bigger Unions (of the Shop-Workers Union—U.S.D.A.W.) also favor this, feeling that if the T.U.C. played a more active part in wage-negotiations, its power to influence the Government would be much stronger. The General Secretary of the National Union of Railwaymen thinks likewise; but he wants the sectional composition of the T.U.C. changed first. At present it is divided, rather archaically, into eighteen sections. Mr. Campbell of the N.U.R. would prefer a single Union representing *all* transport—rail, road, sea, air. This would have two million members

—and would eliminate the present unwelcome competition of ASLEF, TSSA, and to some extent, TGWU.

V. The Lobby and the Political Process

The working paper suggests as topics "public opinion," "parties," "legislature" and "executive"—in that order. As far as Great Britain is concerned, this order is back-to-front. I propose to reverse it for the following reasons:

To begin with, the order would tend to fit the purely "promotional" groups in the Lobby; but these are very weak and poorly regarded in Britain. The influential groups are the interest-groups. Now the first characteristic of these is that they are, pretty well, all "domesticated"— they work, and are expected to work closely with the Ministries, and it would be both impolite and imprudent of them to agitate publicly before first seeing what the Ministry proposed to do about the matter. Hence their relationship to the executive ought to come first. Then, in so far as these groups seek to go further than the Executive has suggested, their next line of attack will be Parliament, where their success or failure will be influenced by their relationship to Party. At this stage they may also appeal to the public. But in Britain the "grass roots lobby" is infrequent and dubiously successful. A selective appeal to public opinion, when this does have to be courted, is the more favored approach. Hence our order will be Executive; Parliament; Party; and Public.

VI. The Lobby and the Executive

For the interest-groups, dealings with government departments take up far the greatest part of the total time they devote to contact with government, and the vast bulk of it deals with minor detail. "The great bulk of the work of government is administration, not policy, and most of what I have called the F.B.I.'s policy work lies in the field of administration." (Sir Norman Kipping, the Director General of the F.B.I.) "Measured numerically," he continues, "the bulk of our contacts with the Government concerns minor, though often important issues."

The departments and the interest groups both have what the other requires, and both require what the other has. The *desiderata*, on both sides, may be summed up as information, consents, administrative convenience. The interest groups want to have the earliest intimation of official policy, and access to those much wider aspects of their own "interest" which only a public department is in a position to give. Next, they often require some alteration in the current policy pursued by the department, and can get this only if the department is consenting. Finally they consistently need to intervene and intermediate in hard cases and anomalies: they require smooth and equitable administration.

For their part the departments require the technical insight of the interest-group. "Collectively, one of these organizations knows far more of Government policy over a wide field than any individual can hope to attain to."[11] Secondly they require consents to the chosen policy, and would sooner negotiate with a representative body and test its opinion than either consult individually, or, alternatively, not consult at all. Finally they often seek an organization's help in actually *administering* policy: e.g. the present structure of agricultural administration depends on certain duties being shouldered by the N.F.U.

There exists, accordingly, the most close, continuous and intimate relationship between the interest groups and Whitehall. The Select Committee on Intermediaries thus characterized it: "There exists between these bodies and the Government Departments with which they principally deal *close and friendly personal contacts* at all levels. The members and officers of the organizations, senior and junior, know their opposite numbers in the Departments and have ready access to them."[12]

This contact operates at two levels, official and informal. At official level it takes three forms:

(1) *Government Committees* on which appropriate interest-groups sit. The T.U.C. sits on sixty such Committees; the F.B.I. on at least one score.

(2) *Ad hoc* Inquiries, (often sparked off by an interest-group) to which they are invited to give their views. These are much more numerous than one might suppose. e.g. The Howitt Committee (patent law); Verdon-Smith Committee (Censuses of Production and Distribution); Mocatta Committee (Endorsement of cheques). Also there are full scale Royal Commissions, or Interdepartmental Inquiries.

(3) *Prior Consultation* of interest groups by the department on all proposed Rules, Orders and Regulations. It is almost unknown for ministries not to consult bodies such as the T.U.C., F.B.I., B.B.C., Association of Municipal Corporations, County Councils Association —indeed, pretty well all those major groups mentioned in Part I—on proposed administrative regulations, on which their comments are politely requested. When a group is *not* so consulted, (this sometimes happens) there is recrimination and ill-feeling.

[11] *Report on the Committee of Intermediaries*, London 1950. Cmd. 7904—an important source.
[12] *Ibid.*, p. 44.

This close relationship is not natural—it has to be earned. "The organizations rely on the prestige they have acquired both with members and with Departments and *on the confidence* which the departments have in the organizations."[13] Both sides have to agree, tacitly, to trust the honour, sense of responsibility, and common sense of the other. An organization that misused confidential information or indulged in sharp practice would suffer immediately: the department would withdraw its confidence, and this would destroy the organization's usefulness to its members.

VII. PARLIAMENTARY PRESSURE

Parliament is sovereign. It is the master of the Ministries. It is the obvious place to turn to, if Ministers and Civil Servants prove recalcitrant.

Except for the eighty Trade Unions affiliated to the Labour Party, and the Co-operative Society affiliated to the Co-operative Party, all interest-groups proclaim that they are "non-political." This has a purely technical meaning. It means that the organization is neither affiliated to, a party, nor takes from or gives to a party's funds. It does not preclude either (a) seeking direct representation in Parliament and participating in the Parliamentary processes nor (b) espousing a general philosophy. (e.g. "Free Enterprise") compatible with only one of our main parties, or (c) "Aligning" with one or other of the many parties on major issues. All "non-political" may mean is that the organization reserves the right to look a gift horse in the mouth, and to bite the hand of the very party that feeds it.

So much for the matter regarded from the Lobby viewpoint. If we look at it from the Parliamentary standpoint, then both Houses may be said to be organized in two different ways viz: (a) into a number of interests (b) into the two main parties. The Lobby's successes in Parliament depend on *both* and *each*.

Parliament and Interests

The degree to which Parliament directly represents interests has passed largely unnoticed, owing I suspect to the fashionable obsession with parties and the still more fashionable preoccupation with so-called *"oligarchy"*. The degree to which Parliament represents interests may be seen, for instance, by an occupational table such as is provided by D. Butler.[14] It is more dramatically illustrated by another table com-

[13] *Ibid.*
[14] See David Butler, *The British General Elections of 1955*, London 1955.

piled by the author. It does not show occupation. It *does* show relationship, present or past, with an outside body and this is much more significant. It is very incomplete—if *"Dod's Parliamentary Companion"* and *"Who's Who"* had been consulted, many more relationships would have been disclosed. It is offered therefore as illustrative only.[15]

For their part, associations of all kinds seek direct representation. They may attain this by (1) Having members or officers as M.P.s. (2) Asking sitting members to interest themselves in the association, either (a) on a definite "Parliamentary panel" or (b) *ad hoc*.[16]

Interests and Party[17]

Interest groups stand in one of three relations to the two major parties viz: (1) Embodiment, or affiliation (2) "Alignment" and (3) Shared favors or No favors. ("Hard to get").

(1) Eighty Trade Unions are affiliated to the Labour Party. The mechanism of their affiliation, the fact that they command about half the Parliamentary seats, and overwhelmingly command the votes in the Party conference, as well as providing the central H.Q. with most of its money—these facts are so well known that I propose to take them as read.

Likewise the Co-operative societies affiliated to the Co-operative Party have a number of joint Co-op-Labour M.P.s, to the number of 16.

(2) No interest-groups are "affiliated" to the Conservative Party but as I have argued elsewhere,[18] the great organizations of employers in

[15] At this point the author inserted into his report a table showing, respectively, the name, constituency and party complexion of Members of Parliament, coupled with the organizations of which they were a member or officer, and the relationship in which they stood to these organizations. It contained 166 M.P.s and enumerated 216 relationships. Since this information was simply copied from *The Times House of Commons*, which is easily accessible to readers, the author has consented to delete the table in the interests of space.

[16] The one political scientist who has fully expressed and written about the importance of this topic is Professor Samuel H. Beer in his "The Representation of Interests in British Government: Historical Background," *The American Political Science Review*, vol. LI (1957), pp. 613–50.

[17] On this topic see Samuel H. Beer, "Pressure Groups and Parties in Britain," *ibid.*, vol. L (1956), pp. 1–23, an admirable and judicious study. I substantially agree with the analysis save that I think the author has overrated the similarity of party policies, and overrated our social consensus. See also S. E. Finer, "The Political Power of Private Capital," Parts I and (more especially) II, *Sociological Review*, vol. III and IV (1955–56), pp. 279–294, and 5–30; and Professor F. C. Newman, "Reflections on Money and Party Politics in Britain", *Parliamentary Affairs*, vol. 10 (1957), pp. 308–332.

[18] *op. cit.* (fn. 17).

industry, trade, commerce and farming must be regarded as *aligned* with the Conservative Party. The link between them is not made by the organizations *qua* organizations but by the fact that the private individuals who compose these organizations, do, as individuals have overwhelming links with the Conservative, and not the Labour Party. This personal behaviour takes the three forms of

Voting. The one-third of a million who make up the "top business section", voted 10–1 Conservative against Labour in 1951.

Presence. This section is heavily represented among Conservative M.P.s (and Peers) and lightly among the Labour Party. In 1951 and in 1955 the proportion of employers and managers on the Conservative Parliamentary Party was 33%: in the Labour Party only 9%. There is a similar identity between prominent business people in the constituencies and on executive committees of the Conservative and Unionist Associations.

Money. Such meager evidence as is available shows that they contribute to the Conservative Party and not to the Labour Party. To this we ought to add three other points. The F.B.I., N.U.M., Institute of Directors and the like, in the same breath as they protest political neutrality, also affirm their devotion to *"Private Enterprise"* and their antagonism to any who oppose it. Secondly, the members of these associations refer in private to the Conservative Party as "their party." Thirdly, they all know that though their party may chastise them with "Whips," the Labour Party will chastise them with scorpions.

(3) There remain huge uncommitted organizations. The N.U.T. offers to support electorally an equal number (4) of candidates from each of the three parties. In other cases, e.g. the farming interest, the textile interest, the motorcar industry, there is a cross-bench *"Interest"* of capital *and* labour which often transcends party allegiances. And some groups like the Legion, or Old Age Pensioners play "hard to get" between both parties.

One major effect of this relationship must be noticed here. It may be termed, the "Esau phenomenon".

It is simply that owing to this relationship, party programs encapsulate the demands of many of the interest groups. The Labour Party, when policy-making in opposition, consults with and embodies many demands of the Unions. Likewise the Conservative Party's Central Office consults with its "aligned" interests and introduces a selection of their demands into its program. Both parties seek to win the uncommitted groups—hence old age pensioners', or women's equal pay demands, find their way into the program. A party is expected to honor this if elected—this is true for both parties today. Hence the vital importance of this interest-cum-Party policy-making. Once adopted in the program the much attested discipline of British parties ensures implementation. Observers conclude that this means that "party is stronger than the lobby". It really means that a lobby in either party is stronger than a lobby outside the party. The party is often speaking for "its" Lobby. "The voice is Jacob's voice; but the hands are the hands of Esau".

The Technical Efficiency of the Lobby

" '*Tis not in mortals to command success.*" Nor in lobbies either. But there are certain necessary conditions, though these may not be sufficient ones.

These necessary conditions may be collectively dubbed the "*technical efficiency*" of the lobby and it consists of three things, viz; Advance intelligence: established access to friendly M.P.s; and facilities for briefing.

(1) *Advance intelligence.* The less well equipped lobbies may pay a Parliamentary agent (a law firm specializing in Parliamentary work) to scrutinize private bills, affecting them. E.g. the National Federation of Property Owners; the Caterers' Association; the Licensed Victuallers' Defence League. Others use special Public Relations firms (there are one or two). But to have good advance intelligence demands at least a well paid professional staff. (The N. U. T. has a headquarters staff, and nine full time divisional secretaries. The F.B.I. has a staff of no less than eighty.) Better still, if as described above, the Department is in the habit of sending draft orders etc. to the organizations and consulting them in advance of Parliamentary action.

The poorer, the less representative, the less reliable an association, therefore, the less well equipped to make a Parliamentary fight of it. Most propaganda and promotional associations are of this kind.

(2) *Established access to friendly M.P.s* I have mentioned the practice of forming or acquiring parliamentary panels. These alone can do little. Their real task is to raise the lobby's problem in the appropriate quarter and win over other M.P.s to their side—i.e. to act as channels. The organization of the Parliamentary Parties into functional specialist back-bench committees, dealing with Agriculture, Education, Industry, etc., facilitates such extension of support. The N.F.U. Yearbook carries each year the following standard phrase: "The Union continued to use the established channels of communication with the Parliamentary Agricultural Committees of the major political parties; and, as occasion required, the principal officers and staff of the Union attended meetings

of those Committees and their representatives, to discuss the issues arising." This practice, I may add, is—for the well established interest groups—a standard practice.

There have been several occasions recently when so-called *"mass lobbies"* descended on M.P.s at the Palace of Westminster. Taximen protesting at the number of licences issued in the London area; 2,000 women (monstrous regiment?) who descended on Parliament to protest at the Budget; the London Schoolmasters' Association; the Peace Committee; and the like. Often the more demonstrative the lobbying, the weaker and poorer in repute the organizations concerned. The best equipped lobbies tend to work silently. E.g. during the passage of the Restrictive Practices Bill the press made a song and dance about the fact that three hundred amendments had been put down. But nobody at the time said that sixty of these had emanated from the joint F.B.I., N.U.M., A.B.C.C. Committee. This fact was only revealed when these bodies published their annual reports!

(3) *Facilities for Briefing.* Access merely puts one's foot in the door; a lobby wants to have both feet under the table. The case to be put promptly and well. Here again the large well established lobbies with their large staffs are at an advantage. In addition, parliamentary agents or professional PRO's are engaged by the feebler lobbies. It must also be remembered that a mere statement of a case is not nearly sufficient; in a major bill legal amendments must be drafted, and alternative amendments should these not be carried. Lobbyists often sit in the Committee rooms or outside them to brief their M.P.s during the discussions.

Parliamentary Success

The lobby frequently wins its battles in Parliament and if it loses, usually gets some sort of consolation prize.

(1) It tends to win if it can pin the Minister between the Opposition and his own backbenchers: thus (*Opposition pressure + Ministerialist pressure vs. Minister.*)

Thus in 1956 the Minister had to postpone the operation of a bill which increased teachers' superannuation contributions, because the whole Opposition opposed him and so did a number of his own backbenchers. This year, in the Rents Bill, the Minister had to postpone the date of decontrol of rents for a group of 800,000 houses, because the Opposition opposed the whole measure, whilst his own backbenchers (afraid of losing the tenants' votes) would have joined the Opposition on this point.

(2) It tends to lose if the Minister can squeeze it between himself and

the Opposition i.e. (*Opposition pressure + Minister*) *vs. Ministerialist pressure.*

Thus in the Transport Bill, 1956, the Road Haulage Association tried to exert pressure in the Conservative Party to defeat the Bill—(this Bill halted the breaking up of the Nationalized British Road Services). The Minister, firm in Opposition support, and with a large number of his own side in support also, isolated the R.H.A. bloc, and could afford to ignore it.

(3) Indeterminate: the straight party line up. i.e. *Opposition pressure vs. (Minister + Ministerial Pressure).*

This is the most usual case. The logic is this. The Opposition will take *any* concession from the Minister, since anything is better than nothing, and the Minister can always vote them down. The "pressures" on the Ministerialist side will take any rebuff from the Minister, since they have still worse to fear from the policy the Opposition is advocating and would pursue if in office. This leaves the Minister as king-pin.

VIII. THE LOBBY AND THE PUBLIC

The appeal to the grass roots is not nearly so important (or obvious) in Britain as in the U.S.A. It will be helpful if I indicate the reasons why. There are four: (1) Campaign expenditures are not only limited by law but this law is fully respected. According to Professor Frank C. Newman[19] the American elections of 1952 cost from 80 to 140 million dollars, the British elections of 1951 about 2.75 million dollars. (2) We spend far less on advertising generally than the U.S.A. Our expenditure was less than 1,000 million dollars in 1956. American expenditure was nearly 10,000 million dollars. (3) The two most potent and expensive media viz broadcasting and TV are barred off "politics" in Britain. In the last three months the Independent Television Agency (commercial) has banned two films by lobbies, on the grounds that they were, in fact, "political." One was a film contrasting roads in Britain and abroad, sponsored by the Road Campaign Council. The other was the mere script of a series of films. "Although the programmes in themselves seemed intended to contain 'unexceptionable factual accounts' of British industrial achievement, the descriptive material seemed to the I.T.V. to suggest "the project as a whole has in some part a political end".[20] (4) The different roles played by interest groups in the two countries. The British work more cordially with the departments and are much more closely embodied in the legislature. In the U.S.A. the

[19] op. cit.
[20] *The Times*, May 29, 1957.

groups are still regarded as piratical; are less rarely directly represented in Congress; and Senate and House may be self divided on party lines, or be both of a party opposing the President. Hence to be effective the American pressure group has to convince the President and the Congress alike from the outside. It is forced into public campaigning.

The "Background" Public Campaign

Nevertheless, a degree of background "grass roots" lobbying does go on. There are bodies like the Peace Pledge Union which hawks its newspapers around on street corners. There are others, like the Roads Campaign Council which holds meetings, shows films and distributes leaflets.

There is also a certain amount of "Private Enterprise" and "Socialism" propaganda going on. The latter finds its chief outlet in the very numerous trade union journals. There are about ninety of these. Their circulation is about one and a half to two millions. On the whole they are pretty dull. Capitalist propaganda is disseminated, of conscious intent at any rate, from two organizations, *Aims of Industry* (founded 1942) and the *Economic League*. (1919) Each uses fleets of loudspeaker cars; distributes leaflets: holds factory-door meetings. "*Aims*" specializes in placing features in newspapers. The following figures may be of interest.

Economic League	1947	1956
Meetings held	14,110	18,069
Group meetings held	63,071	33,500
Leaflets distributed	7 million	20.4 million
Publicity placed	24,000 inches	36,700 inches
Full-time outside staff:	100	
Aims	1948	1956
Publicity placed	80,000 inches	145,120 inches

It may be noticed that "*Aims*" undertakes special assignments for lobbyists, and it is "*Aims*" which is carrying on propaganda on behalf of the Roads Campaign Council. It receives a special budget for this. Otherwise, both it and the *Economic League* get their revenue from members' subscriptions and private gifts. The total expenditure of "*Aims*" in 1955 was £ 156,000.

The "Fire Brigade Campaigns"—Grass Roots Style

This is the name given to the *ad hoc* campaign, launched by lobbies, to support their Parliamentary attack on Legislation. They became quite common during the 1946–1951 period, under the Labour Government. The two most notable were the Road Hauliers' anti-nationalization campaign 1946–7, and "the Cube Campaign" of 1949. The Road Haulage Association, at first alone and later in association with the Railway Stockholders Union, organized its 14,000 members through their Regional and District Committees to defeat the nationalization of long-distance road haulage. They collected a fighting fund, and appointed two Public Relations Officers to help organize the Districts. They organized a petition; distributed hundreds of thousands of leaflets; put sticky labels on lorries (dockers tore them off); put up poster displays; held hundreds of public meetings; and sent two propaganda films touring the country. The *Economic League* helped them with another 7,000 meetings and 30,000 bus-stop and factory-gate meetings. In my opinion the whole campaign was completely unsuccessful. Only about 850,000 people signed the petition—expensive, since the campaign cost   100,000! Also we know that public opinion was unmoved. A Gallup Poll taken in October 1946 showed that as many as 57.5% of those expressing an opinion disapproved of the Government's action; but a later poll, in May 1947—i.e. after six month's propaganda showed that now only 56% were so opposed! And, finally, the R.H.A. won no concessions in Parliament to speak of.

The "Mr. Cube" campaign, directed against the proposed nationalization of the sugar-industry, was technically far more brilliant, though the failure of the Labour Party to get a working majority in the 1950 election precludes judgment of how successful a campaign it was.[21]

The "Fire Brigade" Campaign—Selective Style

The most usual method of public campaigning adopted, in support of a Parliamentary struggle, is a selective campaign. The propaganda is aimed at key-people rather than the public at large. The N.U.T. campaign for higher salaries and against the Superannuation Bill of 1956 is a good example. The N.U.T. drew public attention to itself (and its case) by calling on its members to desist from collecting school-savings. As a result it received 3088 newspaper references and 200 leading articles, much of the background being supplied by the Union. As its Annual Report guilelessly remarks, "The extensive publicity described above was secured at little cost to the Union."

In the meantime however the Union sought to press the matter home. A letter stating the Union's case was sent to every Member of Parliament, while of course the twenty-three N.U.T. members in the House

[21] Since the campaign has been brilliantly described by H. Wilson, "Techniques of Pressure—Anti-Nationalization Propaganda in Britain," *Public Opinion Quarterly*, vol. XV (1951), pp. 225–42 it is unnecessary to say any more here.

(twenty-one on the Labour side) were rallying support there. Simultaneously, the Union decided to spend £100,000 on a press and publicity campaign. One advertisement called "A Square Deal for Teachers" appeared in eleven newspapers, and cost £1,617. But the heart of the campaign was the distribution of half a million leaflets and speakers' notes; these were distributed where it was thought they would do the most good. I give the whole list because it brings my end back to my beginning—the multifariousness of our groups, and the centres of influence in our community:

> County/City/Borough/Urban/Rural Councillors and Aldermen
> Co-opted members of Local Education Authorities
> School Managers and Clerks to Governors
> County Education Officers and divisional executives
> Parent/Teacher Associations and Federations
> M.P.s
> Representatives of the local press
> Professional and Cultural Associations
> Ratepayers Associations
> Trades Councils
> British Legion
> Residents' Associations
> Rotarians
> Civic Societies
> Social and Political Clubs
> Chambers of Commerce
> Women's Institutes
> Women's Guilds
> Business & Professional Women's Clubs
> Soroptimists
> Workers Educational Associations
> Prominent businessmen and business houses including banks
> Ministry of Labour Offices
> Co-operative Societies
> Toc H
> Doctors and Dentists
> Leaders of Voluntary Organizations
> Local clergymen and ministers of religion.

IX. THE LOBBY AND THE PUBLIC INTEREST

The foregoing pages make it apparent that the Lobby plays a major part in the British political processes. It would be very easy to draw false conclusions from this, as, to my mind, Professor F. C. Newman unquestionably has.[22] Professor Newman is apparently so amazed at his discovery that Britain has an extensive, well-organized and powerful

[22] *op. cit.*

Lobby (as British political scientists well know) that he has not paused to ask himself what countervailing influences exist. For the facts are that the British Lobby is *not* a corrupting influence in public life; that it does *not* result in erratic and grossly inconsistent policy; and that it does *not* lead to the oppression of minorities—or, indeed of majorities. There is increasing danger of the oppression of minorities, it is true—but not because (as Newman alleges) some lobbies are rich and some are poor: I have dealt with these dangers and the reasons for them elsewhere.[23] But at the moment by and large the U.K. remains the same tidily and justly governed country that it is usually represented to be. One could say that the Lobby gives our party governments a distinctive bias; they lean towards one set of interest groups rather than another according to whether the Government is Labour or Conservative. But this bias is moderated by the factors now to be mentioned. The final result is that a British Government—Labour or Conservative—might best be described as being like the Irish judge—neither partial nor impartial.[24]

Three sets of factors correct the pressure of the lobbies, and produce reasonably self-consistent public policy. They are (1) *Institutions*, (2) *Processes* and (3) *Beliefs*. All are aspects of one another.

Institutional Checks

1. *The Civil Service: Departmental Policy and tradition.* The department consists of well-trained professionals, with a very high degree of permanence. Its characteristics, compared with both politicians and lobbies, are its disinterestedness, knowledgeability, and permanency. Each department, in the course of its dealings with the lobbies, has formed a set of departmental rules-of-thumb. These, together with past and present ministerial pronouncements, form the *departmental view*.

At the sub-ministerial level, this view is the *sole* operative one.

At political level, it is *one* factor among the others, described below.

The views of other departments. These are often different and even

[23] See ch. IX of my *Anonymous Empire: A Study of the Lobby in Britain*, London, 1958. That particular chapter was reprinted in *Political Studies* vol. VI (1958), pp. 16–32.

[24] The two studies of the relationship between Lobby and British political life which come nearest the truth are those by Samuel Beer, *op. cit.* (fn. 17) and his "The Future of British Politics: an American View," *Political Quarterly*, vol. XXVI (1955), pp. 33–43. I have expressed my own views in my *op. cit.* (fn. 17), and in a broadcast, "In Defence of Pressure Groups," reprinted in *The Listener*, June 7, 1956. I am in substantial agreement with Professor Beer and the very brief notes—almost talking points—following in the text are in supplementation, not contradiction of his thesis of "British Consensus".

antagonistic. It is a rule in the Civil Service that all departments with an interest *must* be brought into full and frank discussion and their views reconciled even if this means "going to Ministers".

The collective Cabinet view. Similarly, at "top level": no Minister may put up a bill unless and until all departments concerned are fully consulted; and then participate in drafting, at all subsequent stages. The Cabinet is collectively responsible for "policy" measures.

Party. The parties encapsulate the claims of some lobbies, to be sure. But these claims are not always compatible—the party has to regulate them. Also, some of the lobbies (e.g. Agriculture, and Labour) *cross* the parties, so that the party has to move some way towards the views upheld by the *other* party. In short, the party system organizes the lobbies' divergent claims into two *coherent* systems. And though in rivalry, these two systems have many points in common.

Also, as Professor Beer points out, it is wrong to try to reduce party programmes to a mere collection of lobby-claims. Party outlook, temperament and philosophy emerge from lobby-claims: But these outlooks and philosophies also act as an antomonous force, as a yardstick, by which some such claims are adjudged worthy of inclusion and others to be rejected. (E.g. The quarrel in the Labour Party over "old fashioned" nationalization, and the "take-over bid" variety. This hinges on the party's sentiments about the morality of profits, and especially, of the Stock Exchange).

Party discipline ensures pretty consistent adherence to the line once it is chosen.

Parliament. Its organization into Government and Opposition turns a pitiless publicity on any deal suspected of being "shady".

It should be noticed, too, that England is governed, in effect, by rotation of office. Since 1832 no single party has ever been uninterruptedly in sole charge of the country for more than eleven and a half years at a stretch. Hence a *"Do ut des"* policy on both sides.

Press. The Press takes sides, often on party lines. It exposes what it thinks are "rackets" but it also rationalizes the views of the lobby it supports into something like a coherent philosophy. c.f. the *Daily Express's* campaign against the Common Market.

Processes

1. The governmental process is based on consultation with all affected interests, at *every* stage.

2. At each stage a sectional view is therefore exposed to the views of the counter-lobby, and to counter-ideologies.

3. A policy, when finally evolved, is the *moral* responsibility of the Minister in charge, even though the Cabinet as a whole espouse it. Now no Minister wants to make a fool of himself; and no Minister wants to be thought of as a compliant tool.

4. Yet the procedure exposes him to searching criticism of just this kind. Hence, even if he does espouse a lobby's viewpoint, he will only do so if it is administratively sound, and morally colorable.

Beliefs

1. Professor Beer talks, rightly, of the "British consensus" and stresses the constrictive influences of our "climates of opinion—" e.g. the common acceptance of Keynes; and the public dedication to "full employment".

2. One ought to go further. Such beliefs are brought together in English political life by the myth of "the public interest". No individual can lay down the criteria for this: but everybody will say that there is a "public interest" different from, or transcending, sectional interests. Hence no lobby can or will ever defend itself by simply saying that the policy is "good for the trade." It has to try to show it is "good for the country." This invites rebuttal in the same terms.

3. To show what is "good for the country" entails invoking precisely such common concepts as "full employment" etc. as form the current climate of opinion. This softens asperities, and also acts as a yardstick by which sectional policies are judged: and thus acts as a cohesive force.

4. George Orwell wrote, in *"England, your England"*: "Here one comes upon an all-important English trait: the respect for constitutionalism and legality, the belief in 'the law' as something above the State and above the individual, something which is cruel and stupid, of course, but at any rate, *incorruptible.* . . .

"It is not that anyone imagines the law to be just. Everyone knows that there is one law for the rich and another for the poor. But no one accepts the implications of this, everyone takes it for granted that the law, such as it is, will be respected and feels a sense of outrage when it is not. . . . The totalitarians' notion that there is no such thing as law, there is only power, has never taken root."

In the same way, though no two men agree on what precisely constitutes the public interest, all agree it exists, must be respected and feel a sense of outrage when it is not.

SUPPLEMENTARY SELECTED BIBLIOGRAPHY

In addition to the references contained in the footnotes to the above report the following publications are of interest:

1. W. J. M. MacKenzie, "Pressure Groups in British Government," *British Journal of Sociology*, Vol. VI (1955), pp. 133–48.
2. ——, "Pressure Groups: The Conceptual Framework," *Political Studies*, Vol. III (1955), pp. 247–55.
3. Allen Potter, "British Pressure Groups: Characteristics and Effects on Government Policies," *Parliamentary Affairs*, Vol. 9 (1956), pp. 418–30.
4. J. D. Stewart, *British Pressure Groups: Their Role in Relation to the House of Commons*, Oxford, 1958.
5. "Pressure Groups in Britain," Special Issue of the *Political Quarterly*, Vol. XXIX (1958), pp. 1–82.

PRESSURE GROUPS IN JAPAN

KIYOSKI TSUJI*

I. Pressure Groups and Politics in Japan

As in all European nations and in the United States, interest groups, in their broader sense, have been found also in Japan, from old times. However, the political phenomenon which might be called the rise of pressure groups in a modern sense is clearly related to the development of representative government and of party politics.

There are three principal causes which gave rise to the pressure groups:

1. As was pointed out by V. O. Key, along with the extensive and complex differentiation of occupational groups in the twentieth century, it has become impossible for the member of parliament, who was elected according to the principle of territorial representation, to adequately represent occupational interests, extending beyond the narrow limit of the constituency. That is: it has become vital that, side by side with the common interests of the voters living within a certain district, the special interests which citizens have in common with their fellow members as businessmen, wage earners or professionals, should be promoted.

For this reason, the respective interest groups, dissatisfied as they are with the legislative activities of a parliament, elected on a territorial base, launch pressure activities in order to induce the members of parliament and the political party to work for the attainment of their particular objectives.

2. As M. Ostogorski and R. Michels have described it, in the twentieth century, the rise of an oligarchy in the system of the political party brought about a stronger control by a small number of leaders over the party: and this has made it easier for them to affiliate with any particular interest groups.

This phenomenon is especially conspicuous in the case when the party leaders take the chairmanship of standing committees in parliament.

3. The third cause is the fact that, with the close of the age of laissez-faire, the government control over social life and economics has been strengthened. For this reason, it has become increasingly difficult for

* The author wishes to acknowledge the assistance of Professor Takeshi Ishida.

an interest group to attain its objectives, exclusively through their ordinary activities. This has resulted in efforts of putting various kinds of political pressure on the executive branch in whose hand enforcing power rests.

Thus, the recently increasing activities of pressure groups are strategically related to the changed pattern of representative government and party politics. In other words, the role of pressure groups in modern politics should be investigated not only from the pathological aspects of corruption, etc., but also from the normal aspects of complementing the processes of representative government.

In Japan, the study of pressure groups from such an angle had scarcely been undertaken before the end of the Second World War. Typically enough before 1945 treatment of pressure groups was completely lacking in books on political science. Of course, this was not due to the negligence of scholars. The reason was rather that, in Japan before the surrender, political power was predominantly in the hands of the military and of bureaucrats, and that the status of parliament and political parties had been very low. It was not rare that the legislation of the House of Representatives, elected by popular vote, was rejected by the House of Peers, the Privy Council (largely recruited from bureaucrats) or the military. Therefore, to put pressure just on the popularly elected House of Representatives was insufficient. Pressures were actually put on the civil and military bureaucrats, but they took the latent form of bargaining between business and government, rather than clearly defined overt action. Accordingly, interest groups themselves hardly engaged in the activities which are ascribed to them by political scientists in democratic societies. In the last ten years, with parliament as the supreme legislative body, the systematization and the activities of pressure groups have been conspicuous, and much attention has focused on them.

II. Various Types of Pressure Groups and their Activities in Japan

Recently the number of pressure groups has increased much. The following is a list of the principal pressure groups in Japan.

Business

Japanese Federation of Employers' Associations (Nikkei-Ren). Founded in April 1948, as an organization of employers to cope with labor unions. The members are employers' associations. It has 45 local sub-organizations and 41 occupational sub-organizations, comprising about twenty-thousand employers. This is one of the most influential pressure groups in Japan.

They hold a general meeting once or twice a year, but usually the business is conducted by the Board of Directors. Besides deciding on the general principles of management concerning labor disputes, collective bargaining, and interpretation of labor regulation acts, the main activities of the Federation consist in making propositions to the government concerning labor policy. It engages also in political activities and has for instance expressed its preference for a two-party system and has published the "Resolution on the Defense of Parliamentary Government" in the face of a growing influence of the Socialist Party. The organization restrains or encourages the conservative parties and their governments and tries to form public opinions favorable to management. It has gained admission to the International Organization of Employers in 1951.

Federation of Economic Organization. (Keidan-Ren). Founded in August 1946. About 850 economic organizations are members and it comprises the principle economic organizations and big companies in Japan. Its field of activities is broader than that of the Federation of Employers' Association. Its main activities are not limited to labor problems, but it acts as a liaison among the various economic organizations, conducts research on economic problems and establishes statistics; it also has various special committees and sends recommendations to parliament and the administration concerning economic policies, economic administration, and reforms of economic regulation.

Japanese Management Association. (Dōyū-Kai). Founded in April 1946. Consists of liberal employers and their staffs. Its membership amounts to about 3000. It is organized with an executive committee, other committees, research sections, etc. It conducts research on economic policies from the point of view of the national economy, and publishes the results. It is especially concerned about the training of future managerial staff, holds seminars, etc.

Political Federation of Japanese Small Business. (Chūsei-Ren). Founded in April 1956. It has 320,000 members. Its aim is to protect small enterprise against the competition from big business, and to improve the social status of the small businessmen. It is very active in the political field to promote the interests common to small enterprise. Its principle objectives are to work for the decrease of taxes on small enterprises, the increase of credit facilities to them, and the passage of social security legislation for small employers. Different from the above two pressure groups, it puts pressure on any political parties to attain their objectives; and its brilliant actions to secure the passage of the Small Enterprise Bill in the recent parliamentary session gained public notice. It is one of the typical pressure groups in Japan.

Japanese Federation of Smaller Enterprises. (Nitchū-Ren). Founded in April 1950. The membership comprises 500 smaller business groups. It represents the opinion of a wide circle of smaller enterprise and aims at modernizing management and techniques of the smaller enterprise. It is not very active in political pressure activities, even though it sometimes makes recommendations to the Government concerning the promotion of the interests of the smaller enterprise.

Labor

General Council of Trade Unions of Japan. (Sōhyō). Founded in 1950, as an anti-communist labor organization, it comprises now both left and right wings. It is the most powerful federation of labor unions, and has about 4 million members. It has set up a political section. It criticized the Peace Conference at San Francisco, and is opposed to rearmament, and to the amendment of the present Consititution, formulating slogans "for peace and independence." The Council is not content with developing a strategy for labor disputes, but protests against amendments to Education Acts and Police Acts, and takes the leadership in the movements against nuclear weapons and military bases. It nominates and backs candidates in campaigns for general elections.

Japanese Trade Union Congress. (Zenrō). Founded in April 1954, at the initiative of four labor unions including the Seamen's Union and the Union of the Textile Industry Labor, who opposed *Sohyo* for being too radical. It has at present about 960,000 members. It maintains that labor should participate in management, but favors a policy of cooperation between capital and labor. Politically, it professes Democratic Socialism.

Japanese Teachers' Union. (Nikkyōso). Founded in June 1947. Membership about 500,000. It belongs to *Sohyo*. However, the activities of this union are especially noteworthy because in Japan the social status of teachers is comparatively high, and the Government has always been particularly prone to tighten its control over education.

Not limiting their activities to the policy of improving the living standard of teachers the Union holds study meetings. Recently, it has been active in opposing legislation which is detrimental to the independence and freedom of education. Using its systematic organization, it nominates a large number of union representatives as candidates for parliamentary elections, and has been successful in many cases.

When in 1956 amendments to the Education Acts tried to abolish the publicly elected Board of Education and to place education once more under the strict control of the bureaucracy, the Teachers' Union put strong pressure on the Socialist members of the House of Councillors in order to prevent the passing of the amendments.

Agriculture and Forestry

National Federation of Agricultural Co-operative Mutual Insurance Associations (Kyōsai-Ren). Founded in January 1951. Its objective is to promote efficient production in agriculture, and to improve the economic and social status of farmers. It comprises at present 76 units of agricultural co-operatives and their federations. In 1949, the Government's deflationary policy, accompanied by the drastic measures for accumulation of capital, brought about the impoverishment of farm economy. This National Federation was then founded with the aim of defending the agricultural producers against this disaster.

National Federation of Agricultural Co-operative Marketing Associations. (Zenhan-Ren). Founded in October 1948, comprising 54 federations of associations.

National Federation of Agricultural Co-operative Purchasing Associations. (Zenkō-Ren). Founded in October 1948, comprising 53 federations of associations. They are respectively engaged in co-operative marketing of agricultural products and co-operative purchasing of agricultural machines and implements, agricultural medicines and fertilizers. The latter Federation aroused much indignation when it became known that it had offered funds to political parties and bribed officials of the Ministry of Agriculture and Forestry.

Japanese Forestry Associations. (Nichivinkyō). Founded in April 1949. It has a membership of 468, including both individual membership and associations. It conducts research on forestry, facilitates mutual communications of the member organizations; it also makes suggestions to the Administration and parliament concerning forestry policies, and tries to see its proposals implemented.

Japanese Farmers' Union. (Nichinō). It was founded as far back as 1922. Though at one time it was the promoting force of proletarian parties, the oppression during the war succeeded in all but destroying it. Resurrected in February 1946, it fought for the re-distribution of agricultural land and for a rationalization of the delivery quota of rice. It also opposed heavy taxation, and strove for the democratization of agricultural and forestry administration. Nevertheless, differences in political viewpoints led to the split of the Union into three groups: *Zennō* (the right wing), *Nichinō Shutaisei Ha* (The anti-communistic left wing), and *Nichino Tōitsu Ha* (the pro-communistic left wing). Recently, the reunion of the latter two groups is being attempted.

The Japanese Farmers' Union was the largest organization of farmers' movements. However, since the number of small landowners increased as the result of post war land reform, it is not as active as it was formerly. Nevertheless it opposes the exploitation of farmers which the monopolistic capital and the conservative government have tried to achieve through the purchase of materials and other means. It is especially important inasmuch as it is the only force fighting against the repossession of land by the former big landowners.

Local Bodies

It may sound rather strange to include local bodies in the category of pressure groups. However, we have a special reason for this. For a long time, bureaucratic centralization of power in the hand of the Central Government, with the ministry of Home Affairs as its central administration, was very strong. In 1947 (the Local Self-Government Law gave autonomy to the local bodies such as the prefectures, and cities, towns and villages; nevertheless a policy of centralizing financial and administrative powers has been adhered to till the present. Recently there is even a strong tendency to abolish the public elections of the governors of prefectures and to return to the method of their appointment by the Central Government. The reason given for the proposed change is the alleged immaturity of the public to take responsibility for voting. Because of such trends, there is a movement to prevent the reestablishment of proposed bureaucratic control over the local governments; and all local bodies have rallied to this cause. Among them the six outstanding groups are the National Association of Governors, the National Association of the Chairmen of Prefectural Assemblies, the National Association of Mayors, the National Association of the Chairmen of City Councils, the National Association of Headmen of Towns and Villages, and the National Association of Towns and Villages, each of them comprising heads and chairmen of local bodies.

These local bodies send petitions to parliament, put strong pressures on the members from their respective districts, and publish journals. Their research division is not yet fully developed.

Miscellaneous

Federation of Housewives. (Shufu-Ren). Founded in September 1948, comprising 250 associations of housewives. Its objective is to defend the interests of consumers, and to improve home life. It agitates against raising the price of rice, the charges for electricity, gas, and water service, and also of transportation fares. By making proposals to the parliament and the government, or by collecting signatures in streets, its members have been successful in arousing public opinion.

Japanese Medical Association. Founded in November 1947, to improve the standard of medical practice, to spread the knowledge of public health, and to protect the interests of the medical profession. With a membership of 65,000, it is strongly opposed to the separation of the dispensary from medical practice. Putting pressure on parliament and the government, the Association at last succeeded in preventing the proposed legislation. The Association nominates and supports candidates for election to the House of Councillors.

Japanese Pharmaceutical Association. Founded in October 1948, with a present membership of 24,000. It aims at raising the standard of the pharmaceutical profession and defending the interest of the profession. They nominate and support candidates for the members of the House of Councillors. In opposition to the Medical Association, it agitates for a separation of dispensaries from medical practice.

Among specialized pressure groups, we could mention the following: The *Japan-China Trading Association,* whose objective is to promote the trade between Japan and China. Established in 1955, it comprises 374 firms.

The *Association for Returning Okinawa Islands to Japan.* Established in 1946, it comprises about 300,000 Okinawians and emigrants from the islands.

The *Japan Federation of Veterans' Associations* whose aim it is to improve the social status of veterans and to organize them.

The *Association of Former Big Land Owners* whose aim it is to promote the movement for repossession of reparation payments and for their land which they have lost as the result of the land reform.

The *National Association for Restitution of Properties in Foreign Lands.* This group has requested the restitution of the properties which they have lost in foreign lands because of the Japanese defeat. Established in November 1952, it has a membership of about 700,000.

III. Peculiarities of Japanese Pressure Groups

The peculiarities of pressure groups in Japan can be summarized as follows:

1. Since the party organizations are weak (as a matter of fact, the membership of the Liberal-Democrats amounts to about 100,000 and that of the Socialists to about 40,000), pressure groups take the role of sub-

organizations of the parties and are apt to be involved in the same kind of activities as parties.

In general it is believed that what distinguishes parties from pressure groups is that only the former put up candidates for elections. In Japan, however, it is not rare that interest groups take an active part in election campaigns. It is known that especially for elections to the House of Councillors where 100 out of 250 members are elected from a nation-wide constituency, pressure groups nominate and support their own candidates. Once elected, the members are therefore likely to be in-fluenced by the views of the organizations that have supported them.

2. Since there are strong remnants of the bureaucratic system in Japan, the number of public bills is far higher than those sponsored by members of parliament. Among the laws which were passed by parliament since the surrender, public bills amount to 1,341 in comparison with 549 members' bills. If we take into consideration that among the members' bills those are counted which the administration had designated for sponsorship by members of parliament, the actual number of public bills is still higher. Under these circumstances, the activities of pres-sure groups are apt to be directed to administrative agencies which have important powers to give licenses and approvals. As a consequence of this situation, we are used to see members of parliament functioning as lobbyists for the pressure groups, introducing them to governmental officials, and requesting special favors for the groups. The officials who had connection with pressure groups are then frequently in-volved in scandals and indicted. Reform legislation to remedy these maneuvers is demanded by public opinion, but it will be quite difficult to pass it.

3. It very often happens in Japan that after their retirement, high governmental officials take important positions in economic organiza-tions and in public associations with which they had intimate con-nections while they were still in government. To give some examples: former officials of the Finance Ministry would become directors of main banks, officials of the Ministry of International Trade and Industry would be given important positions in big steel companies, former officials of the Ministry of Agriculture and Forestry would become advisors of the above mentioned agricultural associations, and former officials of the Ministry of Home Affairs would become leading mem-bers of local public associations. And we may add that there are many former governmental officials who are elected to parliament because of the "sphere of influence" which they have cultivated while in govern-

ment. As a result of the intimate relations between the former and present bureaucrats, there grows a compact bargaining unit among the three, namely the members of parliament, the executives of pressure groups, and administrative agencies, a unit which might indeed be called a Trinity.

INTEREST GROUPS IN SWEDEN: THEIR POLITICAL ROLE

GUNNAR HECKSCHER

I

The problem of interest groups has been rather extensively discussed in Sweden. The literature is however almost exclusively published in Swedish and not easily available to the foreign observer. It is therefore not referred to in this paper. On the other hand, as a consequence of the interest taken in these questions, there is little difficulty in identifying all major organized groups; and on the whole it can be said that no important groups exist without formal organization.

The development of these organizations goes back to the final period of the nineteenth century, industrialization in the modern sense of the word having begun in Sweden about 1880. *The labor unions,* of course, formed in order to establish equality of bargaining power for workers in a period when wages were low and employers still had a somewhat authoritarian attitude. They were comparatively successful from an early date. Employers did not to any important extent receive protection from the state (nor did the workers), and in one case after another they had to recognize unionization of their workers, bargain with the unions and to a greater or smaller extent accept their demands. By playing out one employer against another, the unions towards the end of 1890's actually seemed to be in a strong position which was still getting stronger.

Employers in Sweden reacted to this not by calling for state protection or support, which incidentally might not have been available, but by forming organizations of their own. *Employers' associations* for the various branches of industry began to confront the unions. By this means, it was possible not only to eliminate competition between different employers in so far as wages were concerned, but also to put financial pressure on the unions by exposing them to the danger of widening conflicts and heavy burdens of strike subsidies. On the other hand, the establishment of employers' associations meant recognition by the employers of collectivism in the labor market, and the establishment in 1906 of the state mediation service emphasized this even more strongly. Already at this early period, nationwide or at least regional collective agreements for one or two years were usual, and the abortive general strike of 1909 did not materially or permanently alter industrial relations.

White-collar workers did not join the unions of the workers, since they were regarded as occupying positions of trust within the enterprises. Eventually, this proved a doubtful blessing, and during the 1920's and early 1930's they were in danger of being squeezed between the two powerful organizations in the labor market. The answer, again, was organization, and during the 1930's this group rapidly organized and their organizations gained bargaining power without, however, associating themselves with the unions of the workers. Employers were at first not very willing to accept the idea of such organizations or of collective bargaining rights for this group of employees, so that the legislation to safeguard freedom of association and of bargaining, passed in 1935, was chiefly intended for their benefit. On the other hand, the Collective Contract's Act passed in 1928, in spite of opposition from the unions, mainly codified principles which had in actual fact been accepted for a long time.

Agricultural Producers' Co-operatives began to be established at the turn of the century but became important only some thirty years later. The long and complicated history of this development must be left aside at this point, especially since it is tied up with the development of Swedish agricultural policy in general. But it should be noted that also in this case the objective of the organizations was to establish equality of bargaining power. Particularly in view of long distances within farming districts, the Swedish farmer was frequently unable to influence effectively the prices paid for his products in the cities. Organization seemed to be the answer, permitting farmers to control the output collectively as well as to rationalize distribution, although in actual fact these ideas were finally accepted only in connection with regulations supported by the state.

In many respects the original *consumers' co-operatives* were of a similar character. In this case monopolistic control of the market was certainly not the objective, but the small consumer frequently found himself in the hands of the shopkeeper, especially where, as in numerous rural industrial communities, the shopkeeper had the direct or indirect support of the most influential employer. A consumers' co-operative, combining the scanty resources of the workers of the community, could relieve them from pressures of this type. As in the case of the unions, there was a considerable amount of initial success, but on the other hand the financial position of the co-operatives and of their central organization was shaky until several years after the end of World War I. After that time, however, consumers' co-operatives in Sweden have been uniformly successful. They do not control economic life, nor do their activities in production go much beyond what is required for their own purposes, but on the whole success has been striking and somewhat threatening to the private retail trade.

From the 1920's onwards, *retailers* have tended to respond by establishing organizations of their own in order to simplify distribution and acquire the same advantages of large scale trade as those held by the cooperatives. Retailers' organizations are very definitely defensive in character and have in fact never acquired economic power comparable to that of the co-operatives. On the other hand, they are by no means insignificant and present another example of the general tendency of meeting the problems of organization on one side by counter-organization on the other.

The above should be sufficient to provide a general idea of the development which has fostered the growth of economic organizations in Sweden. As to organizations of the type of *free churches, temperance societies* etc., other causes are obviously much more important. Here, the idealistic objectives must of course be given first place: organizations were established and grew in order to achieve individual or collective improvement of human nature. On the other hand, it must be remembered that especially during the formative period between 1880 and 1914 these organizations also fulfilled another function. The growth of industrialism, coming on top of far going reconstruction of the agrarian society, broke a number of existing social ties and left individuals somewhat isolated. Organizations formed a substitute for the type of contact existing in the village community, now dissolved. This is probably especially true of temperance societies, which offered human contact of a different type than that of the saloon: equally warm, with a better social status and probably less expensive.

In Swedish literature, the term "popular movement" is frequently used in the place of "organization" or "pressure group". True, some of the organizations just mentioned, such as employers' associations and other business organizations do not fall within the term, but on the whole the development of organizations in Sweden has been parallel with the growth of democracy in the political as well as the social sense of the word and can be understood only as part of their growth. Historically, therefore, the term *popular movement* has considerable significance. Although this is less true in the actual environment, the historical tradition maintains some of its importance in this connection.

II

The historical development just indicated covers only some of the major organizations. At present, Swedish society is more completely organized than most Western societies. It is necessary to give some description of the actual situation in the organizational field.

It is in the *labor market* that organized groups have the oldest tradition, and this is still by and large their most important field of activities. With regard to employees, three major organizations ought to be mentioned. The oldest and largest is the Federation of Labor, LO (*Landsorganisationen i Sverige*), which has practically complete control over wage-earners and some salaried employees, mainly those employed by public enterprises in manual labor or comparable activities. The main body of both private and public salaried employees are however organized in the Central Organization of Salaried Employees, TCO (*Tjänstemännens Centralorganisation*). In addition, there is a special Federation of University Graduates, SACO (*Sveriges Akademikers Centralorganisation*), which in many respects acts as a negotiating partner for its members, especially in relation to state and local authorities.

On the employer side the oldest and most powerful organization is the Swedish Employers' Federation, SAF (*Svenska Arbetsgivareföreningen*), representing the vast majority of private employers in industry and related fields. There are independent employers' associations for employers in commerce, agriculture etc. The activities of the latter are however on the whole co-ordinated with those of SAF.

The role of *co-operatives* in the Swedish economy has been widely publicized. The oldest and most important organization is that of the consumers' co-operatives, KF (*Kooperativa Förbundet*), which works through a very great number of technically independent local units but also carries on production of certain commodities, mainly for the benefit of member associations. Housing co-operatives are also very important, and most of them are organized centrally in HSB (*Hyresgästernas Sparkasseoch Byggnadsförening*). In agriculture, almost complete coverage has been obtained by producers' co-operatives for all major commodities. They also have a central organization, *Sveriges Lantbruksförbund*.

For various parts of *economic enterprise,* there exist special organizations. Among these are the Federation of Swedish Industries, (*Sveriges Industriförbund*), and its branch organizations, the Chambers of Commerce, the Swedish Export Association (*Sveriges Allmänna Exportförening*), the Association of Crafts and Small Industrial Enterprise (*Sveriges Hantverks- och Småindustriorganisation*), the Swedish Retailers' Association (*Sveriges Köpmannaförbund*) and the Swedish Wholesalers' Association (*Sveriges Grossistförbund*).

Cartels exist in a number of fields, and while there is no legislation against combinations in restraint of trade, cartels are required to register and action might be taken against them if it is found that they are concluding agreements which are contrary to public policy. It seems safe to say that the importance of such combinations has diminished in recent years, largely owing to favorable conditions on the Swedish market.

Other organizations of economic importance include the National Association of Swedish Farmers, RLF (*Riksförbundet Landsbygdens Folk*), and certain other non-co-operative organizations in agriculture, the Association of Tenants (*Hyresgästföreningarnas Riksorganisation*), and its counterpart the Association of Real Estate Owners (*Sveriges Fastighetsägareförbund*).

In addition to these, there are a great number of non-economic organizations and movements. While sometimes more difficult to identify, these are yet of very considerable importance. Most noteworthy are perhaps the free churches, organizing religious dissent in a country where the Lutheran church is specifically recognized by the state and has for a long time maintained its position as the established church of Sweden, and the temperance movement, including a number of different organizations which used to compete eagerly in the past but are today co-operating closely among each other. Educational organizations, such as the Workers' Educational Association, ABF (*Arbetarnas Bildningsförbund*), and a number of comparable associations organizing other social or ideological groups for educational purposes are an important factor in the cultural life in the country. Sports associations exist in great number, although frequently with a rather floating membership. Their activities are regarded as being of first class importance, but on the other hand they do not as a rule act very strongly as organized pressure groups. And finally there are a number of women's organizations, some of them attached to other political or interest groups, but some of them, chiefly those dating from the time when women's suffrage was still a goal to be attained, entirely independent.

The membership of some major organizations in Sweden as of January 1, 1957.

Labor Unions (LO).	1,404,000[1]
White-collar employees organizations (TCO)	345,000[2]
Employers' organizations (SAF).	16,000
Employees of members	826,000
Consumer co-operatives (KF).	1,103,000

Housing co-operatives (HSB).	125,000
Agricultural co-operatives.	
Aggregate membership of all organizations:	1,120,778
Membership of largest member organization:	272,000
Probable total membership, approxim.:	360,000[3]
Free churches.	340,500
Temperance associations.	362,000
Educational associations.	689,000

[1] The total number of "workers" (*arbetare*) in 1950 is estimated in the official statistics at 1,661,000.

[2] The total number of "white-collar employees" (tjänstemän) in 1950 is estimated in the official statistics at 843,000. Some of these, however, are affiliated with LO.

[3] The total membership cannot be exactly estimated, for technical reasons. This figure applies to the circulation of the magazine of *Sveriges Lantbruksförbund* (*Jordbrukets Föreningsblad*).

With a system of organizations as wide-spread as that—and indeed far from completely catalogued here—it is obvious that there must be very considerable overlapping membership. For instance, LO and KF have to a large extent identical memberships, although their activities and even their philosophy are widely different. In the labor market, SACO members frequently belong to TCO as well. And it is obvious that housing co-operatives, tenants' associations, educational groups etc. draw a very large part of their membership from groups also organized along different lines. It is difficult to estimate the average number of associations to which a normal Swedish citizen is apt to belong, but it seems safe to say that nobody interested in organizational activities need yearn hopelessly for positions of trust within organizations once he has reached the mature age of 30.

Organizations are practically exclusively financed through membership dues of various types, with the exception of the different co-operatives, who are of course in business for themselves and therefore not normally dependent on dues. Outside financing is practically unknown except that subsidies by the state or local authorities are sometimes given for specific purposes, chiefly to non-economic organizations.

The *legal position* of organizations in Sweden is slightly obscure. The law distinguishes between "economic associations" and others, not on the basis of the objectives of their undertakings but on the basis of the type of work actually carried out. Thus, the legal term "economic association" is much more narrow than the term "economic organization" as used in this paper. Labor unions and employers' organizations, for instance, are non-economic associations in the eyes of the law and it is mainly the co-operatives which are legally regarded as "economic", since they are the only ones which are directly engaged in economic activities. Their legal situation is regulated by special legislation, dating back as far as the 1890's and providing guarantees for orderly accounting and registration as a pre-requisite of legal personality. In many respects this legislation corresponds to that governing limited liability companies, although economic associations are less strictly regulated and more favorably placed from the point of view of taxation. For the "non-economic" associations, on the other hand, there is no legislation at all. Courts recognize their legal personality in so far as they have some kind of by-laws and other indications of permanence, and they may thus acquire property and appear in court without previous registration and regardless of their internal organization. This is true notwithstanding the fact that for instance the unions and the employers' associations control very large funds, and are at the same time extremely important for the general economic life of the community.

On the other hand, legislation concerning the activities of group organizations is very meager. The labor market legislation is limited to activities directly connected with bargaining and collective contracts. In certain other fields, such as that of co-operative insurance and co-operative housing, there is special legislation. But the general character of the organizations is hardly regarded as a matter for the state at all. There is no legislation concerning "lobbying" nor has anything of that type ever been suggested.

III

The role of organized groups in Swedish society is such that they are always very much in the public eye. Their meetings and resolutions as well as their leading personalities receive wide publicity in the daily press, on the radio and in similar connections. On the other hand their activities are frequently the subject of debate in the press and are often criticized by independent organs as well as by papers attached to political parties. The larger organizations have established press services of their own and the trend in that direction has been increasing in recent years. On the whole, groups are acutely conscious of the importance of their public relations and quite prepared to do their best to deal with the problem.

A number of organizations issue periodicals of their own. This is true not only with regard to such journals as *Fackföreningsrörelsen* (LO), *Industria* (SAF) and *Jordbrukets Föreningsblad* (*Sveriges Lantbruksförbund*), but there are also a great number of branch organizations and smaller associations who publish periodicals both in order to keep in contact with their members and to explain their activities and views to the public. Their articles are frequently quoted in the daily press. LO alone is in addition the owner of daily newspapers, at present one morning paper (*Stockholmstidningen*) and one evening paper (*Aftonbladet*) in Stockholm.

Practically all organized groups are taking great interest in education. Many of them work together with one or more of the educational organs: LO with ABF, TCO with TBV (*Tjänstemännens Bildnings-versamhet*), the agriculture co-operatives with SLS (*Svenska Landsbyg-dens Studieförbund*). A number of them have organized specialized educational activities for their members and sometimes maintain their own educational institutions to house their courses and conferences. As a matter of fact, a number of older and newer Swedish mansions have been applied to this purpose: Bergendal is owned by TCO, Yxtaholm by SAF, while LO has established schools of their own at Brunnsvik and Runö. Finally, the folk high school movement is connected with these tendencies. A number of schools are owned by the "movements": Sigtuna by the church of Sweden, Tollare by the temperance movement, Brunnsvik and Viskadalen by the labor movement, Sånga-Säby by the agriculture co-operatives and Jakobsberg by the consumers' co-operatives.

Work at these educational institutions plays an important part in the development of the ideologies and the formulation of long-range objectives of organized groups. It seems likely that this has been an important factor in maintaining an idealistic attitude even on the part of group organizations chiefly concerned with representing the material interests of their members.

IV

The interaction between parties and interest groups in Sweden is intelligible only on the basis of at least an elementary knowledge of the party structure. For a long time, Sweden has had a multi-party system, and it is only for a very brief period that a single party has been able to command a majority in Parliament. On the other hand, the number of parties has never been excessive, and the establishment of new parties has always met with considerable difficulty. There are at present five parties, in order of magnitude Labor (Social Democrats), Liberals (The People's Party), Conservatives, Farmers, and Communists. The Communist Party is very small and has never held a significant representation in Parliament, although it has on the other hand always been represented. Of the other four, Labor is at present in power, while Liberals and Conservatives co-operate more or less closely in opposition and the Farmers, who until October 1957 were members of a coalition Government with Labor, occupy an intermediate position.

Political parties in Sweden

	Number of votes polled in 1956 election to Lower House	Members of Lower House	Members of Upper House
Conservatives	664,000	42	16
Liberals	923,500	58	30
Farmers	367,000	19	24
Social Democrats	1,729,500	106	78
Communists	194,000	6	3
	3,878,000	231	151

The basis of parties has always been closely connected with the social structure of various organizations. On the whole, there is great stability in the electorate, and changes in votes are usually fairly small from one election to another. It seems safe to say that the choice of party is frequently determined by group allegiance rather than by ideological reasons. On the other hand, party policies are as a rule rather clearly determined, although the span of difference between democratic parties is limited and a great number of problems are solved in agreement between all political groups.

The closest group-party relationship exists between the Labor Party and the labor union movement (LO). Most unions are affiliated to the Labor Party, the position of members being that they have the right of contracting out, but failing any such "reservation" automatically pay dues to the Labor Party through the union. The vast majority of union membership votes labor, although some have always voted communist and the number voting liberal or conservative has probably increased somewhat in recent years.

In the first decades of the Labor Party—which was founded in 1889— a similar relationship existed also with the consumer co-operatives. But in that respect a great change has come about in recent years. A great number of members outside the so-called working class have joined consumer co-ops, and the leadership of KF has strenuously worked to emphasize its political neutrality. TCO has always remained neutral from the point of view of political parties, and probably all parties (with the possible exception of the Farmers' Party) have a considerable number of their members among those adhering to TCO.

The Farmers' Party has never represented farmers to the same extent that the Labor Party represents union labor. It is probable that the other parties between them receive as many farmer votes as the Farmers' Party or even more. The situation is reflected in the relationship between that party and producers' co-operatives in agriculture. In principle, agricultural co-ops maintain political neutrality, and this is also in fact the case with regard to the great national organizations in this field as well as of The Association of Swedish Farmers. But in local co-operatives there are not infrequently conflicts between farmers belonging to the Farmers' Party and others, especially those belonging to the Conservative Party. In a number of cases, the Farmers' Party has managed to gain control of local producers' co-operatives, and this has also resulted in a certain amount of financial support to the respective local organizations of the Party. It is at present impossible to say whether this trend is going to continue or whether neutrality will again be more firmly established within the movement.

An interesting example of co-operation between parties and groups is that of the post-war program of the Labor Movement, which was issued jointly by LO and the Labor Party (and afterwards accepted *in toto* by the Communist Party). There is also very much current co-operation between LO and the Labor Party. At one time it was stated that leading members of the LO secretariat met weekly with leading members of the Labor Cabinet; at election time the support given to the Labor Party consists in conducting, within the unions, a vigorous and on the whole successful fight against communist influence, and it can safely be stated that LO and the Labor Party together are acutely conscious of the necessity of keeping communism down at a minimum of influence.

On the other hand, organizations like SAF, the Federation of Swedish Industries, etc., make no secret of it that they—or their members—are giving financial support to Conservatives and Liberals. These contributions are not channelled through the organizations themselves but are either provided by individual enterprises or through a special fund established for this purpose. But it is quite clear that the organizations take considerable interest in resisting the power of the Labor Party; in fact they are opposed to political labor much more fundamentally than to the power of the labor unions.

Non-economic groups are on the whole less closely related to politics. There was a time when both the free churches and the temperance movement were definitely connected with the Liberal Party and did in fact provide that party with a basis differing in degree and form rather than in substance from that provided by the unions for the Labor

Party. Although something of this connection still remains, the situation today is rather different. The temperance movement is now exercizing considerable influence on the Labor Party as well as on the Liberals, and the free churches are represented among Conservatives and Farmers as well as in the Liberal Party. Both these types of organizations are thus able to influence the whole field of political parties rather than being tied up with one of them, and this is all the more striking since their actual influence in the social life of the country has diminished rather than increased. On the other hand, they are not giving financial support to any political party except very rarely at the local level.

A fundamental problem in this connection is that related to the nomination of candidates for parliamentary and municipal elections. Sweden has for almost 50 years had a system of proportional representation at all elections, the parliamentary constituencies corresponding roughly to the counties. This means that electors vote for a list (or lists) of candidates presented by the party and not for individual candidates. The nomination system is regulated by the parties themselves and there is no legislation whatever in this field. Actually, although the formal procedure differs from one party to another, the main tendencies are the same: parties provide their members with an opportunity of participating in nominations, but members rarely avail themselves to any very considerable extent of these possibilities. In fact, the nomination lies in the hands of the executive committees or representative assemblies of party organizations in the constituency. For various reasons the central party organization exercises hardly any influence at all. But since the success or failure of the party in the constituency depends to a large extent on the attractiveness of the list presented to electors, parties are very anxious to make these lists as attractive as possible. There is even in Sweden a not inconsiderable floating vote which all parties are out to capture, and the voting of anybody belonging to a group organization (and most voters do belong to one or several such organizations), is supposedly influenced by the appearance on the party lists of candidates representing his group. The lists are composed largely with such considerations in mind and candidates are frequently being selected on the basis of their group affiliations rather than of their personal abilities. This tendency is strengthened by the character of electoral campaigns, where there is practically no "canvassing" and where speeches are made just as frequently by national figures of the parties as by the candidates actually proposed for the constituency. On the whole, both during electoral campaigns and between elections there is comparatively little direct contact between candidates and voters, and whatever contacts take place within organizations are therefore of very considerable importance.

Obviously, these tendencies have a considerable effect on group representation in parliament. In fact, this is a problem which has been largely discussed in Sweden. The tendency is for each party to try to nominate candidates having an appeal in marginal groups as well as in major groups related to the party. Since the membership of most groups votes for more than one party, this means that the parties are most eager to have a maximum of group representation among their candidates. In fact, one of the difficulties of Swedish politics is that candidates who represent no important group may find it difficult to get the nomination, even if they should be personally suited for political work and are extremely loyal members of their parties.

V

It follows from what has been said that interest groups have every opportunity to influence parties and thus, indirectly, the legislative process. Since parties are eager to bring forward candidates with important group attachments, all major groups can count on having spokesmen in one or more parties, and the system of proportional representation applied in Sweden means that it can often easily be estimated whether a candidature will in any given case be likely to lead to election or not. This applies to both the Upper and the Lower Houses of parliament, and there is no preference on the part of the groups to have their spokesmen in one house rather than the other. Another consequence is that while the idea of an Economic Council for group representation has sometimes been discussed, this has been not in order to provide the groups with better possibilities of influence, but in order to avoid their predominant influence in parliament as such by transferring it to a special body.

Since group representatives are elected on party tickets, and since party allegiance is usually quite strong in all major political questions, it frequently happens that parliamentarians or councilmen from the same organization may find themselves on different sides in a division, even on matters affecting the interests of their organization. But as long as the question is not one of major political importance, the reverse possibility also exists: group representatives may come together across party lines and try to affect the result in the interests of their organizations regardless of party affiliation. In many respects this makes for a more complicated relationship within the legislative process, while at the same time it paves the way for co-operation between parties as well as between groups.

But the actual influence of organizations on the legislative process is by no means limited to that exercised through members of parliament. In many cases, organizations—both economic and non-economic—appear to a more or less considerable extent as pressure groups. However, due to the general legislative and administrative system of Sweden and its traditional procedures, this influence is exercised rather openly and before the eyes of the public, although it is by no means less common or less dominating than in other countries.

In the first place, royal commissions play a very great part in Swedish legislative and political work. Practically all important questions which are brought before parliament have at one time or another been studied in a royal commission, the report of which is made public well ahead of the bill which is presented to parliament. Groups and interest organizations are given very full representation on such commissions and are thus able to use this device already at an early stage in order to reach agreement with political parties, with other groups and with administrators. The tendency is to attempt the greatest possible amount of agreement already at this stage, since proposals can more easily be carried if the commission has been unanimous.

But this is only the first stage, and of course not universally applied, since a number of decisions by government and legislature are not based on any reports by royal commissions. Organizations are able to make their views heard by other means as well. Most important are the memoranda officially presented on the demand of the government in the form of *"remissyttranden"*, that is comments submitted on the basis of actual proposals whether by royal commissions or otherwise. Such memoranda are requested from various administrative agencies but also from the relevant organizations, and on the whole the views expressed by organizations such as LO, TCO, SAF, KF and the farming co-operatives are taken equally or more seriously than those presented by government organs.

If the problem under discussion relates to a bill to be presented to parliament, a summary of the views expressed at the preliminary stage is included in the justification attached to the government proposal. Thus, a governmental bill frequently contains a considerable number of arguments presented against its own conclusions, although of course the Minister will present his own counter arguments as well.

But the system of *"remissyttranden"* applies not only to legislative proposals presented to parliament. Reports are also asked for and considered by the government in other matters, as well as before the decision is taken as to whether a legislative proposal is to be submitted on not. These reports and memoranda are particularly important in view of the fact that under Swedish constitutional law the documents of public agencies, including those of the ministries, are freely available to the public as long as there is no legal rule to the contrary. Exceptions exist mainly in order to safeguard documents which are properly speaking of a secret nature. The publicity of official documents is particularly important to the press, which informs its readers rather fully about the views expressed in *"remissyttranden"*, whenever they come in.

Even this, however, is not the end of the matter. Parliamentary committees may establish similar contacts both with administrative agencies and with organizations. These contacts sometimes take the form of hearings, but these hearings take place in closed sessions and their contents are thus not available to the public. On the other hand, the parliamentary committee may also call for *"remissyttranden"* by administrative agencies and organizations, and these are made public and referred to in the committee reports. Thus when the houses of parliament have to take their final decision, they have before them officially the views expressed not only by the government and the relevant committee, but also by agencies and organizations consulted at the preliminary stages.

It is of course rather difficult to evaluate how important views expressed in this way are for legislation and other parliamentary decisions, as well as for government decisions. Much depends on the character of the organizations involved.

A number of decisions by government and parliament are taken on a non-party basis, and in these cases reports of substantive importance presented by organizations with independent experience of the matters concerned seem to be taken very seriously. If the matter is one involving party politics, the situation is of course different. Here it is chiefly the major organizations that count, and particularly those more or less closely connected with the party or parties in power. Labor Ministers will be strongly influenced by whatever is said by LO and Farmer Ministers by the comments of the agricultural co-operatives. But this is not the whole truth. Constructive comments, even if coming from an organization normally adverse to the party in power, are rarely altogether neglected. In many cases, even in those involving party politics, the execution of the decision will depend to a larger or smaller extent on co-operation between the state and the groups, and this is a fact which has to be taken into account already at an early stage.

Thus, interest groups are given very full opportunities for influencing the legislative process at all different stages. On the other hand, organized pressure through "lobbying", letters to members of Parliament etc., while by no means unknown, are actually far less important. This is not due to any superior moral attitude on the part of organizations but chiefly to the fact that these activities are largely unnecessary in a system where the opportunities for open participation are as great as in Sweden.

VI

The *administrative system* of Sweden is in many respects unique. It is based on a clear distinction between the ministries, which are small units chiefly concerned with legislation and budgeting, and separate administrative agencies appointed by the government but with independent power of deciding administrative questions. Thus, under the Ministry of Social Affairs, there is a Board of Social Welfare, a Board of Pensions, a Board of Insurance, a Labor Market Board, etc., each of which acts independently and is on the whole not subject to directives from the ministry. Interest groups are to some extent represented in independent organs of this type. This is especially true of labor market organizations, which are represented for instance on the Labor Market Board and its local organs, on the Board of Vocational Training, etc. Some special administrative courts, the Labor Court (*Arbetsdomstolen*) and the Rent Court (*Statens Hyresråd*) also have group representatives among their membership.

But this representation indicates only a minor part of the points at which the administration co-operates with interest groups. On the other hand, the state has by many means and for a long time recognized group organizations, for instance, through the mediation service in labor conflicts, established already in 1906, and by the form of subsidies given to agriculture in the 1930's. Moreover, in all matters affecting the interest of a group there is both official and unofficial co-operation with administrative organs, who may ask a group organization to state its views officially or ask informally for its advice. Whenever an organization finds that the administration is about to decide a question of interest to them, it will as a perfectly normal thing and without attempt at dissimulation demand consultation, and this is invariably granted. The whole process works rather smoothly, perhaps largely because Sweden is a small country and this type of contact therefore very easy to establish.

It should be clear from what has been said that organizations in

Sweden are politically very important and recognized as such by parliament and government. Obviously, this will influence their relations with the administration as well. In negotiating with government agencies they are in a position of strength, and the agencies know that lack of co-operation on their part will frequently lead the organizations to appeal over their heads to political authorities, who are just as likely (or perhaps more likely) to follow the advice of organizations as that of civil servants. Moreover, organizations are often useful to the administration both by assuming, as in the case of agriculture, more or less direct administrative functions on behalf of the state, and by lending their authoritative support to the administration in its relation with citizens. In these circumstances, it is very definitely in the interests of the administration to co-operate, and on the whole also in the interests of the organizations. Conflicts are rare and usually resolved by compromise. Individual interests, on the other hand, might occasionally suffer from the close relationship between the administration and the organizations, since both tend to take account of the effects of a measure on the majority of those concerned rather than on the individual. Precedents rather than special considerations acquire predominance in these circumstances.

Another tendency should be mentioned at this point. The recruitment of high officials in the Swedish civil service has always been somewhat informal, probably also due to the fact that the country is small enough to make it possible for those in power to know personally about likely candidates for any high administrative office. In recent years, it has not been unusual to recruit from among leading people in the organizations both governors of provinces ("*landshövdingar*") and for instance directors of central administrative boards. On some occasions this practice has been criticized, for instance when the vice-president of LO was appointed to be director general of the Labor Market Board. But the criticism has rarely if ever been warranted by the results. There is obviously a strong sense of responsibility among group leaders, when they sever the ties with their original organization and pass into government service. On the other hand an official with this type of background is frequently able to command loyal co-operation from his erstwhile group in the performance of his new functions.

In the working paper submitted by the rapporteur, the question is asked whether there is ideological and social affinity between bureaucrats on the one hand and groups on the other. The question is not an easy one to answer in general terms. Quite obviously bureaucrats will feel a considerable amount of affinity with group organizations such as

TCO or SACO of which they may have been or still remain members. On the other hand, there exists a considerable amount of suspicion between people in group organizations and bureaucrats, such suspicion being based on general principles. Although with their increased importance the work of organizations is becoming more and more bureaucratic, they are traditionally distrustful of State interference. To some extent this is true even of labor unions, which may be in favor of increased state activities in principle but have so far strenuously opposed state interference on the labor market.

VII

The Swedish Government has been characterized by the term "politics of compromise." Indeed, there is hardly any point at which this term seems more definitely warranted than with regard to interest organizations: an equilibrium is maintained chiefly through the willingness of each of them to make concessions in order to achieve important results rather than using force in order to gain all or nothing.

Moreover, the "pluralist" character of Swedish society is openly accepted on all sides. There is no attempt to get rid of powerful organizations or indeed even to curb their activities. At least, no such attempts have been made for a very long time. It is regarded as more or less inevitable that groups of this type and other organizations should exercise a power almost equal to that of parliament and definitely superior to that of parliamentary parties.

This applies chiefly to those organizations which are important and powerful in economic life. To some extent, it applies also to the temperance movement, which is in many respects one of the strongest pressure groups of Swedish political life, if only because of the limited number of questions interesting the movement. For instance, recently a government bill permitting the manufacturing and sale of a new type of beer which was strongly supported by at least one of the two opposition leaders and regarded with indifference by the other, failed to pass in either of the two houses of parliament exclusively because of the opposition of the tee-totalers. On the other hand, the State Church and the religious groups rarely act as pressure groups. In the circumstances of Swedish religious life, they are so strongly concerned not to lose any possibility of religious influence on the various groups of society that they refrain from even attempting political pressure which might be held contrary to their ideas and antagonize important sections of society.

The organizational structure of interest groups is on the whole very stable. Organizations are recognized even by opponents: labor unions would not like to be rid of employers' associations, nor would employers like a weak union structure. Public opinion takes organizations for granted, although specific actions by organizations might occasionally give rise to protests. There is thus little need for anonymity in the activities of organizations. The political and administrative system includes certain tendencies to corporativism. But this does not go to the length of breaking up the democratic system as a whole. Obviously, organizations exercise political pressure, but this is mostly taking place in the open, not secretly.

Still, this should not be understood to mean that no problems are involved. Although organizations jealously guard their independence, they are not infrequently working as organs of the state rather than as representatives of the immediate wishes of their members. This is defended by the argument that they are in fact furthering the long-range interests of their members in acting for the good of the public as a whole, for instance when labor unions keep down wage demands in order to counteract inflation. So far, this policy has on the whole been accepted by the membership, but this may chiefly be due to the fact that living standards have been rising in Sweden in any case. In less fortunate circumstances, there might be more widespread dissatisfaction and it is difficult to say to what extent this might even undermine the authority of powerful organizations in relation to their own members.

The internal work of organizations is influenced by these conditions. Decision-making within the organizations becomes centralized, largely because this is necessary if they are to fulfill their functions. Moreover, since membership is often virtually though not formally compulsory, a number of members are apt to be indifferent in their attitude towards the organization and to identify themselves with it to a much smaller extent than they used to do during the formative period. The organization tends to be regarded as something external, as an administrative agency similar to those of the state and the municipality rather than as a body expressing and realizing the members' wishes and aims.

Also, within various "movements," a considerable amount of bureaucratisation has taken place. Members do not participate in the actual work of organizations except to a very limited extent. They have to be satisfied with electing officers and leaving the actual decisions to them. Here, as in so many other fields, Swedish democracy is rigorously representative rather than direct.

While there may be certain dangers in this situation, these dangers should not be overestimated. It is an interesting fact that group leaders are almost invariably drawn from the rank and file of their own group.

And on the whole, many factors, including the great interest taken in educational work, tend to maintain the interest of members in the problems handled by their group organization if not with the details of its activities. So far, the system has been quite successful, and no immediate signs indicate any important change in its fundamental characteristics.

SELECTED BIBLIOGRAPHY

Bolen, B., "Organization och riksdagen," *Tiden,* vol. 46 (1954), pp. 9–13.

Bonow, M.: *Kooperationen och folkförsörjningen.* Stolkholm 1936.

Childs, Marquis W.: *Sweden: the middle way.* New ed. New Haven 1947.

Childs, Marquis W.: *This is democracy. Collective bargaining in Scandinavia.* New Haven 1938.

Cole, Margaret & Smith, Charles: *Democratie Sweden.* London 1938.

Croner, Fritz: *Tjänstemannakåren i det moderna samhället.* Uppsala 1951.

Fusilier, Raymond. *Le parti socialiste Suédois.* Paris 1954.

Guesde, Jules: *La Suède d'hier et d'aujourd'hui.* New ed. Stockholm 1957.

Heckscher, Gunnar, "Group Organization in Sweden," *Public Opinion Quarterly,* vol. 3 (1939), pp. 130–35.

Heckscher, Gunnar, "Pluralist democracy." *Social Research* vol. 15 (1948), pp. 417–461.

Heckscher, Gunnar: *Staten och Organisationerna.* New ed. Stockholm 1951.

Johansson, Hilding: *Folkrörelserna och det demokratiska statsskicket i Sverige.* Lund 1952.

Johansson, Hilding, *Folkrörelserna.* Stockholm 1954.

Karlbom, Torvald, *Den svenska fackföreningsrörelsen.* Stockholm 1955.

Norgren, Paul, *The Swedish collective bargaining system.* Cambridge, Mass. 1941.

Robbins, James, *The Government of Labor Relations in Sweden.* Chapel Hill 1942.

Rustow, Dankwart, *The Politics of Compromise.* Princeton 1955.

Tiljo, J., "Painostusryhmät ja painostuspolitiikka," *Socialistinen Aikakauslehti,* vol. 53, pp. 416–20.

Westerståhl, Jörgen: *Svensk fackföreningsrörelse.* Stockholm 1945.

Westerståhl, Jörgen, and others: *Svenska metallarbetareförbundets historia.* Stockholm 1948.

Våra folkrörelser. En läsebok. Stockholm 1946.

AMERICAN INTEREST GROUPS: A SURVEY OF RESEARCH AND SOME IMPLICATIONS FOR THEORY AND METHOD

SAMUEL J. ELDERSVELD

Everywhere today interest groups have become the research vogue, recognized by scholars and political analysts as critical centers of power in the political process. In his day, Lord Bryce perceived the parties as "the great moving forces" of politics[1]; today, interest groups would certainly share this status. Tentative explorations of the political group patterns in other countries have led to claims that interest groups may be more influential in the governmental process in Europe than here. Samuel Beer has recently maintained, after sketching the British pattern, that "If we had some way of measuring political power, we could quite possibly demonstrate that at the present time pressure groups are more powerful in Britain than in the U. S."[2] And Bernard Brown concludes from his survey of French groups that "Pressure groups continue to be of greater importance in France than in Great Britain or even the U. S."[3] Although these views may be open to question, the spate of "working" and "strategy" papers for orienting interest group research throughout the world has recently mushroomed to new heights. Serious scholars here and abroad are demonstrating a long-range comparative interest in such research.

The question might be parenthetically, if gently, raised at the outset, of course, as to whether all the research goals in this area are realizable. Given the apparent direction and objective of research in this field as indicated—an objective to discover, describe, and analyze regularities between and within interest group phenomena from country to country—one wonders whether the stage has been properly set for the ambitious program of research contemplated. In any field the pro-

[1] James Bryce, *The American Commonwealth*, 1916 Edition, p. 5.
[2] "Pressure Groups and Parties in Britain", *American Political Science Review*, vol. L, (1956), p. 3.
[3] Bernard E. Brown, "Pressure Politics in France," *The Journal of Politics*, vol. 18, (1956), p. 718.

gress of knowledge has followed five stages, from observation to the taxonomic to the structural to the dynamic to the holistic. Before ambitiously approaching the holistic stage at once, as one recent report suggests,[4] political science may have to assure itself that it has properly developed observational techniques, adequate categories for analysis, and convincing "lower level" propositions for analysis. This is not to say that we should not aim at the total process of politics. Rather, we cannot afford to ignore the requirements of knowledge and the perfection of a convincing research technology.

The widespread interest throughout social science for a careful study of interest groups is significant. Sociologists, economists, as well as political scientists are interested. The implications of this for broadening the base of our inquiry into interest groups should be readily accepted. Franz Neumann perhaps stated this need in typical fashion, when he said that "the translation of economic power into social power and thence into political power becomes the crucial concern. . . ." Pressure groups, as "organizations . . . by which (social) power is translated into political power" need intensive study he claims. And, he adds, "really sophisticated, comparative analysis is still lacking." Further he makes the point that this process of the "translation of power" is one which "differs from country to country and from historical situation to historical situation."[5] The point is well taken. It must be re-emphasized that we must not be concerned merely with interest groups *qua* interest groups. Our aim must be to analyze them in the broad context of social and economic change, and by studying their impact on the decisional process to move toward answers to questions posed by a theory of the democratic political process.

TYPES OF AMERICAN INTEREST GROUP STUDIES

The study of American interest groups may have some value for those interested in comparative research. The American experience may suggest certain methodological and theoretical guideposts, but it may also serve as a *caveat*. It illustrates the stages of political inquiry through which we have passed and the major questions which yet remain.

By well-nigh universal agreement the classic discussion of interest groups was presented in 1908 with Arthur F. Bentley's *The Process of Government*. Coming at a time when the insights of American scholars were rooted in the legal basis and formal structure of government and

[4] Gabriel A. Almond, "A Comparative Study of Interest Groups and the Political Process," *American Political Science Review*, vol. LII, (1958), p. 271.

[5] *The Democratic and the Authoritarian State*, 1957, pp. 12–14.

when there was an alienation from systematic theory, this original work found poor receptivity. Bentley turned from structural formalism to what he called the "raw materials" of politics, seeing these as the activities and interactions of social groups. It should be recalled that Bentley did not perceive these groups as conglomerates of unarticulated interests, but as "collectives of action," pressing, demanding, conflicting, mediating. These collectives had taken on "temporarily, or with some permanence, a fairly definite form—definite enough, at any rate, for us to handle, describe, and value in terms of other activities."[6] And, to Bentley, "the balance of the group pressures *is* the existing state of society."[7] Despite such a dynamic conception of political group process, Bentley had no influence until rediscovered within the last decade. In fact, it was not until the Twenties that any scholarly studies of pressure groups were made in the United States.

There are now at least thirty solid studies which are of relevance for an understanding of interest groups in this country. In addition there is a large body of monographic literature, journal articles, and unpublished dissertations. It is interesting to note that very little of this writing antedates the Great Depression, with the decade 1935 to 1945 being perhaps the most prolific. Since David Truman's rediscovery of Bentley and his publication in 1951 of the *Governmental Process,* studies employing systematic theory and employing empirical materials have been appearing more frequently.

Although our literature on interest groups has been generously interspersed with speculative philosophizing about the nature and importance of these groups, speculation which has been both objectively interpretive and value-oriented, the primary form of investigation has been the case study. Three major types of studies are found in our literature—the study of a single interest group; the study of interest groups as they operate in a single arena, especially the legislative arena, over a comparatively short time-span; and the study of interest groups concerned with a particular law or policy-conflict.

Illustrative of the first type is the ground-breaking study by Peter Odegard in 1928 of the Anti-Saloon League. Odegard clearly traces the origins of this group from 1832 on, its transformation from a social movement to a national organization, the character and roles of its leadership, its complicated tactics and pressure techniques, its financial basis, and some of the counter-groups ranged against it. It is an extremely interesting description, exciting to read again even

---

[6] Arthur F. Bentley, *The Process of Government,* new ed. 1956, p. 182.
[7] *Ibid,* pp. 258–9.

today, including rich insights into the operations of such an ideological movement a half century ago.

Many other studies which concentrate attention primarily on a single interest group exist, including Kile's study of the American Farm Bureau, Lorwin's book on the American Federation of Labor, Rutherford's work on the American Bar Association, Brady's analysis of business associations, Duffield's early study of the American Legion, and a variety of others. There are two such studies which seem to me to deserve special attention. Oliver Garceau's *The Political Life of the American Medical Association,* published in 1941, was a pioneer contribution employing relatively rigorous theory and techniques in "illuminating the always obscure relationships within these societies." He is concerned almost exclusively with the internal organization and political relationships of the AMA, exploring particularly the character and technology of the "active minority" and its problems in producing membership unity as well as in moulding public opinion generally.

The other study of this type which I would like to call to your attention is *Union Democracy,* by non-political scientist Lipset, a careful analysis of the Typographical Workers Union. This brilliant book utilizes available empirical evidence to describe and explain the internal processes of the union, especially its unique two-party system, in terms of a set of carefully developed, interrelated hypotheses. Its contribution to theory is considerable.

In the second category of studies are those which are descriptions of "lobbies" or interest groups operating in one policy arena. An early scholarly effort of this type was E. P. Herring's *Group Representation Before Congress* (1929). Herring studied the lobbies of more than 100 associations, collecting much of his material by personal interview. His classification of these types of groups and his explanation of the reasons for their rise are still widely used. Furthermore, his concern with these groups as being "signs of a 'restructuralization' in human relations,"[8] although not pursued in his work, suggests a theoretical standpoint which might well motivate our research today. Studies on state legislatures, such as those of Belle Zeller (New York) and Dayton McKean (New Jersey) were further milestones in our research on the legislative arena. Both studies were goldmines of factual information and insights revealing the decentralized and dispersed nature of interest group activities under the federal system. Two studies on the developing relationships between interest groups and the administrative process should not be overlooked. Herring's *Public Administration and the*

---

[8] E. P. Herring, *Group Representation Before Congress,* 1929, p. xi.

Public Interest, and Avery Leiserson's very useful contribution to theory, *Administrative Regulation* (1942). The latter is a study which has not been given adequate recognition in my opinion. It is much more than mere description and taxonomy, being above all an attempt to generalize and hypothesize about the consequences for the "democratization of authority" of the integrative process by which interest groups have deneutralized the governmental bureaucracy.

Finally, we have had some interesting attempts to study the role of interest groups interacting with a single policy-conflict situation. Such studies have traced proposed legislation from the initial idea stage through to the stages of policy adoption and implementation. Such studies are particularly necessary in view of the complicated character of the American legislative system and the system of checks and balances. The early outstanding effort of this type was E. E. Schattschneider's *Politics, Pressures, and the Tariff* in 1935. In studying "the political behavior of economic groups in the tariff revision of 1929–1930," Schattschneider not only describes the facts of pressure group tactics carefully, but develops some interesting categories for analysis (especially categories as to the type of pressure group activity). He also attempts to test some theories implicit in the pressure group process, especially the theoretical expectations based on an economic interpretation of politics. His discussion of the bargaining process, the "process of the confrontation of official with nonofficial leaders," with particular reference to the Congressional hearing as a forum for such negotiation, is one of the earliest presentations of this interpretation.

Other studies of this type merit equal accolades, especially Stephen Bailey's *Congress Makes A Law,* a study of the passage of the Employment Act of 1946. Of particular importance in this study is the documentation of the close practical relations between the liberal-labor lobby and Congressmen in the development and execution of political strategy. Considerable light is also thrown on the nature of interest group coalitions, the circumstances which make such coalitions expedient, and their political effects.

Reference to the above studies is not meant to disparage by implication the many other solid studies which have added to our information about interest groups in the United States. I have cited here types of studies and examples of each type, with indications of only a few kinds of contributions they have made.

One type which has not been included so far is the study which employs survey research methods in order to discover the attitudes, political predispositions, and political orientations of interest group members. A significant example is *When Labor Votes,* by Arthur Korn-hauser, Albert J. Mayer, and Harold L. Sheppard (1956). This survey of UAW local union members in the Detroit Area was conducted with a random sample of 828 workers. It is packed with valuable data about the political interest, voting patterns, and attitudes of the members of these locals. Particularly interesting are the four basic types of UAW members, a set of categories distinguishing members on the basis of their political and union orientations. Such interpretations and pre-dictions as the following are particularly interesting: labor union po-litical activity will be widened and there will be "an accentuation of pressures and needs ... toward greater political participation";[9] mem-bers will go along with the "idealism and social reform in the auto union's politics";[10] labor union members need not necessarily become more conservative politically as they become better off economically and more upwardly mobile;[11] and there is at the present no tendency among union members to prefer "individualistic" to "collective" po-litical action alternatives.[12] This type of study has immense value for providing us with the kind of data about internal perspectives which were not realizable with studies utilizing primarily documentary and observational techniques for data-collection, supplemented by a limited number of relatively unstructured leadership interviews.

EVALUATION: THE PROBLEM OF CONCEPTUALIZATION

If one surveys this body of literature, impressive by its volume alone, one finds himself reflecting with mixed feelings. There is no question that there is here an imposing descriptive research. The case studies have uncovered important facts about the origins, formal organization, and operational techniques of pressure and interest groups. Further, there is no question but that, if one reads carefully, intermittently one picks up fugitive insights which may have relevance for a theory of interest groups. What one does not get from this reading of the literature is a clear understanding of the intrinsic nature of the interest group, the reasons for the diversity in style and tactics, or the implica-tions of organization for interest group effectiveness. Certainly, one finds it difficult to find a real understanding of interest groups in the context of political and social change. One still asks the same basic questions concerning the role of these groups in the policy process, the

[9] Arthur Kornhauser, *et al, When Labor Votes,* 1956, p. 268.
[10] *Ibid,* p. 289.
[11] *Ibid,* p. 278.
[12] *Ibid,* p. 283.

political system generally, and the social order. What may be some of the reasons for such feelings of interpretative inadequacy or frustration?

One explanation is that we have not yet satisfactorily solved the problem of conceptualization, and we have not met the need to develop proper categories for analysis. There can be no question but that we have certainly striven mightily for a conceptual position, but the results have not produced clarity, in the sense of delineating the unique and distinctive character of interest groups *vis a vis* non-interest groups. Perhaps the fault or credit initially was Bentley's. He claimed that "the term 'group' will be used throughout this work in a technical sense."[13] Yet, he had no interest in combining conceptual differentiation with an exercise in taxonomy. Herring's early work did not solve the problem. The groups he studied are merely called "new agencies for the expression of opinion and for the protection of specific interests" ... which "partake of the characteristics of both the typical 'society' and the minority party."[14] Schattschneider's early study distinguished defensive-offensive, negative-positive, and primary-secondary types of interest groups. And these are the kinds of categories we used, until Truman opened up the question in 1951 again. In summarizing and codifying preceding developments in sociology, social psychology and political science, he attempts a definition, saying simply that a "political interest group" is a shared-attitude group making claims through or upon the institutions of government.[15] This is a short-hand statement which no doubt is helpful. It simplifies some previous confusion and interrelates social-psychological developments with political analysis. But it has by no means settled the age-old controversy as to the difference between interest groups and political parties. It has questionable analytical utility, and above all, does not indicate to us the conceptual categories needed for significant research. Truman's further identification of the "potential group"[16] as a collectivity of present non-interaction but possible future interaction, and the "association"[17] as a group of "tangent relations" bridging two other groups, are interesting contributions, but scarcely peculiarly adaptable to political research.

Our literature, today yet, abounds with new terminology, new attempts at definition, new indications that we are still groping for some meaningful conceptualization. Thus we speak, erroneously I feel,

[13] *Op. cit.*, p. 211.
[14] *Op. cit.*, pp. 2–3.
[15] David B. Truman, *The Governmental Process*, 1951, p. 37.
[16] *Ibid*, p. 36.
[17] *Ibid*, p. 39.

of "policy aspiration groups" (interest groups) and "power aspiration groups" (parties);[18] of "power groups" as contrasted to "demand groups"; of "associational" and "nonassociational" interest groups;[19] of "expressive" versus "social influence" voluntary associations;[20] of "veto groups"[21] and "peak associations"; of groups for "tangible interests" and "intangible interests".[22] It is apparent that we still need a conceptual orientation from which would emerge critical categories of political group types. There is some question, of course, as to whether these would be analytically valuable for investigating the basic relationships at issue.

Political science is not the only discipline confronted with this problem and challenge. Sociologists have been grappling with the distinction between group types for some time, plagued with a recognition of variations in institutional systems, but finding consensus difficult as to the basic characteristics of each. The terms are still used interchangeably. Essentially the confusion seems to arise from the use of such terms as "social movement", "organization" and "structure". Reading current sociology one discovers some confusion in the use of these terms. At most we can say that certain distinctions are being made by some writers, distinctions which, incidentally, may have some value for political scientists wrestling with the self-same problem in another context, the interest-group context. The distinctions seem to be of this order: a "social movement" is a social collective whose members voluntarily participate and for which the basic unifying factor is the psychological identification of the members with the movement. Its members normally share attitudes, values, perspectives toward the social process. But a social movement may or may not have an organization, although organizations generally stem from social movements. (Perhaps for us a case in point would be the Anti-Saloon League, a social movement which developed an organization. Similarly, third party movements in the United States have taken on this character). A "structure" develops within each social movement, structure meaning the social (or political) roles played by the participants in the movement. Every social movement has a "structure" or a population of roles by necessity,

[18] "Report of the Inter-University Summer Seminar on Comparative Politics, Social Science Council," *American Political Science Review*, vol XLVII, (1953), p. 649.

[19] Almond, *op. cit.*, p. 272.

[20] Arnold M. Rose, *Theory and Method in the Social Sciences*, 1954, p. 52.

[21] David Riesman, "Who Has the Power?" in *Class, Status, and Power* (R. Bendix and S. M. Lipset, eds.) 1953, p. 154–162.

[22] Bernard C. Cohen, "Political Communication on the Japanese Peace Settlement," *The Public Opinion Quarterly*, vol. 20 (1956), pp. 30–31.

and these positions become critical for analysis. (For example, it is very difficult to understand the labor union movement in the United States unless one analyzes carefully the roles of men like Gompers, Lewis, Green and the Reuthers. Any amount of concentration on the bare bones of formal organization will still leave one wanting in knowledge of the movement itself.) The term "organization" is familiar to all political scientists. It develops when some of the members in the movement are designated to make decisions for the group. The development of organization is the process of delegation and distribution of power, the establishment of mechanisms of control, and the elaboration of all the apparatus of the decisional process. There are obviously various degrees of organization and types of organization. What is important to notice in the elaboration of this distinction is that every social movement has a structure but not necessarily an organization, according to the sociologist. Further, that role structure is as, if not more, important than organization. Structure precedes organization and cannot be ignored. For the study of political-social movements as interest groups this may be a critical distinction which we have overlooked.

The sociological literature has proliferated other conceptions about group types. For example, Robert Angell describes one particular type as the "struggle group", made up of persons who feel they have a common cause but with some diminution in "sense of moral community". For such groups, he says, when "the struggle becomes one between conflicting systems of ultimate values, rather than between subsidiary immediate ends or means, the elements of moral community vanishes."[23] This type of group, perhaps illustrated by the White Citizens Councils in the South versus the NAACP, can be contrasted possibly to what Turner and Killian call the "control movement", "a movement devoted to dominating the ... society ... while leaving its value objectives flexible or undefined."[24] This distinction may have value in goal terms for understanding certain labor and business organizations, or the developing trend in such groups in the United States. The ideological "struggle group" in contrast to the expediency-oriented "control movement" is a conceptual differentiation which may have merit for the study of interest groups, over time and comparatively. The labels themselves, of course, are unimportant.

Reconceptualization of interest groups and their relation to politics in the United States involves a reexamination of the definitional components which we have almost accepted as axiomatic. The first of these

[23] Robert C. Angell, *Integration of American Society,* 1941, p. 63.
[24] Ralph A. Turner and Lewis M. Killian, *Collective Behavior,* 1956, p. 361.

deals with motivational theory and concerns our preoccupation with the term "self-interest". It is still the vogue to refer to interest groups as uniquely impelled by a body of members who are seeking to implement their "self-interest", as if this meaningfully distinguishes interest groups from other groups. The particular variant of this which has been employed is economic self-interest. James Madison in *The Federalist* is usually credited with having originated this observation. The trouble with this type of observation is that, although a beginning, it stops too soon and says very little. Yet, we have continued this tendency of characterizing these groups as sharing a self-interest, without elaborating the concept carefully for research purposes. In a recent attempt at reformulation Latham isolates two aspects of the concept—the desire for "self-expression" and the impulse to seek personal and collective "security",[25] implying also, however, that the "chief social values cherished by individuals in modern society are realized through groups."[26] To Truman, "the shared attitudes . . . constitute the interests."[27] The assumption underlying our use of this term is that we can differentiate types of political groups on this basis, or political groups from other groups on this basis, and further that we can account for their behavior and their impact on politics in these terms. It is my opinion that we have not done so. I am particularly interested in this connection with the interpretation of Schattschneider, who applied economic determinism theory to his study of pressure groups and the tariff. His expectations were not borne out—pressure groups with equal economic stakes did not produce equal pressures and many economically affected groups were politically inert.[28] The terms "self-interest", "shared attitudes", "security" and the like are elusive and need specification and differentiation. The attempted distinction between the group which seeks to satisfy interests and the group which "propagates faiths" is also really no help.[29] These terms may have utility in the task still confronting us, namely the development of a set of categories of goal-orientations or goal-motivations of political groups which can be useful for analytical purposes. The terms "demand" and "power" as components of the interest group conception suffer the same criticism, it seems to me. Unless one specifies the variations in power achievement status or level aspired to, and the substance, as well as, the range of demands to be expected, no categories of goal-setting which can be used will emerge.

[25] Earl Latham, *The Group Basis of Politics,* 1952, pp. 28–9.
[26] *Ibid,* p. 1.
[27] *Op. cit.,* p. 34.
[28] E. E. Schattschneider, *Politics, Pressures, and the Tariff,* 1935, pp. 162–3.
[29] Harold D. Lasswell and Abraham Kaplan, *Power and Society,* 1950, p. 40.

A second area in which reconceptualization may be necessary involves the use of the term "legitimacy" to characterize political groups. One of the unfortunate circumstances surrounding the early public discussion and non-scientific literature on pressure groups was the tendency to question their propriety for the political order. They were considered, by scholars as well as muckrakers, as engaged in questionable techniques and pursuing questionable goals. They were not considered as sanctioned by the community nor as having a legitimate regime status. There is still a certain amount of thinking of this type, both in this country as well as in Europe. Lasswell and Kaplan in their recent contribution to theory, *Power and Society*, seek at one point to distinguish political parties from pressure groups as follows:

". . . a party is an internal power group whose status has been formalized—it functions as part of the regime. There may be other internal power groups (private armies, pressure groups) whose practices are not sanctioned by the political formula . . . (The distinction between private armies, pressure groups, and parties is, of course, a matter of degree)."[30]

This is an important problem in political theory, and one which can easily be argued at great length. It seems to me, however, that this position either subsumes too many of the kind of groups we call "interest groups" under the rubric "political party", or it misconceives the roles which these groups play today in the political system. Further, it implies different sets of political practices which are mutually exclusive. It is the kind of conceptual approach which is unrealistic and inhibits a holistic view of the functioning political process.

A third area for reconceptualization is in organizational theory, with particular emphasis on the use of the idea of "latency" or "potentiality" of interest group. This raises the basic question: How wide is the term interest group? In the employment of the component "latency" our attention has been focused on the inclusiveness of the phenomenon, not on the problem of abstracting from group phenomena those which are uniquely relevant to political analysis. It is a concept which was alien to Bentley who emphasized the group as a "collection of action" with a definite perceivable and analyzable form. While we are interested in the problem of affiliation and the processes of association as political scientists, with the members and probable "fellow-travellers" for an interest group, it seems to me that we should not be diverted in interest group research from concentration of attention to groups as structures of power. The distinction between categoric and interactional collectivities is important to make, the phe-

[30] *Ibid*, p. 170.

nomenon of latency cannot be ignored, but these have analytical value primarily for studying such developments as the mobilization of mass support, the activation of counter-groups, and related phenomena.

"Self-interest", "legitimacy", "latency", "demand"—these, then, are not the distinguishing marks of the interest group. Perhaps *a priori* distinctions are useless to search for, and conceptual differentiation will only emerge as a concomitant to the formulation of a set of theoretical propositions about the adaptation of political groups to social and political change. Some suggestions along this line will be made shortly.

The Problem of the Identification of Relationships

American interest group research can be evaluated also from the standpoint of the isolation and testing of important theoretical relationships. Although the work has been primarily descriptive, there has been a definite undertone of interest in the development of causal theory, a searching for data which would help to explain the interrelationships between interest groups and the political process. An infinite number of research questions could, of course, be asked, but there are three major relationships which one naturally could expect such research to investigate:

1. The influence of the changes in the governmental structure, political system, and society on the nature and functioning of interest groups.

2. The influence of internal organizational form and structure on internal process.

3. The influence of interests groups on the policy process and institutional system.

There has been a wealth of speculation in the United States in the first of these areas, particularly with reference to the impact of formal governmental organization on interest groups. It is contended that the institutional arrangements such as federalism, separation of powers and the presidency conditioned the development of a special type of two-party system which, in turn, due to its decentralized and undisciplined nature contributed to the emergence of an interest group system with peculiar characteristics. Political scientists speak quite bitterly about this sometimes. Rigorous testing of this type of proposition, of course, has not been undertaken, and in truth it would be difficult in the absence of careful comparative analysis. Very little attention in this country, on the other hand, has been devoted to demonstrating the roots of the interest group system in the social structure, and to exploring the implications of social change on interest group organization, ideology, membership, role structure, and internal process. We frequently have recognized the social basis for politics, but as yet have not perfected the tools for analysis. Herring said long ago that the interest group is "but one manifestation of a movement which reached back to the very foundations of the social structure."[31] But beyond that generalization we have not progressed far.

The second type of relationship has been more ardently studied. Garceau's study of the AMA, Lipset's study of the Typographical Union, and earlier, Odegard's study of the Anti-Saloon league are some of the outstanding contributions in this area. Aside from these, the literature is mostly descriptive and rarely even attempts to develop a theory about the factors of internal group process. Political scientists tend to distinguish unitary from federal group forms, and then defer speculatively to Michels' law of oligarchy without rigorously testing Michels' propositions. We have discussed in intelligent terms the nature of group cohesion, the problem of overlapping and heterogeneous membership, the existence of the "active minority," and its manipulation of group machinery. Thanks to Truman we have generalized our approach to these matters, even though the data are scant. But the critical intra-group relationships which specify the conditions under which types of leadership emerge and power is exercised, the factors responsible for bureaucratic development, the effects of this on leadership ideology, and the impact of schism and factionalism on leadership and membership—these are relationships which have not been carefully explored. To a certain extent paying homage to Michels was defensible. A theoretical orientation which emphasizes that the goals and leadership of the organization are modified, expanded, or abandoned in terms of the group's changes in internal process, was and is valuable. But we have not implemented this orientation with our research. Rather, we have tended to regurgitate the oligarchical model without empirical verification, and without recognizing that certain components in the oligarchical concept and certain alleged effects of oligarchy may not be applicable to the American scene.

There are two basic questions concerning intra-group process which remain, as Lipset has pointed out: (1) What are the conditions responsible for the institutionalization of oligarchy in interest groups? (2) What are the conditions under which democratic organization and process develops and is sustained in an interest group?[32] On the latter

[31] *Op. cit.*, p. xi.
[32] S. M. Lipset, M. A. Trow, J. S. Coleman, *Union Democracy*, 1956, p. 13.

question, Lipset's own work is the only significant contribution. He has pointed out how commonality of interest, non-stratification, ideological differences, early recognition of the legitimacy of opposition, membership interests and participation were related to the development of a democratic two-party system within the ITU. Rigorous analysis of the factors leading to and sustaining oligarchy in interest groups remains to be done. We have isolated some of the important variables, but we have not tested the propositions. Some questions which need critical analysis here are: What is the extent of membership passivity in interest groups and how does this facilitate leadership control? What is the extent of overlapping membership, is its nature changing over time, and what effect does this have on group cohesion and, consequently, on the development of bureaucratization? Doesn't this tendency reduce leadership control? What are the characteristics of interest group leadership, particularly its skills, and how is this type of variable related to group cohesion, goal achievement, and perception by members of group tactics? Since, even in presumably oligarchic interest groups in the United States there is recognition of the legitimacy of opposition, how does such a norm develop, what effects does it have on leadership control, how is it overcome by the elite? Does "circulation of elites" actually occur, by what process, and with what effects on leadership skill and ideology? Above all, it seems to me, there should be more emphasis on reorientation of goals, historical bases, and the nature of the changes which group processes undergo.

This is a legitimate field for investigation by the political scientist as well as the sociologist, for the nature of the group leadership, organization and process must be understood if we are to know something about the impact of these groups on the political system. It may well be that American interest groups are undergoing a transformation. The simple dichotomy of types which we assume—oligarchic and democratic—are no longer the exclusive models for research design. The changing character of social stratification, the diffusion in ideology, social equalitarianism, the acceptance of the concept of intra-group opposition, the changing nature of group membership and affiliation, as well as the power context in which these groups operate today may be inducing a third model type which should be recognized. We cannot assume the inevitability of the oligarchic model.

Here I am concerned with the primary motifs which recur in our theory of interest group influence, as well as the absence of categories for analyzing such influence. Our literature has a tendency to assume that "access" is the critical problem. "Access" is almost equated with "influence." We emphasize the "door-opening power" of group leaders. not the "decision-making power." Truman says, "The produce of effective access ... is a governmental decision."[33] The influence relationship is a much more profound relationship than "access" implies. The influence of a political interest group, even if one wishes to look at its impact immediately only in terms of legislative votes on a given bill, is a product of such factors as: group organization, leader skill, cohesion (as Truman has pointed out); its symbolic public status; its power status and bargaining potential *vis a vis* other interest groups; its "social politics" strategy, or penetration into the influence levels of the social groups not directly involved with politics; the subtlety of its manipulative tactic for the enlistment of mass support; its capacity for mobilizing political support. Although we recognize these elements from time to time (Truman's statement that group access is a function of social status),[34] we still primarily are concerned with horizontal relationships (i.e. interest groups and Congressmen, interest groups and political parties). We then feel frustrated when Bailey tells us at the end of his discussion of interest groups that "it would be difficult to prove that the direct pressures of the Lib-Lab lobby changed a single Congressional mind."[35] We need a research design to test propositions about indirect influence and vertical relationships if we are really interested in analyzing influence. Such a design must recognize assumptively the extent to which interest groups in America are inter-woven with the social, economic and cultural system.

Eventually, we need to develop categories of differential influence. There is considerable suggestion in our literature that interest groups do have differential power status. The specification of these statuses has not emerged, however. Perhaps, we can hierarchize interest groups for certain periods or for certain issues into the following types:

1. Penetration into formal policy roles.
2. Maintenance of Close Political support and referral relationships.
3. Unchallengeable veto status.
4. Attention, Representative, and Pressure relationship.
5. Potential Reprisal Relationship.
6. Rejection by Power structure, Agitational and Resistance Role.

Regardless of the acceptability of these more or less off-hand distinctions, sophistication in our distinctions is necessary. There are too many hints in our literature of interest groups which indicate the in-

[33] *Op. cit.,* p. 507.
[34] *Ibid,* p. 265.
[35] Stephen K. Bailey, *Congress Makes a Law,* 1950, p. 97.

adequacy of the simple distinction between those groups with influence, in a power status, and those with no influence or minimal impact, in a pressure status.

The roles which interest groups perform in the political system and social system provide fascinating speculation, but as yet little real research. We are still not certain what the effect of interest groups is on our two-party system. A recent report suggests that American political parties "aggregate" group interests.[36] Although I am not sure what "aggregate" implies, if it means that group claims are mediated effectively within the Democratic and Republican parties, I doubt it. There is considerable speculative insight which leads one to the hypothesis that a more or less independent interest group system operates in large part outside the party system. Similarly, there is some theory which suggests that the interest group system has meant categorically an intensification of political competition, without looking at the counter-evidence which may imply the hypothesis that the strengthening of interest groups results in a kind of political bargaining, imperfect competition, or oligopoly. Again, the social impact of interest groups has not stimulated any significant body of theory. We have operated usually with a "conflictual" theory, that interest groups pit group against group and thereby exacerbate social relationships and promote tension. There are some, however, who have emphasized the "integrative" function of these groups in our pluralistic society. These conceptual positions have yet to be clearly spelled out and researched. The role of interest groups in the long-run in distributing power, in inducing social change, and in helping the individual identify with political authority, as Rose has pointed out,[37] are ultimately the most important relationships for political analysis.

THE PROBLEM OF EVIDENCE

It remains to say briefly a few things about research technique. Much of what has already been said is methodological. Careful design and specification of the relationships to be investigated must remain as the critical area of concern for those searching for regularities in American interest group phenomena. Two observations about technique might also be made. The first relates to the problem of evidence; the second to the problem of comparability. Data-collection is a singularly trying operation when it comes to interest groups. Securing access to an interest group, interviewing its members and leaders,

[36] Almond, *Op. cit.*, p. 275.
[37] Rose, *Op. cit.*, p. 51.

observing internal processes, ferreting out non-public negotiations with political parties and indirect connections with policy makers—these requirements of research procedure are hard to meet. In our investigations in the Detroit Area of the political action techniques and organization of the UAW-CIO, although presumably we had maximized our rapport with the upper leadership there were still PAC coordinators who were unwilling to give us interviews. This type of problem requires a reassessment of research strategy. Related to this is the problem of the objectification of research techniques. The informal, unstructured, even casual type of interview is the type of data relied on in the past to supplement observation and documentary sources. This type of interview is considered most feasible even today. Yet, paradoxically, this is the most unsatisfactory type of data from the standpoint of scientific requirements. Unless one has highly trained and well-coordinated interviewers this type of interview process is bound to be quite subjective and unreliable. It is useful for exploration but not for proof. Our experiments in the past few years with a questionnaire schedule applied identically and openly with all interviewees has given us a rich body of data on political leaders and union activists. It is my feeling that there is no substitute for this if one seeks rigor, objectivity, proof. If we do not meet these requirements for knowledge, we will forever be making probabilistic statements about reality, we will be presenting "findings" which are not demonstrable and which evoke controversy. We will be forever saying "Although the evidence is weak, it appears that ..." A content analysis of Truman's summation of knowledge about interest groups reveals the weak evidential basis for most of our propositions. In Chapter 10 "Interest Groups and Elections", on 18 occasions the author reports the absence or negligible amount of evidence. Thus: "we know almost nothing of a systematic character about how nominations are made ..."; "Although evidence on (the effectiveness of endorsements) is slight, it is probable ..."; "the semi-contractual theory of contributions thrives on the dearth of evidence ..."; "the evidence does not tell us the extent to which members' votes are 'deliverable' ...", etc. It must be recognized that "presumptive evidence" is not sufficient except for speculative philosophers.

The other technique problem, that of "comparability", is one that will plague us constantly as long as we rely on case studies in which there is no coordination of design. I certainly do not deplore these case studies. They have given us all the information we presently possess, and they are responsible for the few theoretical clues which we are working with. But their limitations must be apparent. I have personally tried, for example, to study side by side three studies by Odegard, Garceau, and Lipsett, to see what regularities or equivalencies I could tease out of these discreet inquiries; to discover, for example whether the form of organization determines the types of strategies utilized. I am tempted to say that these studies demonstrate that organization is unimportant and not the basic variable for an understanding of strategy. But further study reminds me that these three men went at their work with quite different assumptions, objectives, and data-collection operations. They raise different questions; they consult different bodies of data. I am not sure, therefore, whether their findings are "additive" in any real sense at all. This I feel is the real challenge for comparative research, whether within a country or among countries—the challenge to produce reliable data testing identical theoretical relationships which have emerged from a replicable design.

INTEREST GROUP ADAPTATIONS TO "FLUID POLITICS" IN AMERICA: SOME INTERPRETATIONS AND HYPOTHESES

I should like to conclude with some remarks about the changing nature of interest groups in American politics. I do this not only to characterize recent developments, but also to illustrate some of the distinctions already made in this paper. These remarks attempt to reflect some of the recent speculation and investigation in this area, as well as my own observations.

It is the growing complexity and fluidity of American society, with its consequences for power distribution, which must be recognized first. The great technological changes in the U. S., accompanied by specialization, social pluralism, social mobility, and equalization of status, suggests to many an amorphous, diffuse, "open" society. In such a society, the "interconnections between the legal and social framework" are more intimate than ever before, the struggle for power is central, political group relationships are with difficulty "stabilized". Diversification of power sources mean that the decision-making process is more indirect, non-public, and obscure.

This "amorphous" distribution of power in our society results in change for the governmental system, political leadership, and the political group system. Scrutiny of the governmental bureaucracy raises the question as to its "neutrality"; the legislative arena's character raises the question as to its "representativeness". Governmental decision-making is seen either as group bargaining or as stalemate. Political leadership undergoes transformations in the face of political group pluralism. The "influentials" take on new characteristics. Wealth is not as powerful as in the past.[38] There is less certainty that a "decisive ruling class", to use Riesman's term, exists. The fashionable phrase becomes the "multiple elites".[39] Although the two-party system is retained, the role of the party politician begins to be specified differently, and party-interest group interaction takes on a new pattern.

These social changes and modifications in the power context have been accompanied by new interpretations of the norms and prerequisites of the democratic political process. New popular theories are spawned about the nature of group competition, the significance of elections,[40] the role of public opinion,[41] the meaning of the "public interest",[42] to mention only a few. Above all, the question is raised as to whether our governmental institutions are adequate to cope with these changes in the dynamics of political decision-making.[43]

If this is accepted as an apt description of developing social and political trends in America, how are interest groups adapting? What are the current developments in, and expectations as to the probable future of, interest group politics? In the short-hand sketch presented here it will be seen that this adaptation is not single-directional but one which can be seen often as trend and counter-trend. The propositions presented will deal with five aspects of the problem: the political action context, goal-orientations, structure, strategies, and the consequences of interest group development for the political and social order.

First, so far as the *context* is concerned. In the United States there is greater recognition today of the meaningfulness and efficacy of collective approaches to political action as compared to individualistic approaches.[44] The individual citizen working by himself despairs of effective access or influence. Our political vocabulary comes more and more to see group action as vital, even though less simple and less

---

[38] Riesman, *op. cit.*, p. 162.

[39]. See Bell, ed., *The New American Right*, 1955, p. 178, and Riesman, *op. cit.*

[40] For example, Joseph A. Schumpeter, *Capitalism, Socialism, and Democracy*, 1942, Ch. 22.

[41] Among others, see Bernard Berelson, "Democratic Theory and Public Opinion," *The Public Opinion Quarterly*, vol. 16 (1952), pp. 313–330. Also, Walter Lippmann, *The Public Philosophy*, 1955, and, for an earlier revision, Donald C. Blaisdell, *Economic Power and Political Pressures*, (Temporary National Economic Committee Monograph No. 26) 1941, Chs. 1 and 2.

[42] See Glendon A. Schubert, Jr., "The Public Interest' in Administrative Decision-Making," *American Political Science Review*, vol. LI (1957), pp. 346–368.

[43] E. P. Herring, *The Politics of Democracy*, 1940, p. 107; See also House Select Committee on Lobbying Activities (81st Congress Second Session—"Buchanan Committee") *Interim Report*, 1951, pp. 3–4, 62–65.

[44] Kornhauser, *op. cit.*, p. 283.

direct. A second general proposition is that although multiple and over-lapping group membership still exists, and indeed is a major phenomenon of our time, there may be a perceptible trend towards closer group identification. The individual begins to "choose up sides", to resolve his overlapping and cross-pressures in one direction, and to decide which group is more politically representative and potent for him.[45] A third general proposition I would make is that the diffuseness of political society is gradually observable as taking on a certain order, though certainly an imperfect order. In our society the struggle for power position among groups becomes more important, and a stratification or hierarchizing of groups maybe taking place over time, and with reference to particular policy issues. Earlier mention has been made of certain types of power positions which might be hypothesized. Such political stratification is inevitable and one which will be formalized over time in the image which the public as well as formal policy-makers have of the interest group complex.

So far as *goal-orientations* of interest groups are concerned, I would suggest these developments: The goals have become more than mere representation, or "articulation" of the group viewpoint. The desire is for something more than "access"; perhaps the term is "consideration." Although historically representation and access may have been the goal, the shift in objectives has led to groups concerned with ongoing political and social relationships, desiring to penetrate deeper into the political and social structure, not periodically and intermittently, but continuously and for the purpose of developing and sustaining contact and influence with the significant opinion and action leadership of the community.[46] The group perspectives are no longer merely specific and limited, but long-range and comprehensive. The basic motivation is still no doubt expediency, but an ideological-rationalizing element has been introduced in the communication of these perspectives to the public. Finally, while historically centered around economic self-interest (a motivation still basic today, since groups are interested in sharing in economic rewards in a prosperous society) a counter-trend has developed.[47] The trend towards social and economic equality has directed groups into setting goals concerned with the development of a

[45] See, e.g. Martin Kriesberg, "Cross-Pressures and Attitudes," *The Public Opinion Quarterly*, vol. 13 (1949) pp. 5–16.

[46] *Interim Report, op. cit.*, pp. 24 ff.

[47] This point was discussed at considerable length at a Conference on the Comparative Study of Pressure Groups called by Professor James K. Pollock at the University of Michigan, February 28–March 1, 1957 (Report in preparation).

"social politics", preoccupation with issues such as social equality and issues with a secondary economic importance.

Interest group *structure* is also undergoing change. There are fewer social movements and more structures of power. The interest group has become a formalized, independent action system, attempting to maximize its political strength and durability. But the old categorization of groups as oligarchic or democratic no longer seem to fit. A new type of "managerial group", highly professionalized and expert at the top stratum and attempting to maintain a body of mass support and mass membership at the lower levels is developing.[48] Cohesion of a tightly organized membership is less the ultimate aim. Internal factionalism, present to some extent in many of our interest groups for some time, may even increase.[49] Leadership control directed at a mass public may find itself increasingly confronted with internal schism. This possibility is especially portended in the trend toward the recruitment for leadership of the professional public relations expert, on the one hand;[50] and the cooptation of nonprofessionals, on the other hand. Lobbyists with technical legal skill[51] and professional publicity experts plus coopted non-professional (coopted for appearances of non-specialization) being to participate in policy-planning for the group. The organizational technician gives way to the technician in bargaining and persuasion.

The *strategies* of our interest groups are of course being modified in this adaptive and adjustive process. First, it has become apparent that the indirect approaches to power may be more efficacious than the direct approaches. Manipulation replaces domination or outright demands.[52] Whereas in the past emphasis was on "all or none" demands, this is now no longer overtly the case at least. Second, great emphasis is placed on the strategy of proper public presentation of demands, of selling the group and its objectives to the public, of mobilizing a long-run mass support. The objective is to picture the group in a favorable

[48] Neumann, *op. cit.*, p. 9.

[49] Lipsett, *op. cit.*, p. 407.

[50] Stanley Keller, *Professional Public Relations and Political Power*, 1956.

[51] See Joseph A. Schlesinger, "Lawyers and American Politics: A Clarified View," *Midwest Journal of Political Science* (1957), p. 31; also, Lester Mulbrath, "Lobbyists and Campaign Politics," (Paper read at Fifty-Third Annual Meeting of the American Political Science Association, New York City, 1957), who found that three-fourths of a sample of 100 lobbyists interviewed had been trained in the law, p. 19.

[52] This distinction is made also by Morris Janowitz in "The Military Establishment as a Social System" (Paper read at 1957 Annual Meeting of the American Sociological Association, Washington, D. C.

light, a task requiring important persuasive skills. But a counter-trend should not be overlooked. This is the insistence on secrecy and privacy, the determination not to be investigated, the desire to be left alone, the preference for obscurity and in a sense for irresponsibility.[53] Finally, the group strategy in relationship to other groups is one of bargaining, negotiating, coalescence, reciprocation, even combination and continued alliance.[54] Such attempts to limit competition result in less group autonomy. The negotiations necessarily take place often "out of sight" and "behind the scenes", whether with political parties or other interest groups. As a consequence, the visible relationship between interest group and party may be completely misleading. The processes of sharing expertise, intellectual resources, financial resources, personnel, as well as attitudes has become much more prevalent and important than formal organizational liaison and cooperation. This inter-group bargaining process has become much more essential today in the United States in our fluid power context. In the process, bargaining potentials gradually emerge and group goals must be modified.

What are the *consequences* for the political and social system of these developing trends? Many might be foreseen, but only a few of the most significant will be hypothesized here. In the first place, a kind of checkmate system among interest groups is materializing, especially among those in the upper strata of the group hierarchy. The tendency for groups to behave more circumspectly in terms of what they perceive they can presently achieve, and the tendency for "bargaining" indicates an awareness of the limitations on their power. Thus, open and autonomous group competition decreases in intensity. A counter-trend to this (the product of an economic or social breakdown in certain group relationships) may be the rise of radical, extremist, and even violent

---

[53] This concept of "secrecy" has of course been observed and commented on by many writers. See, particularly, Franz Neumann, *op. cit.*, p. 9–10; Avery Leiserson, *op. cit.*, discusses interest group preferences for being left alone and for "irresponsibility" p. 135. See also Oliver Garceau and Corrine Silverman, "A Pressure Group and the Pressured: A Case Report" *American Political Science Review*, vol. XL (1954), which reveals the "extremely low level of recognition of interest group activity" in a state legislature, p. 685; Blaisdell, *op. cit.*, p. 7.

[54] The "bargaining" concept has been outlined well in Robert A. Dahl and Charles E. Lindblom, *Politics, Economics and Welfare*, 1953, Part IV. Other specific references are found as follows: Schattschneider, *op. cit.*, p. 221: Belle Zeller, *Pressure Politics in New York*, 1937, pp. 230, 237–8, 249–50; Leiserson, *op. cit.*, p. 269; Herring, *Group Presentation Before Congress*, p. 75; Bailey, *op. cit.*, pp. 91 ff; Keller, *op. cit.*, pp. 81–211; Schlesinger, *op. cit.*, p. 31; Truman, *op. cit.*, p. 170; Garceau, *op. cit.*, pp. 678–681; Garceau, *The Political Life of the American Medical Association*, 1941, p. 107; Brogan, *Politics in America*, 1955, pp. 356, 362.

groups denied a demanded power position. Such groups when they emerge are likely to be social movements led by individuals, such as the fringe groups which appeared during the depression of the Thirties, or the "White Citizens Councils" in the South today. Such groups perceive themselves as rejected by the system, as operating against the system. They may become "struggle movements" which lose their sense of moral commitment to the community, although rationalizing their techniques in moral terms.

Another observed consequence is the increasing transformation of legal policy-making arenas through informal relationships with interest groups. In the long-run this may mean the transformation of administration and the legislative process into an informal and functional type of representative system. Interest groups become indirectly, rather than directly, responsible for policy planning and for political support. This type of "syndicalism" while explicitly recognized and taken for granted, does not, however, become formally institutionalized. Over time this may mean either the transference of the check-mate system to the bureaucracy and legislature, a development which we already have noticed in this country on certain types of issues, or it means the alternation in power status and thus in policy control from era to era.[55]

The scope of operations of the two-party system is restricted, with these trends in interest groups. Parties lose their functions of bargaining and goal-setting, and become primarily formal agencies for the the recruitment of governmental personnel. The function of the boss or party leader at the local level becomes atrophied, with primary emphasis on winning votes through an organizational machine.[56] Elections thus become primarily a contest for personality. Parties do not really "aggregate" and mediate group claims. Interest groups restrict and neutralize their capacity for leadership and policy control while maintaining indirect relationships with them. But, in all this, our chances for keeping the two-party system are maximized, because group

[55] On "bureaucratic neutrality" see particularly Reinhard Bendix, "Bureaucracy and Power Relations," In *Reader in Bureaucracy* (Robert K. Merton, et al, eds.), 1952, pp. 114–135; Also, Samuel P. Huntington, "The Marasmus of the ICC: The Commission, The Railroads, and the Public Interest," *Yale Law Journal*, vol. 61 (1952), pp. 467–509. The general question of the "permeability" of the party system by interest groups has been discussed widely. A recent discussion of interest in Jean Meynaud, "Essai d'analyse de l'influence des groupes d'intérêt," *Revue Economique*, (1957) pp. 217 ff.

[56] See E. P. Herring, *The Politics of Democracy*, p. 327, and Stanley Keller, *op. cit.*, p. 210.

conflict is legitimized and institutionalized outside the party arena. The "third party" is perceived as an avenue of influence only by the group rejected for the checkmate system, and this perception is an irrational miscalculation.

It is obvious from this that the rules of the political game become subtlely modified. We merely develop somewhat different modes of conduct and we modify the roles of interest groups and parties in the political process. The political process may actually become less "conflictual", with interest groups assuming more of the "integrative" functions ordinarily conceived as performed by the parties—"integrative" so far as the public, group interaction, and legal policy-making is concerned.[57] We come to need interest groups more than ever in the democratic society.

These are some of the current trends and future possibilities which can be advanced about American interest groups. They suggest a frame of reference for viewing this system as interacting within the total political process and as responding to the changes in the social order. Whether this type of model is applicable to the study of interest groups in foreign countries is not for me to say. This depends of necessity on the nature of the political institutions, the character of social change, and the norms of political behavior which exist in any society. As Bacon said, "We see all governments are obscure and invisible. . . ."[58]

BIBLIOGRAPHICAL NOTE

The American literature on interest groups is so vast (and still constantly growing) that even a selected bibliography would exceed the limitations of this volume. In addition to the works cited in the footnotes to the foregoing report the most important publications in the field will be found listed in the bibliographies of two recent standard works on the subject: David B. Truman, *The Governmental Process*, New York, 1951, pp. 537–44; and Donald C. Blaisdell, *American Democracy under Pressure*, New York, 1957, pp. 280–288.

[57] A somewhat opposing interpretation to this is presented in the last chapter of Sigmund Neumann (ed.) *Modern Political Parties*, Chicago, 1956. Neumann in stressing the developing "party of social integration" (p. 404) and the relative roles of party and interest groups in "this crucial problem of national integration" (pp. 412–13), foresees a larger and more necessary role for parties.

[58] Quoted in Franz Neumann, *op. cit.*, p. 19, fn. 1.

INTEREST GROUPS AND THE POLITICAL SYSTEM OF YUGOSLAVIA

JOVAN DJORDJEVIC

I. Introductory

It is a well-known fact that various political systems, often fundamentally different from each other, have existed in the world and continue to exist. By a political system we understand here the institutions exercising governmental authority and those which, in one way or another, participate in or influence the political process taken as a whole, together with public activity and the rights of citizens inside and outside those institutions. Differences in the political system give rise at the same time to differences in the positions of interest groups and in conceptions of them, and in the same way differences are revealed in the relationship between a political system and interest groups, and in the very conception of those relations.

Despite all those differences of nature and magnitude between various political systems, differences which can to a certain extent hamper comparative studies in political science and make them more difficult if they are not treated and explained scientifically, political systems and interest groups and their role in politics do lend themselves to comparative study. This is due to the existence of certain universal laws relating to the movement and formation of human society into a political community. These laws, tested in present-day political practice, indicate that, in spite of differences between them, no political systems, even those which are built on differing relations of ownership of the means of production and a different class structure, are so far apart from one another or so unlike, as not to lend themselves to objective scientific comparative research.

A common feature of all political systems is that they are political systems, more accurately that they have as a common factor the existence of authority, a struggle for self-assertion and the perfecting or changing of the system of authority, and the activity of the people and their organizations trying to set in motion, to perfect or change the mechanism of government and the political institutions and social relations. A political system exists precisely because the material, social and moral conditions are still lacking for human society to govern itself and for men to dedicate themselves to public affairs in a manner transcending politics, that is by identifying their own interests with those of the community.

Sociologically speaking, political systems and policies spring from the structure of society. In all countries human society is not homogeneous, but heterogeneous. The individual social structures are characterized by antagonistic contradictions between the basic economic, social and political interests, but within each such structure today there occur differing interests and a series of larger or smaller contradictions at the various levels of inner social relations between citizens. Given that fact, there also exist in every political system individual "interest groups," regardless of the differences which exist regarding the position, significance and other aspects of those groups in the political system of a country.

Taking these considerations as our basis, we are able to establish three fundamental premises in connection with the study of interest groups in Yugoslavia; first, the problem of interest groups exists in this country as in others; second, the study of interest groups in each specific country must be closely allied with a general familiarity with the conception and structure of the political system of that country; third, it is essential that in objective, comparative scientific studies, every effort should be made to avoid analogies, mechanical comparisons and the application of a rigid system of ideas and sense of values arising from the conditions of one political system to another with a different political structure. This means that the same problems of interest groups do not occur in every country, nor do the same problems have the same meaning and significance in every country, and this applies to Yugoslavia as well as to other countries.

The social economic basis of the political system of Yugoslavia is represented by social ownership of the means of production in the spheres of industry, transport and commerce, and by private individual tenure by farmers which is the most prevalent form of ownership in the agricultural sphere. In the field of craftmanship privately owned workshops are similarly predominant. The social character of ownership, as distinct from State ownership, finds itself reflected in what is termed the right of self-government of the producers. This self-government operates within the framework of a relatively free market, of limited economic planning, which is in effect a scientific-directive and not an administrative-regulative act, and an abandonment of the conception and practice of the ownership by and directive rights of the State in the sphere of the economic process and the division of the fruits of human labor. Self-government of the producers means the right of both factory and office workers as well as members of co-operatives to plan and carry out economic projects independently and arrange their internal relations in an enterprise or co-operative by mutual agreement within the framework of the laws and economic plans and other norms ordained by the highest state organs. This includes their right to decide on their own share of the proceeds of their economic operations, since, after obligations to the community have been met, salaries are fixed relatively independently.

Political philosophy in Yugoslavia is based on the conception that a political system which places the materially and morally interested citizens, and particularly the active working man, not only in the position of a voter and "observer of the political scene," but into the position of an ever more active and more complete manager of social affairs, must exist and be developed. "The political system of a State of the transitional period must be so developed as to enable the most progressive material and spiritual movements of the working people, whose consciousness is already being formed under conditions of social ownership of the means of production, to express themselves daily and contribute towards a ceaseless changing of obsolete forms. This is the meaning of the demand for democratization which is being heard today as the principal demand in the many countries which find themselves on the *road of socialist* development".[1]

On the other hand, this philosophy is founded on the concept that the political structure is a relatively independent and significant factor which does not appear solely as the reflection of economic relations. This means that without a democratic structure there is neither economic democracy nor socialism. "The political system of socialism must be built up in such a way as to enable the working class and other working people to have a direct influence upon it and not merely through some ruling party susceptible to bureaucratization. New political forms can only appear and develop normally under conditions where the progressive aspirations of the working people, which grow up parallel with the development of the material basis of socialism and the adoption of socialist relations, are really able to be expressed in the appropriate democratic organs of social and state management. For that very

[1] E. Kardelj, *Socialist Democracy and Economic Policy in the Further Socialist Development of Yugoslavia*, Beograd, 1956, p. 8.

reason there is no socialist progress without a constant advancement of democracy in all social relations; of course, as we have said, this democracy must correspond to the movements and progress of socialist economic and social-political factors. That alone is the course which makes possible a gradual removal of the elements of bureaucracy from social relation which appear in the transitional period on the basis of social ownership of the means of production".[2] The same political philosophy also forms the basic premise of the current Yugoslav Constitution adopted in 1953.

In order to put this basically anti-totalitarian and non-etatistic conception into practice, the structure of the political system is founded on the following principles:

First, the essence of socialist statehood lies in its *reduction and weakening,* not expansion and strengthening. Accordingly, the political system is not identified with the state, nor is the state the patron and organizer of that political system. The state is reducing its earlier functions of nationalization and the management of the economy through the state administration which were apparent in the period of the revolutionary taking-over of state power by the working people. This process of de-etatization is being pursued in several directions, the following being the most important: a) separation of the economic organization and its autonomous functioning on the basis of the self-government of the producers in the basic economic organizations and higher economic bodies (economic associations, chambers and the like); b) schools, cultural and educational institutions, scientific institutions, social insurance bodies, social institutions and those institutions devoted to "public service" are organized and managed on the principle of "social government"; this means that they are managed by the interested citizens or the citizens working in them together with the representatives of "society" as elected by the citizens themselves or the representative bodies of the country, or as delegated by the associations concerned; c) in the basic social communities (in the towns and the rural districts) local self-government has been set up and developed. This is considered to be the basic cell of the political organization and operates through elected representative bodies as differentiated from direct democracy (the referendum, the assemblies of voters and the like); d) the mechanism of the State (the system of authority, government) finds itself in process of de-etatization. This is reflected among other ways in the fact that a series of bodies responsible for the performance of executive and administrative tasks (the so-called councils

---

[2] *Ibid.,* p. 36.

in local self-government and the organization of authority of the people's republics) are made up not only of the members of representative bodies and of public functionaries, but of citizens who are delegated by autonomous institutions and associations.

Second, this political structure is starting to differ essentially from the "classical" one, whether "liberal" or "totalitarian". This means that the political society appears, neither as the mechanism of influence of "free groups" upon a system of authority restrained in its functions nor as a mechanism for the management of society and public affairs by means of a state mechanism increasingly expanding its functions in relation to society.

The Yugoslav political system represents a new political symbiosis of the state and a relatively autonomous social mechanism; the state and the non-state mechanism are independent within the framework of their rights and powers and as such are the bearers of specific general and public interests. It is true that those rights, or, more accurately, that degree of autonomy and freedom of action, has been fixed by the Constitution and the laws enacted by the central representative bodies belonging to the state mechanism in the narrower sense. Those representative bodies, given the fact that, by the method of their election, they represent the "political society," as a whole are empowered to determine what are the interests of society as a whole, and decide upon the respective rights of both the state apparatus and the autonomous social mechanism of government. To restrict the possibility of separation of the highest representative bodies from society, from social and political reality, all members of those bodies are subject to recall and direct representation of the basic economic interests is introduced into the structure of representative bodies (the so-called councils of producers, as will be shown later). The highest representative bodies possess largely regulative powers as established by the Constitution and, finally, the political executive function has been entrusted to specially elected bodies and the administration to responsible officials.

Third, within this kind of political structure the status and role of political organizations (political parties) change. Yugoslavia never belonged to those countries where the Party constitutes the core and the sole motive force and directing power of the State mechanism and political process. No monopoly of the Communist Party has ever been proclaimed. Alongside it there also exists a general political organization of all citizens regardless of the philosophical and other outlooks they might entertain (the People's Front).

It is understandable that the present-day political structure of the country should also have called for fresh changes in the status and role of the two basic political organizations: the League of Communists and the Socialist Alliance of the Working People. The League of Communists is not a party organized to exercise authority. It is a voluntary political association of citizens bound by a common political philosophy and the unity of ideology. This political association is outside the mechanism of authority and performs none of its functions. By championing specific standpoints through free discussions between people of differing viewpoints and by the concrete activity of its members, the League of Communists sets itself the task of promoting an over-all socialist orientation and of winning the largest number of citizens to it.

The Socialist Alliance is a general political organization which serves as a political forum for examining public issues and as one of the organizers of the political process. It is a voluntary organization to which citizens belong irrespective of their philosophical, religious and other differences; the essential point is that they accept the general socialist orientation and the broad outlines of the program for the country's development and its struggle for independence, peace and peaceful coexistence and co-operation between the peoples of the world.

Both those political organizations are oriented towards the political process and participate in it, but they are neither a component part of the state apparatus nor of the other political institutions of the country.

Fourth, outside the authorities and the social organisms performing definite functions of government and public service, there are also free associations of citizens. These associations form part of the political system. They do so not only because they serve to bring into being a number of interests which the different groups have in common but also because the former individual functions of the state system have been de-etatized to such an extent that these associations perform the functions and tasks of free organizations of citizens. They do this all the more since it is in keeping with the philosophy of the political system that not only "private," but public tasks be performed by the interested and free citizens on their own initiative and within the framework of and through their multifarious free associations.

II. THE TYPES, THE ROLE, AND THE SIGNIFICANCE OF INTEREST GROUPS

The Concept

The concept of "interest group," if we adopt it for reasons of international communication and comparative research, can assume a broader or a narrower sense. The broader sense would be sociological, and the narrower political. In the sociological sense, society is a mosaic of larger and smaller, and highly different, interest groups. These groups, in the final analysis, are linked together through the interests of those groups that occupy strategic positions in social production. Here there obtains a wealth of varying groups and sub-groups from the social classes and from different segments within the classes and outside them to the *ad-hoc* social agglomerations which are formed to satisfy temporary interests. The more a society is developed materially, socially, politically, culturally and spiritually, the more complex, richer, and more "pluralistic" will its structure be. Actually this is a law already discovered by the English sociologist Herbert Spencer and elaborated by modern sociologists, especially since Marx.

In the narrower, or political, sense, we are concerned with those groups that participate in the political process directly or indirectly. In reality, the sociological and political aspects of interest groups cannot be separated. Generally speaking, political groups are organizations for the realization of economic, political, ideological and other interests (conceptions, attitudes, aspirations and the like) of the groups in the sociological sense. The groups in this narrower political sense form the subject of political science. However, political science cannot neglect or underrate this relationship between the sociological and the political groups.

The relationship between interest groups in the sociological and political sense is complex and not one-sided, dialectical and not mechanical. The groups in a sociological sense provide the basis for groups in a political sense; through programs and ideology political groups rationalize the aspirations, the character, the needs and demands— more simply, the "interests"—of these basic social groups and actuate them by their action. Political groups, more accurately groups in the political sense, influence those groups of a sociological nature and themselves create definite interests, which they ultimately adopt as long as the first do not betray the fundamental interests of the second. In addition, groups of a political nature can not only separate themselves from the interests of the basic groups they represent, but may also begin to pursue their own narrower and selfish interests, becoming a force in their own right. This separation and emancipation of groups in the political sense is not an exceptional phenomenon: it is known in all social organizations and political systems. If a political system affords fewer material and spiritual conditions for free activity and man's freedom, that process of estrangement of the political force from the social force becomes easier and more universal.

In this, one should emphasize, as a universal tendency, the phenomenon that every political group, every organization of interests of certain social groups, acquires interests of its own as well. Thus in each of these groups in the political process there occurs a complex mixture of narrower and broader interests: in the action of these groups we find represented both the interests of the groups in the sociological sense, i.e., groups that are being represented, and those of the groups doing the representing, the latter appearing more or less as the official representative of the basic groups. This phenomenon is ordinarily termed bureaucratization of a group. However, besides bureaucratization, which constitutes a systematic estrangement of the political force from the corresponding sociological group, we also find here, as a well-nigh universal phenomenon, an "invisible" estrangement, one characterizing every political organization, every organization for purposes of representing interests and political action. Escape from such an estrangement is provided not only by democratization of the internal organization of a group, but by a constant fostering of direct democracy, by the gaining of political activity and political influence on the part of the groups proper and the citizens.

Such would be the general appraisal of the concept and significance of interest groups.

Classification

Every classification of interest groups in the political sense is inevitably expressive of a definite political philosophy, one drawing its elements from the political system or systems closest to it. Hence, inescapably, it is arbitrary and artificial from the point of view of concrete truth and scientific political theory.

From the standpoint of Yugoslav political experience, interest groups in the political sense could be broken down into these three basic categories:

(1) *Groups participating directly in the political process of government.* Here one can distinguish two sub-categories. First, the groups having the status of autonomous economic organizations and social institutions and those performing definite functions of social government and public services. Belonging here, as already indicated, are the economic organizations that are managed by the producers themselves, the social institutions in the domain of education, culture, sciences, public health and social services that are managed on the principles of social self-government. Second, we have the groups occupying their place in the very structure of the representative bodies. Thus the pro-

ducers elect their representatives to the councils of producers, which are independent chambers of the people's assemblies and the people's committees as the basic representative bodies of Yugoslavia.

(2) *The groups holding a basic position in the political system.* This category obviously covers the political organizations (parties).

(3) *The organizations representing the different interests of the citizens.* Among these organizations three categories can be distinguished: a) the mass-membership social organizations; b) the social organizations representing the narrower and special interests of citizens; c) organizations of a private character as recognized by society and the laws (the churches).

Analysis of interest groups in Yugoslavia on the basis of the stated classification could certainly provide a number of more concrete and more conceivable analyses and conclusions. It would indicate once more that certain general classifications in the social sciences call for advance preparation and familiarity with more concrete classifications which are nearer to the essence of the political system and to the interest groups of each individual country.

With a view to finding scientifically more acceptable and perhaps more justified scientific classifications, one can adopt as the point of departure one of those classifications which are featured in the individual studies of a comparative character. It seems best to accept the classification which was proposed by Prof. David Truman in his work, *The Governmental Process* (New York, 1951).

According to that classification, the structure of interest groups in Yugoslavia reveals the following picture:

(1) *Groups holding a strategic position in society.* In Yugoslavia, these groups can be understood to include the groups which, while occupying an influential, or even strategic position in the political process, do not find themselves within the structure of the mechanism of government. Not only are they not a part of the apparatus of government, but they do not even form a part of that mechanism which is termed social self-government, or the mechanism performing definite public functions. Accordingly, only the Socialist Alliance and the League of Communists (political organizations) can be included here. The status and role of these political organizations has already been dealt with; and the question of the relations of these political organizations with other interest groups will be treated later.

At any rate, the religious organizations and the Army do not belong to this category of interest groups. In Yugoslavia the church is separated from the state. All churches, whether the major (the Serbian

Orthodox, the Catholic and the Moslem) or the minor ones (the series of Protestant churches ad sects), enjoy equality and freedom in the field of worship and religious rites. On the other hand, the Constitution bars the church from interfering in politics. The church as such does not form a part of the political structure, nor does it participate in the political process. None the less, this does not preclude the individual churches, notably the major ones, from influencing the political concepts and constituting a certain political force. In Yugoslavia that political force lacks a strategic position, and it exercises no essential influence upon the political process. Not only are the rightful interests of the Church as a religious community recognized, but it has the right to represent certain interests of its own. For the regulation of those interests, special political bodies exist within the framework of the Federal Government and the republican governments (the commissions on religion).

The army is the organization of national defense and a constituent part of the federal administration. It is an organ of the political organization, but it is no independent political and interest group in Yugoslavia. This status of the army represents one of the characteristics of the political organization of the country. The army has never represented special interests and much less has it had the possibility of pretending to represent the general interests. The independence of the army in military matters and its subjection to political control constitute the characteristic of the position and role of this important organization in the political system of Yugoslavia. The army, therefore, holds no strategic political position, nor has it ever shown the ambition to assume it. This, at the same time, forms one of the characteristic features of the political system of the country and of the democratic nature of the system.

(2) *Interest groups within the general mechanism of government as a whole.* These groups constitute one of the original features of the Yugoslav political system. Included here, first of all, are the economic organizations wherein the producers, acting directly or through their representatives, manage the process of production and exchange. In any society, and in a socialist one particularly, management of the economic process is a component part of the political process. Economic enterprises and co-operatives are managed directly by the workers and other employees, or agriculturists engaged in them. To advance the individual branches of the economy the country's economic organizations join together in institutions of common law called economic associations. The economic organizations and economic associations of

the individual branches of the economy are affiliated with chambers which represent the highest form of independent organization in the economy on the basis of the self-government of the producers.

Alongside the large numbers of economic organizations throughout Yugoslavia, there are also eight Yugoslav economic chambers. Some of these chambers constitute a unified organization of economic associations and enterprises (the Federal Chamber of Industry, the Federal Chamber of Foreign Trade, the Federal Chamber of Transport and the Federal Chamber of Building Trades). Others, again, represent federations of territorially organized chambers (the federations of chambers of agriculture, chambers of commerce, chambers of catering, and chambers of arts and crafts). Co-operatives are affiliated to their area associations and finally to the Central Co-operative Union of Yugoslavia.

In addition, the producers elect their political representative body in the form of councils of producers. The council of producers exists in all representative bodies of the state mechanism.

Lastly, management in the sphere of education, culture, science, public health and other public services is performed through autonomous social institutions by citizens who are directly concerned with those services or who work in the institutions and by those who were delegated to the organs of management of those institutions.

The status and role of all the autonomous social organisms is indicative of the phenomenon of institutionalization of interest groups. This institutionalization signifies a radical curtailment of management by the state; it stands for the emancipation of a series of public functions from state monopolism, the latter being a particularly dangerous feature where the means of production are nationalized and within the framework of socialist society. At the same time the institutionalization decreases in this way the phenomenon of statism or "etatism," and also the possibility of uncontrolled and sometimes irresponsible influence of "pressure groups".

(3) *The groups representing special interests.* The Yugoslav political system is characterized, as already mentioned, by the existence and constant growth of a large number of associations of citizens.

The Yugoslav Constitution guarantees "the free association of citizens with the object of pursuing democratic political, economic, social, scientific, cultural, artistic, sporting and other common interests."

Over 1,000 such associations exist in different parts of the country and with different aims. There are over 100 federations affiliating the territorial or national associations.

The general characteristics of the above associations are as follows:

All associations represent democratic organizations with their own statutes, registered with the state authorities, and governed by autonomous bodies which manage the affairs of the associations (assemblies, managing boards and executive boards). They regularly hold meetings within periods of 1 to 3 years, to elect their organs of management, so that the officials, in so far as there are any, have practically no influence upon the policies of the associations. No association at all is organized as a pressure group, but nearly all of them participate, directly or indirectly, if not in the political process, in the performance of tasks of public interest.

From the point of view of the role and significance of these associations in the political process and the performance of public functions, they could be classified as follows:

Associations with the character of social organizations. As a rule these are mass-membership bodies which, by their numbers and character, influence the political life of the country. They include the Federation of Trade Unions (1,550,000 members), the People's Youth (over 1,000,000 members), the Federation of War Veterans of the National Liberation War (1,200,000 members), the Federation of Disabled War Veterans (350,000 members), and the Federation of Women's Societies (affiliating 1,000 societies). The remaining societies have smaller memberships and narrower programs and aims.

Associations performing certain public functions. Here first of all, there is the Federation of Trade Unions which performs certain public tasks as determined by law, such as participation in different commissions serving to approve the salaries in economic organizations, considering the dismissal of workers or specific important issues affecting public officials etc. The Federation of Disabled War Veterans operates institutions and services for assisting mothers and children. The Federation of War Veterans organizes assistance for the families of war veterans and victims of fascism. The People's Technological Organization cares for the technical education of citizens. The Federation of Physical Education "Partizan" attends to the physical training of the people. The Federation of Journalists concerns itself with the status and the advancement of the work of journalists. The Federation of Firemen is an affiliation of the volunteer-firemen's societies, which, in addition to the appropriate technical services of the towns and districts, perform the public service of fire protection. The Central Hunting Society organizes both the sport and the economic aspects of hunting in the country.

Associations with the status of organizations under common law and those performing major public functions. Here, for example, we have the legal chambers which as the associations of lawyers look after the interests of the legal profession and the advancement of its work as an independent public function performed by the individual lawyers in their offices. In addition, the legal chambers are also managed by the individual public servants who have been elected to the Council of such a chamber by the republican assemblies.

Associations delegating their members to the executive administrative organs of the people's committees and the republics (the councils) or the organs of administration of the individual public services. Here one should note, particularly, the associations of educational workers, physicians, engineers and technicians, jurists, social workers, scientists and the like.

Associations providing the enjoyment of special rights and protection for their members. So, the associations of clergymen and the associations of artists make, in conjunction with the institutions of social insurance, arrangements for the health, pensions and other insurance of their members. Associations of authors, again, establish their institutions for the protection of copyright.

Over and above those categories there are also interest groups that can have an influence upon the policies and the political process. There are two such basic groups: the national groups, including the national minorities; and the local-territorial groups.

The national groups in Yugoslavia are able to realize their political rights and aspirations in two ways. All Yugoslav nationalities have their own State organizations with the status of a federal unit within the Yugoslav Federation. As such, they are also represented in federal organizations, particularly in the Federal People's Assembly in which the representatives of the republics have special rights, through the Council of Nationalities, to veto all decisions that violate the principle of national equality and constitutional guarantees. The national minorities have their rights secured through the existence of a political territorial autonomy in those areas of Yugoslavia where they live (Vojvodina and the Kosovo-Metohija Region).

In addition to this institutionalizing of the *interests* of the nationalities and the national minorities, the same groups influence the political process as well. The *characteristic* of the political system of Yugoslavia is the absence of any privileges or inequalities in the activity and influence of those national groups.

The local-territorial groups appear in two basic forms, as organized local self-government and as compact groups of a regional character having certain traditions, aspirations, interests and needs which distinguish them from other similar groups.

Considering the position of self-governing local communities in Yugoslavia, these communities affect the political process in dual fashion. There are cases, where the narrow local interests seek precedence over the over-all interests of the country in the wide domain of "local matters," the manifestations of "localism" as a form of influence and pressure by local groups. On the other hand, the representatives of local self-government also have the tendency to exert influence upon the handling of general social matters, participating as they do in the making of appropriate decisions.

In a similar, but often subtle and "invisible," manner narrower and wider local and regional groups exist which are brought together by virtue of their loyalty to their native district, of childhood friendships, common habits and even prejudices.

It is understandable that the influence of these groups is not *a priori* negative in all circumstances. The interests of the community as a whole are, more often than not, a more or less harmonious synthesis of the majority of the varying interests pursued by the individual groups. Likewise there also exist certain group interests that are well conceived and really represent the interests of society as a whole, provided their imposition is not contrary to rightful interests of the remaining groups. Only an undemocratic and underhand influence of individual groups upon the decisions of public interest makes them like pressure machines, disfiguring the free democratic process of government and decision-making.

The problem of the relationship between the membership and the executive bodies of associations in Yugoslavia gains in importance the more these associations are able to influence policies by performing definite public functions. This holds true not only for the trade unions, but for nearly all associations of a public nature. There are cases of disagreement between the central organs of administration and local organizations, just as there occur instances of differences and even clashes between the interests and attitudes of the membership, or its majority, on the one hand, and the leadership of an organization, on the other. It is hardly necessary to mention that the highest and specialized bodies sometime make decisions that should really be made by the wider representative bodies and that executive organs make decisions which belong to the assemblies of members. In the individual associations these phenomena also assume the character of bureaucratization when the executive bodies separate themselves from the mass of the membership and begin to pursue a "policy" of their own. Bureaucratization can accompany the organization of human society in all its forms.

All major organizations in Yugoslavia are of a federal character. This is partly the consequence of the federal structure of the political organization of the country. That the associations have this type of structure also acts as a barrier to centralization, which frequently accompanies and aids bureaucratization. The possibility that the individual organizations may unite themselves to form associations for purposes of wielding influence is not to be excluded, but it is certain that the formation of these associations into federations and confederations has been determined by their aims and the part they play in society.

Connected with these and other questions is the familiar problem of finance, or that of "money in politics" in general. This problem is of a different nature in Yugoslavia from what it is in many other countries. Here there is no possibility of financial assets being used to further the interests of individual groups. (Exceptionally, such a possibility might occur in the influence of economic organizations upon the decisions of local authorities.)

Important for associations in Yugoslavia is the question of independent material means. It is necessary that associations found their activity primarily on the resources of their memberships. At present a number of enterprises depend on grants—made by the state and, partly, by economic organizations. Substantial funds are being allocated to that end corresponding to the political role and significance of the associations. One characteristic of the contemporary political system of Yugoslavia is that, in this way, the associations have not become incorporated into the mechanism of authority, and are immune from any direct influence on the part of the grantor. However, to an increasing extent, the public is seeking a way to emancipate these organizations. This, depends ultimately on the raising of the material standard of the people and on their material autonomy. It is true that only on this condition the inner democracy of these organizations of citizens can be strengthened.

As shown above, the structure of the political society in Yugoslavia is not founded on the public rights of the different interest groups. Those rights are in the form of authority, or of participation in "social government," or of a free public function and service. This is the consequence of the series of factors and changes that have modelled the social and political organization of the country.

Social, not state, ownership of the basic means of production has transformed the function of management of the economy from a "private" into a "public" function; this public function is not of a state order, but a social one; and it is being realized in significant proportions by independent economic organizations managed by the producers. Since management of the economy is founded not on the private or the collective ownership right, but on "social ownership," economic authority, as a public function, has passed in considerable measure to the active participants in the economic process themselves, to the producers of material value.

Another factor that has contributed to this "pluralism of authority" is the democratization of the political structure, that is, curtailment of classical authority and the delegation of a series of public functions to the communes (local self-government), to autonomous social institutions and associations of citizens.

As a result, the basic characteristic of these interest groups in Yugoslavia lies not in their appearance as pressure groups, but in their participation in the active political process. They do not seek to gain authority, nor do they impose decisions through the weight of their material influence, or their political activity and diverse public and private, recognized and unrecognized, skills and "pressures". In view of their place and role in the process of production or in the social and political division of labor, these groups are the bearers of public functions and services fixed by the Constitution.

It is true that these and other groups also appear as factors influencing the policies and decisions of other organized political public bodies, including the state apparatus. But that influence can never change essentially or disfigure the political process, the premises and functions of the mechanism of government as established by the constitution.

However, disfigurements of the political process and the process of government are not excluded, on a different basis. The individual factors of this complex mechanism of self-government (economic enterprises, local self-government, the people's republics, the social institutions and so on) might benefit by their rights predominantly for their own good, regardless of the over-all interests or of the interests of wider sections of the community. The producers can clash not only with the interests of the consumers, but with those of the producers of other branches of the economy. Phenomena of "particularism" are not excluded in such a political system. Local self-government, which is the executor not only of local, but of general functions, can shut its operations within the boundaries of its area, behaving as an "autarchic" unit. Manifestations of "localism," and general conflicts between the over-all and group interests, are all possible in such a mechanism of management of public affairs.

Constant democratization of society, struggle against all forms of political monopoly and bureaucracy, publicity of the process of government and the political process generally, the raising of the culture and consciousness of groups and individuals, human and functional co-operation between varying state and social organisms, promotion of human solidarity—those are some of the remedies for manifestations of particularism, localism and other like tendencies that threaten to weaken the essential social and political unity of a democratically organized socialist society.

But that is not all. If one wishes to perfect the democratic political structure of a socialist society, only considerable further development of the material productive forces and production, the wealth of the community and the prosperity of individuals can provide the most vital base on which the over-all, the group and the individual interests can be co-ordinated without pressures and without hierarchy. From the angle of the present and the near future, in such a political structure the existence of political forces, including the mechanism of the state is necessary to act as arbiter at a definite level and to determine the interests of the community as a whole. But it will rely more and more, on the existing democratic mechanism and the ideas and interests of the largest number of active and progressive social forces and groups, of the majority of citizens.

III. Interest Groups and the Legislative process

1. Characteristic of the political system of Yugoslavia is the introduction of interest groups into the very structure of the highest representative bodies of the country, from the Federal People's Assembly to the republican people's assemblies to the people's committees of the communes and districts. Those interest groups belong to the category termed producers. The producers actually represent citizens directly and indirectly engaged in the process of production, transport, and distribution. From the point of view of property relations, the structure of the productive interests represented in the Federal parliament of Yugoslavia and in other legislative institutions of the country is as follows: all the workers and office employees engaged in socialist economic enterprises and those operating the means of production which are individual or private property are regarded as producers. In Yugoslavia the latter still account for the majority of active producers in the sphere of agriculture and arts and crafts.

All these producers are represented in the parliament as organized producers, on the industrial or production principle, viz., the workers and other employees engaged in economic enterprises, the agriculturists who are members of various co-operatives, and the artisans who are affiliated to their chambers.

A negative facet is that at present the category of producers does not include the following groups of active citizens: intellectuals, namely the producers of spiritual wealth, the officials engaged in the state apparatus (civil servants) and the institutions outside the economy and the representatives of the professions (lawyers, journalists, physicians and the like).

It follows, then, that the producers of material values are directly engaged in the organized political process. They have the right to elect their representatives to the second house of the country's representative bodies which is called the Council of Producers. Hence, those representative bodies are composed of two houses. In addition to the general political representative body, which is elected, on the basis of universal suffrage, by citizens who have attained the age of 18 years, the people's assemblies and the people's committees also have a representative body of the producers.

The basic characteristics of these houses of producers, from the point of view of the theory of interest groups, are as follows. First, here it is not a question of consultative bodies of the type of social economic councils such as were known during the Weimar Republic in Germany and such as exist in some other countries (France, Portugal, and elsewhere). The councils of producers, in effect, are equal to the general political parliaments. However, they do not participate in the solving of all questions within the jurisdiction of the Federal People's Assembly and the other representative bodies. As bodies with equal rights, the Councils of Producers deal with all questions relating to the economy, to finance and the problems of labor and social insurance. (Thus the Council of Producers of the Federal People's Assembly takes part in the enactment of the Federal Economic Plan, the Budget, the economic and financial legislation and labor legislation). The meaning of this restricted competence lies in the fact that the councils of producers are the representative bodies of *active* producers (who remain in production and decide only questions directly affecting them, i.e., those associated with the allocation of the national income and with labor relations). All these tasks of theirs are dealt with by the councils of producers in their separate sessions and no bill may be passed without complete agreement being reached on it by both houses. There exists no priority whatever in favor of one of the houses, nor is there an arbitrator to settle possible differences between them. Where no agreement can be reached on a given bill, and the arbitration procedure provided by the Constitution has been implemented, the national parliament as such (or any other representative body) is dissolved and new elections are ordered.

Besides these rights of the Council of Producers, the most important questions within the jurisdiction of the Assembly are solved in joint sessions of the two houses. Such questions include amendments to the Constitution, election of the President of the Republic and the Executive Council (the Cabinet), election of judges of the republican supreme courts and the like. Finally, the Council of Producers also has exclusive jurisdiction in some cases. It may issue certain decrees regarding the work of economic organizations. In this respect the Council of Producers appears as the highest representative body of the workers' self-government, characteristic of the economic and the whole social system of Yugoslavia.

This brings us to the second basic feature of this representative body of the producers. It is fairly well known, that in Yugoslavia the principle of what is called the self-government of the producers in economic organizations (not only in economic enterprises in the fields of industry, mining, transport and commerce, but in the field of agriculture, as exemplified by state farms and by co-operatives) has been introduced. Self-government of the producers is the consequence and the guarantee of the socialization of the means of production. On the basis of this right, the collectives control the economic organizations. On the basis of the fight for self-government, the collectives are able to make their own production plans independently within the framework of the basic proportions of the general economic plans passed by the highest representative bodies of the country, to determine the production costs and the prices of their products in accordance with the market laws and to regulate their internal social relations including their wages and salaries. These rights also incorporate elements of disposition and appropriation, yet they are no longer property rights. They are exercised within the general social norms as laid down by the Economic Plan and the laws.

Considering the above points, the self-government of the producers in the economy would not only be restricted from outside, but be forever uncertain, if the producers themselves did not participate in the enactment of those general social norms. Thus the councils of producers have grown organically out of the process of workers' self-government and represent a political institution of the producers for the further realization of their self-government in the economy.

The third characteristic relates to the representation of the producers, and thus to the political role of that body. Producers are not represented on the principle of "one man, one vote," but according to the economic norm that the producers shall possess as many representative rights as correspond to their contribution to society, which in turn is expressed in the value of the portion contributed by them to the national income. In the Yugoslav parliament today that ratio is such that the producers engaged in industry, commerce and crafts account for two-thirds, and the farmers for one-third, of the total membership of this House. Given the higher degree of material and technical development of the first mentioned branches of economy, which, in the main, have been socialized, the working class, integrally speaking, has a decisive role in those Houses of Parliament even though in a series of communes and even districts of a rural type the agricultural producers are in the majority.

Generally speaking, the councils of producers express the political theory whereby the most active citizens of the country, the producers, have the right as such to pass decisions on the most important questions of social life, and of the economic system and economic and social policies in particular. The working class as such, not only its political representatives, constitutes itself an authority. This should ensure a more positive influence of the working class and the producers, thereby reducing the dangers of bureaucracy. Only the social economic forces which with their consciousness, interests and status in society uphold the social system (socialism) can continue to build and establish it in a "purer form"; in this instance they are able to create and defend a more genuine economic and political democracy. On the other hand, also the remaining producers, those still operating individual means of production, and, under Yugoslav conditions, in particular the peasants, are able through the council of producers to gain their political representation, being thereby enabled to express and defend their particular interests. This aspect of the councils of producers is of vital interest for the liberalization and democratization of the political process under the conditions of a Socialist society still in the process of construction on the basis of socialized industry and of private property in such an important branch of the economy as agriculture.

The councils of producers can also be viewed as an institution of economic democracy and as the introduction of economic representation into the highest representative bodies of the country. This "duality" is the expression of the unified process of fusion of the political and economic sovereignty on the basis of the means of production representing social property, the principle of self-government of the producers, and a fitting democratization of the political system.

The councils of producers are relatively new institutions but their comparatively brief history has demonstrated their positive value for the mechanism of government and the political life of the country. The discussions between the political houses and the councils of producers vest the laws and decisions of the representative bodies with greater authority and realism. They do away with a major clash of interests, facilitate the application of laws and realization of policies. Besides, the councils of producers serve to introduce a larger measure of independence into the working of the representative bodies and contribute towards legislation that is more in the nature of a synthesis of interests than compromise, legislation that is more a measure of politics than an abstract rule of conduct.

2. In Yugoslavia there is no popular initiative in legislation in the classical form. All the same, considerable development has been made in the *democratization of the legislative process,* more accurately, the process of preparation of laws, economic plans and other political decisions. Prior to being introduced as bills, the rough drafts of bills are subject of wide examination. Observations on and criticism of the drafts are made not only by the law courts, by local self-government units and the specialized administration, but by associations and other organizations, such as the university faculties, the learned societies, academies of sciences and the like. The preliminary drafts are published in the press and the press itself frequently carries the opinions and observations of organizations and citizens. The draft Economic Plan and the more important economic legislation are made the subject of examination and discussion by economic enterprises, co-operatives, economic associations and various chambers. In such "public discussions" a very significant place is occupied by the trade unions.[3]

In addition, as a general rule, the organizations concerned also participate in the preparation of laws and acts (motion picture enterprises and film workers participated directly in the preparation of the Film Act, the lawyers in the preparation of the Lawyers Act and so on).

Admittedly this democratization of the legislative process complicates and regards the work of legislating. But it is considered to be indispensable, not solely from a political point of view, but for the sake of

[3] See J. Djordjevic, "Economic and Financial Policy Making", *International Social Science Bulletin,* vol. VIII, (1956), pp. 295 ff.

passing better, more satisfactory and more practical legislation. It is a constituent part of the quest for the forms and methods of what in Yugoslavia is termed direct democracy. Likewise there often occur sharp conflicts of ideas and interests between the factors participating in such a preparation of legislative and other acts. The Government and, ultimately, the People's Assembly acts as the final umpire and co-ordinator of those interests. But it is not impossible that those who are better organized, more persevering and more influential may translate their interests into the overall interest.

It is a commonplace of political science that a greater or lesser amount of the subjective and the arbitrary inevitably enter every measure. The same is true of laws. But the right of all those interested in publicly, openly and in due time expressing and defending their views and interests, is one of the familiar guarantees which in a democracy brings the individual and subjective interests closer to what we call, if not common, then general interests. ("Common" is best, and the objective is to attain it.)

IV. Interest Groups and Other Forms of the Political Process

Interest Groups and Public Opinion

As in most countries, public opinion in Yugoslavia is expressed and shaped through the press, broadcasting, the educational system. But also different organizations and groups, the political organizations, the trade unions and the basic democratic forums of citizens (referendums, assemblies of voters, political meetings and the like) hold a very important place in shaping public opinion. There is in addition that "inarticulate" public opinion representing the aggregate of the opinions, the ideological and mental attitude of wider or narrower categories of citizens, as well as what is termed "the opinion of the people."

In the process of de-etatization, that is, when cutting down the former state functions and fostering self-governing institutions on the basis of social self-government, we come upon certain new elements of the relations between interest groups as well as the citizens in their political forums, appear in the system of social self-government and direct democracy as a part of the structure of government and decision making. Here the phenomenon we witness is a kind of institutionalizing of the directly interested public opinion. This minimizes the breadth of the free influence of interest groups. They are placed in a position which compels them to translate their views and interests into deeds. The boundaries of this institutionalizing of groups and public opinion are the laws, the measure of powers, on the one hand, and on the other the conception that their is a "social" role, that in pursuing the interests and needs of the institutions they actually appear as part of the public service, as the representatives and delegates of the community. Of course, all this is but the "ideal pattern." Public opinion and the decisions reached under these conditions also represent the interpretation of the general interest, namely the individual interest in relation to the general interest; and in that interpretation not only individual interests but the selfish interests of groups and individuals may prevail. Generally speaking, under the conditions of the social and political system of Yugoslavia, groups which organize themselves to influence public opinion in favor of their interests and to manipulate public opinion do not exist. Groups and organizations actually influence public opinion by their activity and the activity of their individual members. Frequently they take a public attitude, seeking publicity of one kind or another for their point of view.

The political and informative press is as a rule in the hands of social organizations. The most important of the newspapers are the organs of political organizations. But the trade unions, the army and a series of organizations also have their newspapers which, besides the special questions of interest to the members of those organizations, also treat broader issues, including political questions. The broadcasting stations are self-governing institutions founded on principles of social government. The appropriate state organs exercise only a limited control over the legality of their operations: the Federal Government has the right to ban radio programs which are against the Constitution and the foreign policy of Yugoslavia.

Social government in the field of schools and other educational institutions means that teaching, scientific and educational problems are the responsibility of the educators themselves. Their freedom of decision and opinion has been ensured. But, at the same time, the scientific and professional associations, as well as the political organizations, represent definite conceptions in the sphere of education, the basic premise of which is to educate free individuals possessed of initiative and capable of participating in the material and spiritual construction of the socialist society. Such conceptions are not being imposed; however, their supporters have the right to strive for their adoption and application. Conceptions tending to encourage hatred among the races and peoples or some anti-democratic (notably fascist) ideas, in so far as they are overtly advanced, are sharply condemned by the public, and in certain cases the law permits the banning of publications promoting such conceptions.

The political system of Yugoslavia demands and stimulates an enlightened, free and independent public opinion, one separated from all forms of the political structure of society. Thus a public expressing the conceptions and interests of the most conscious groups and individuals constitutes a necessary factor of socialist democracy, of the self-assertion and participation of the man and citizen. One advantage of such public opinion lies in its resistance to the groups seeking to abuse it, or given to opinions which retard the emancipating political process or defend backwardness, conservatism, privileges and the egoistic interests of any social or political segment.

In order to enable the press and public opinion to function in this way a large effort on the part of the collectivity and individuals, as well as special relations between interest groups and public opinion are called for. It is easy to say that only the rightful interests of groups and individuals (in Yugoslavia, those serving socialism, democracy, freedom, social progress, peace and cooperation between nations) should be the prime mover and inspiration of public opinion. In political action it is difficult to separate the rightful from the selfish, since the contradiction and equilibrium of differing interests harbor the danger that interestedness may serve some and not others, i.e. that it may not be general.

The solution of this question consists in enabling public opinion to be more and more of a social and less and less of a group factor and this in turn depends on the development of society, that is, the creation of such property, material, political and spiritual relations as would bring public opinion closer to the interests of "all citizens," or at least to the interests of a large enough majority able to secure the direction of the movement and the life of human society to the least possible exclusion of the minority.

The two political organizations operating in Yugoslavia differ in a number of their characteristics from the classical multiparty and uniparty systems. They are not political parties fighting for power and in opposition to one another. They are neither the organizers nor the managers of social affairs. What they do is to unite citizens for the purpose of examining not only basic policy, but a series of other social issues which are solved by state and social institutions. They contribute to the organizing and actuating of the political process and of political activity, the basic bearer of which should be an ever more conscious and freer citizen.

This role of providing a forum for the examination and initiation of different political and social questions is performed particularly by the Socialist Alliance (membership over 5,000,000, out of a population of 17,000,000). The existence of this political organization illustrates the fact that the construction of socialism is not a monopoly of the working class or its political organization. On the contrary, the Socialist Alliance stimulates an organized united activity on the part of all active citizens in the country. It represents an association of all social organizations, the League of Communists included. The Socialist Alliance organizes elections and its relation to its membership is based neither on firm ideological allegiance nor on special "party discipline".

The League of Communists is a political organization with a definite program, an open and clear-cut ideology, an organization founded upon the principle of "democratic centralism". It is not a party of cadres, but an association of co-thinkers bound together by a non-dogmatically conceived *program* of the construction of a socialist society. The League of Communists (membership 687,000) recognizes and stimulates free thinking among its members and free discussion and criticism prior to the adoption of fixed decisions. In the preparation, application and realization of those decisions, which predominantly have a general and programmatic character, the members take up positions freely and may not only differ on a series of issues, but adopt different positions.

All this shows that in Yugoslavia there is no problem of the influence of individual interest groups upon the political organizations as such and upon their basic policies. Different groups, organized into associations or otherwise, have the opportunity to promote publicly and at the meetings of the Socialist Alliance their views and seek their acceptance by the membership.

Because of this character and this role of political organizations, it is understandable that the individual members of organizations who are deputies in the assemblies or belong to some other political and social organizations, as well as the individual local organizations, may be under extraneous influence and accept such influence. Any man, even one with a developed consciousness and completely dedicated to the political program of his organization, represents at the same time, "the aggregate of all the complex social relations" in which he lives, thinks and acts. Under Yugoslav conditions these influences as a rule do not appear as the product of the mechanical pressure by a particular group upon the concrete action of the individual. Everywhere, and here especially, these influences are far more complex and more subtle, but this does not mean that they have to be *a priori* "negative". Every man belongs to one or more narrower and more specific groups which have their "natural" and public specificities and interests. He may be receptive to the influences of those groups and environments consciously or unconsciously. Some are able to filter these influences "adequately" through the ideology and the interests of the party, while others may be blind to the eventual contradiction between the programs and interests of the groups, or they may consider that they are complementary, or they may even accord priority to the interests of a group. The ideological and psychological mechanism of sublimation of all these influences and interests and of the reaction to them is highly complex and subtle.

In any case, there occur situations in which the individual representatives of the political organizations in Yugoslavia—when participating in the process of making political decisions and acts of authority—are receptive to the influence of definite interest groups or behave as though they were. It is not a rare occurrence, not only in the assembly committees, but at the meeting of the people's assemblies and the people's committees, for members of one and the same political organization to vote differently, revealing traces of the influence of the individual interest groups.

Far more characteristic influences upon the behavior and public activity of the members of different political organizations are found elsewhere. There is the influence of a backward environment, as well as of bureaucratic and authoritarian groups and the personal notions of individuals. If that influence turns the scales, then it may also favor the interests of the individual groups.

To date, no social political system has been immune to all these influences and phenomena. It is essential that, if and when they occur, such influences should not disfigure the basic political organization or the political process in Yugoslavia. This again corroborates the value of and need for a solid democratic political structure in a socialist society.

Certainly, in principle and looking at them from the outside, such manifestations can be removed by a political organization founded on a precise and strictly dogmatic program and firm, disciplined ranks dominated by a hierarchy and a centralized leadership. But in such a political organization there is no freedom of thought and activity of the members, and it is also not impossible that individual, backward and conservative influences might impose, not the official, but the practical policy. The risk of backward and interested influences upon the activity of individual politicians and public persons is a risk implied in every recognition of the freedom of the person and the thinking of individuals. Adoption of this political philosophy in Yugoslavia has not only led to atomization of the over-all policy into different individual interests policies, but has lent strength to the whole political system and the authority of the political organizations and of their leaderships which, consciously and perseveringly, espouse and realize this new democratic political philosophy in the organizing and operating of a socialist society.

Interest Groups and the Executive

As already emphasized, executive authority in Yugoslavia has been invested primarily in associate bodies composed either of the members of the people's assemblies (in the federation, in a people's republic and an autonomous unit) or of the members of the representative bodies and the elected and delegated citizens (in the councils of the people's committees, the autonomous units and the people's republics). In the councils and the executive-administrative bodies, the individual members represent the delegates or elected members of definite interested social institutions and associations. Likewise the principle of "administrative pluralism" has been implemented in the organization of executive authority. Within the Federal Executive Council and other executive bodies there are different specialized councils, not only on economic and social, but educational, cultural, scientific and other matters which are dealt with by the executive organs of authority. These councils, composed of individual specialists and representatives of the services, institutions and organizations concerned, offer their advice to the Federal Executive Council and the other executive organs of the administration. Such councils also exist within the administration. The opinions of the individual councils have to be heard. If they are not, the relevant acts of the executive and administrative authority cannot be implemented.

It has already been stressed how wide is the participation of interest groups and organisms in the preparation of laws, economic plans and other acts that are presented by the executive organs as their proposals to the people's assemblies and the people's committees. The same is also true regarding the preparation of the specific major acts which are passed by the executive organs (especially where federal and republican decrees are concerned). Besides, specialized employees from the administration, together with the representatives of the interested institutions and organizations, acting in the form of commissions or informally, cooperate in the process of study and preparation of different acts which are passed by the executive organs or which are proposed by them to the representative bodies.

There would be no justification for describing these forms of penetration and participation of extraneous organisms and groups in the process of executive authority as an influence by "pressure groups," much less as some kind of bid for power on their part. It is not impossible that an individual acting within those extraneous factors may succeed in having his ideas and his interests turn the scales; this may be "warranted" or "unwarranted". From an organizational-political point of view, the groups can exert influence, but it is not they who decide. Decision rests in the hands of the organs of executive authority which are directly responsible to the representative bodies.

In all these phenomena, under the conditions prevailing in Yugoslavia the essential thing is that they represent democratization and a political expansion of the work and decision-making of executive authority. At the same time those phenomena represent a trend towards minimizing bureaucratic decision-making, especially within the framework of the working of the administration and its employees. The political philosophy underlying those forms of "executive and administrative pluralism" is distinguished by the conception that all the interested factors are a part of the public, participating in the solving of a public matter (res publica). Of course, this is a premise based on the social relations prevailing in the country. But it does not exclude the interested viewpoints and respects the differences and even conflicts between the general and the group interests. Even if the group interests were to prevail in individual acts, they would not be capable of creating major and more durable privileges or of alienating authority from the organs to whom it has been entrusted by the constitution.

For the question of the relations between pressure groups and public administration, it is characteristic that in Yugoslavia as a rule every vacant government employee's post is filled on the basis of public competition, the applications being handled by disinterested commissions.

Finally, it is well worthwhile to study the influence of "pressure groups" not only upon the appointment and promotion of public officials, but on the issuing of different administrative and purely operational acts, especially those relating to the various rights of groups and individuals. In Yugoslavia such phenomena have brought about the establishment of judicial control of the acts and measures of the administration—with the aid of prosecution under criminal law—against the phenomenon of "abuse and exceeding of powers" by officials and all cases of violation of the equality and the rights of citizens.

V. Conclusions

The comparative study of interest groups and their place and influence in the political system of various countries has a two-fold significance. First, such a study makes it possible for us to learn to know the political system, even the civilization of the individual countries and the world as a whole more concretely and fully. It also helps to bring nations together, to have them understand one another better and to establish relations of intellectual co-operation and exchange. Second, such a study is of interest for the development of political science. Political science cannot be raised to the degree of learned generalization and cannot assume the force of scientific truth unless founded on concrete analyses and data regarding interest groups in countries with diverse social and political systems. And it is a familiar fact that no identical political systems prevail even in countries which are very similar as to the type of their organization. Every country has something specifically its own, over and above that which is more or less general in a number of political systems, or even in all of them.

Historical and empirical research, on the one hand, and theoretical generalizations and conclusions, on the other, cannot rationally be separated in this aspect of sociology. Discussion on whether the orientation should be toward empiricism or toward theory only connotes reiteration of the old "philosophic riddle" on what precedes and is more important—"the chicken or the egg". Science has provided the answer to this question, and that is what has made it science. One cannot separate empiricism from theory, nor theory from empiricism. These are two sides of unified scientific thinking and working. Without empiricism, as rich and as diversified as possible, theory is one-sided and empty. Without theory, elucidated and as concrete as possible, empiricism only presents a "pile of facts" devoid of orientation and rational meaning. In the absence of theory empiricism is blind and confusing, and in the absence of empiricism theory is abstract and formal.

It is true that in the initial phases of theoretical work, predominantly concrete study of interest groups, the gathering and classifying of information in different countries is not to be excluded, nor should it be useless. In this respect, signal efforts have been made by the individual research workers in various countries, especially in the U.S.A., Great Britain and, in more recent years, France and Belgium. Elsewhere the interest in the problems of interest groups has been less, if it has been evident at all. In Yugoslavia these questions have not been systematically elucidated as such. The basic reason for such variations in the concern of political science for interest groups lies in the fact that there is no identity of the role and significance of these groups in the political life and system of all countries in the world. But today the need already exists to proceed, while continuing comparative studies on the international level, to certain theoretical generalizations and clarifications as well. This task, particularly, can be performed by the co-operation of the competent scientists of various countries.

One of the first questions requiring theoretical clarification is the concept of interest groups. In this respect there are a number of discrepancies and arbitrary views. It amounts to oversimplification if the problem of interest groups is reduced to organized influence of the organizations of capitalists and the working class, or of the individual segments and groups of those classes. It is also unsound to reduce the interest groups to pressure groups.

It is a well-known fact that interest groups are not merely economic groups, nor merely groups having economic interests. Groups exist with different non-economic interests which represent factors in social and political life, and thus in the political process of the individual nations.

From the point of view of method, here, too, one has to proceed from the "concrete" and the "individual," to the general. On the basis of historical and empirical data and analyses, certain generalizations have to be made within the framework of the political system of each country or within similar political systems (as has been endeavoured in the present paper). Next, from those narrower generalizations, one should pass to certain more universal ones, providing a theoretical definition of interest groups.

Only definitions of interest groups thus established can serve as the point of departure for theory on the typology and classification of interest groups. Great as their significance is for this process of theoretical development, all definitions and classifications of interest groups prevailing hereto suffer from incompleteness and one-sidedness. In fact, they reflect the condition of international and comparative study of the problem.

The very fact that we emphasize the role of interest groups in the political process and their empirical study already command a theoretical value. Such study has served once more to refute the value of the metaphysical, absolutist and romantic theories and conceptions about the state and politics. Even if individual views on the state as the "representative of society," "general interests," of the "spirit of the people," or similar conceptions inspired by Fichte's romantism or Hegel's metaphysics, and sustained by the class, group or bureaucratic interests of the ruling circles of the individual countries, still have a place in ideology and political practice, they have at least been removed from the agenda of contemporary sociology. The spirit of the 19th century must make way for the spirit of the 20th century in the realm of science as well. The scientific spirit of today is the spirit of critical rationalism, of dialectics, relativism and discovery of the essence of matter and society, and concrete truth.

Accordingly, further theoretical research on interest groups and their place and influence in political systems will of necessity contribute to the perfecting of scientific thinking and theory on the state, the political organization of society and policies. At its current level of development human society is complex and heterogeneous and the individual classes, groups, social and political organisms form its sociological content. The differences between the individual political systems occur because some stand for open and others for closed societies. Societies organized in an absolutist and autocratic way screen this inner complexity. Democracy is an open political society and incorporates that complexity in its political system. Heedless of the diversity of the importance, role, form, and influence of interest groups, this complexity occurs both in the countries developing predominantly on capitalist lines and those developing on socialist lines.

In each of those societies, notably in democratic societies, certain forms of equilibrium exist between classes and social groups, and the individual forms of "political pluralism". Sociologically, these relations and forms are found even in those social and political systems which are temporarily founded on the "absolute" monopoly of a particular class or group which is ruling "on behalf of the class".

That, however, does not signify that the study and theoretical generalization of the existence and role of interest groups should and could lead to the revival of the theory of "equilibrium" or of Laski's philosophy of political pluralism, which the more mature thinking of that author discarded.

The rational grain in Laski's pluralism is the negation of political pluralism and etatism, which he noted in the insufficiently conceived idea of sovereignty (such as developed by the Prussian-Hegelian theory of the state and the British metaphysical, positivistic and political philosophies). All pluralistic theories base political organization on the federation of large organized groups and their centres. Hence, even unconsciously, they are non-democratic. In addition, they are formal too since they do not look for the differentiation and the role of the groups in their status within the basic social economic relations, and notably in relation to the class structure of society.

However, from the point of view of the study of interest groups, the scientific weakness of pluralism lies in its ignoring a certain necessary monism as the component part of every political organization, and of the state in particular. Because it fails to recognize the existence, and the necessity of the existence of certain general interests and social groups, of political forces and organizations which in the democratic process can and should carry and assert those interests, the purely pluralistic interpretation of the political organization of contemporary society remains unrealistic, contrary to historical truth and, thus, non-scientific.

It has not been the purpose of the present paper to develop a general theory of politics and political organization of society in connection with the study and understanding of interest groups. That would have been contrary to the scientific method adopted in this paper and its object of establishing and promoting scientific theory concerned with these important social-political phenomena and problems of contemporary society. It has only endeavoured to shed light on some of the key questions and to reiterate the need for and justification of theoretical generalization and theoretical concepts in this domain of political science, as certain authors have already done.

At the same time, and above all, this paper wished to indicate a series of new aspects and problems of interest groups within the framework of the social and political system of socialist Yugoslavia. It hopes to have furnished thereby a contribution to the comparative study of interest groups and political organizations and ultimately to theoretical generalizations that may enrich political science and political practice at large.

III. PROCEEDINGS OF
THE ROUND TABLE

GREETINGS AND OPENING REMARKS

September 10—Morning Session

Professor Edward Litchfield, Chancellor of the University of Pittsburgh, opened the meeting by welcoming the delegates to the Fifth Round-Table of the International Political Science Association. He expressed his wishes for a successful meeting both as the Chancellor of the University that had invited the participants to the first gathering of the Association in the United States and as a member of the Executive Board of the International Political Science Association.

Professor James K. Pollock: As president of our Association I am happy to open this first session of the International Political Science Association Conference on Pressure Groups. Thanks to the generosity of the Ford Foundation, the University of Pittsburgh and the Falk Foundation, we are able, for the first time, to have an international meeting of this Association in the United States. We are exceedingly fortunate that so many of you have been able to come from the four corners of the earth, representing as you do, no less than fourteen different nations, to participate in and contribute to our deliberations. We are sorry that it has not been possible for others who were invited to be with us. I particularly deplore the absence of our old friends, Professor Robson, Professor Duverger, Professor Meynaud and Professor von der Gablentz.

Due to the splendid organization and arrangements of the Conference for which we are particularly indebted to our secretary-general, and the University of Pittsburgh, I trust that we shall be able, with appropriate interruptions, to carry through the discussions on the agenda as prepared by the rapporteur-general. I find the contributions which have been made by the various national rapporteurs, to be excellent; with the help of the gentlemen I have asked to preside over the various sessions, and with that of the rapporteur-general, I trust that our deliberations will not only be stimulating, but also amount to a real contribution in the development of the subject of the Conference. I think you will be interested to know that the Falk Foundation has made it possible for the Association to publish a volume of the proceedings, and that Professor Ehrmann has consented to be the editor. We trust therefore, that the papers and the proceedings, when properly edited will be published in time for use prior to the Rome Congress for which we have scheduled a Round Table on the same topic of Pressure Groups.

As an old worker in this vineyard, I trust that I shall not be kept too busy with the management of the Conference so that I may listen and participate in the various discussions. The important thing, however, is for the chairmen and the rapporteur-general to keep a guiding hand on the deliberations so that they will form a reasonably coherent pattern. Without further ado, I now call on Professor Ehrmann to explain his plans for the Conference.

Professor Ehrmann: With the aid of our colleagues in the Political Science Department of the University of Pittsburgh we have been able to circulate all of the country reports among the participants of this Conference. Therefore, it seems appropriate that these reports are not presented orally so that we can immediately launch upon a topical discussion this afternoon. We have listed those problems that seem particularly worthy of systematic discussion in the agenda that is before you. Let me express the hope that the participants who have been unable to submit reports will avail themselves of the opportunities offered by the topical discussions to "fill in" the experiences of their countries.

I would like to suggest only one exception to the procedure here proposed. Professor Eldersveld's report could not be circulated in time among all the participants. Moreover, it had been our intention from the very beginning to ask Professor Eldersveld for a somewhat different piece of work. His is not so much a report on interest group activities in the United States as a survey of research and an appraisal of methodology in the field. For these reasons I have asked him to present his paper to us this morning. I do not think that it will be necessary or advisable to engage in a discussion following his report, since all the questions he raises will come up for your consideration as the round table proceeds.

Professor Sam Eldersveld then presented his report, "American Interest Groups. A Survey of Research and Some Implications for Theory and Method."*

* See above, p. 173.

Discussion: IDENTIFICATION AND INTERNAL ORGANIZATION OF PRESSURE GROUPS

September 10—Afternoon Session
Professor Gunnar Heckscher, *chairman*

Professor Ehrmann: Having been asked to introduce each of our sessions by listing the problems we might fruitfully discuss, I would like to refer, first of all, to the questions which I raised in the working paper submitted to you earlier.* In addition, my introductory remarks will reflect observations made in the various country reports and consider their implications for the study and theory of pressure groups.

Professor Eldersveld opened his paper by stating, "Everywhere today interest groups have become the research vogue." Our French colleague, Professor Meynaud, made a similar point though introducing a *caveat:* "The activity of interest groups," he wrote in a recent article, "is now considered one of the essential factors of explaining politics. But, especially in European countries, its systematic analysis has hardly begun and permits at best a formulation of a certain number of working hypotheses." M. Meynaud's conclusion may well serve as a maxim for our discussions during the coming days: "In order to achieve progress (in this field of study) it will be necessary both to formulate a conceptual framework and to assemble a mass of facts. . . . We are only at the very beginning of a collective effort which must be immense; but interest groups, perhaps even more than parties, are now the central phenomenon of our political societies."

This last remark suggests some aspects of the problem we are to consider this afternoon—is there a need for defining what pressure groups really are? Should we try to differentiate them clearly from other phenomena and especially from political parties, generally better known and long studied? Do we wish to accept the suggestion made by our colleague Professor Djordjevic who, in his paper, distinguishes a broader (sociological) and a narrower (political) concept of interest groups? Is there validity in a definition describing pressure groups as the main agents for translating economic and social power into political power, or is that definition too narrow, especially when we also want to look at non-Western societies?

* See above, p. 1.

Once we have arrived at a satisfactory definition, a classification of groups may be necessary. Should the openly proclaimed objectives of the groups be a valid criterion? Should we differentiate according to the groups' access to the centers of decision-making, especially as to whether such access is direct or indirect? Or should we seek a classification according to the "style" of group activities? Groups may express movements of struggle or of protest; they may raise accepted or widely rejected demands; they may act either moderately or immoderately. Obviously, as soon as we deal with "styles" our comparison of pressure groups cannot neglect the differences that exist between political cultures. But is it not true that the study of interest groups is considered a promising field for comparative investigation precisely because it may lead to a more complete and realistic picture of the political process and thereby provide new insights into different political cultures?

Professor MacPherson: I hope we shall not spend much time on identification and definition. True, there are hazy margins. Some pressure groups become parties, or virtually such, and organized *incivisme* may be almost a pressure group. But we should not start at the margins. It may be said that definition is essential for analysis even in the center of such a new field. But what will it lead to? Definition here involves putting in one's assumptions about the whole nature of society, generally some variety of liberal pluralism. Serious discussion of definitions then becomes discussion of these assumptions. We cannot expect such discussion, at this stage, to be a cutting edge for analytical work.

Professor Leiserson: I agree with Professor MacPherson, if he means that definitions alone will fail to show the relationship of interest groups to the political system. However, we must distinguish between the interest group system and the party system. In the United States we differ as to whether interest groups or political parties are more important. We must seek to specify the relationship of interest groups to other forms of political action as well as to the larger political system, and must develop adequate models for understanding the internal structure and function of interest groups as well as the relationships between interest groups, parties and government. Everywhere interest groups form a system, or perhaps one should say a series of subsystems, of decision-making that is non-governmental though perhaps tied to the governmental structure.

Professor Akzin: To arrive at a proper indentification we may distinguish the areas within which interest groups operate. These will easily differ in various countries. Let me give you some examples from the experience of Israel. There parties (i.e., organizations established to compete for public office) are characterized by distinct ideologies. Specific interests play a subsidiary role in party life. Interest groups, on the other hand, are primarily concerned with special economic interests or with the representation of people who feel connected occupationally, linguistically or by country of origin—what the Germans would call *"Landsmannschaften."*

Because Israel has adopted proportional representation, even relatively small interest groups have a chance to gain a voice in parliament. In addition, the coalition system which prevails in the national government as well as in municipalities allows even a small group of deputies or municipal councillors to exercise considerable influence. Therefore, interest groups in Israel are asking themselves whether they should remain lobbies or constitute themselves as political parties asking for voters' support.

Professor Townsley: In Australia, interest groups and political parties are so closely related that it is sometimes difficult to separate the ones from the others. From the start trade unions have had overwhelming influence in the Labour Party, just as the farm interests are closely tied to the Country Party. The Liberal Party claims to be different because it does not represent a special interest, but we know that it derives support from industry, commerce and banking. Hence, all of these parties give expression to economic interests.

Professor Finer: I wonder if we could agree on some neutral word to describe the groups we are discussing. At the moment we use the word *interest* groups. As I see it an "interest" means some economic or social stake in the community, much as we used to talk of "the church interest" or the "landed interest." However, some groups don't stand for a strict "interest" in this sense but stand for a cause, such as pacifism or feminism. We want a word to cover both types of groups. I have tended to use the word "lobby"; but in some countries, for instance France, this term is loaded with bad meaning. Likewise, "pressure group" has unpleasant overtones. In one sense "private association" might meet the difficulties, but the trouble here is that sometimes we have to deal with certain influential groups, for instance, the Officer Corps in Germany which had a *public* character.

Professor Heckscher: Professor Finer seems to reserve the term "interest group" for economic interest groups.

Professor Finer: Is the church an interest group?

Many Members: Yes!

Professor Odegard: I'm surprised that Professor MacPherson thinks that we could do without a precise definition. How else can you delimit the field of inquiry? To sociologists, for example, the study of pressure groups embraces all of society, and does not merely scrutinize group influence on issues of public policy.

Professor Leiserson: Does not the discussion of the morphology and typology of interest groups bring out the political scientist's method of breaking down what the sociologist calls social structure? Don't we need a conceptual scheme to examine interest groups and a satisfactory theoretical structure within which we can operate?

Professor Neumann: It seems to me that the study of politics has entered a new stage. We realize that many of the old categories are too static, but we still rely on them and hesitate to formulate new concepts. In order to establish a satisfactory theoretical structure, following Avery Leiserson's suggestion, the growing concern with interest groups must be seen in connection with the fundamental changes in the character of political science during the last quarter of a century.

This silent revolution which has taken place in the modern study of politics is threefold in its emphasis on dynamic processes, comparative approaches, and systematic integration. It has something to do with the fact that in our developing mass society, whether at war or at peace, in democracies no less than in dictatorships, the people have become potent participants and protagonists. Our interest, therefore, has turned away from a merely formal, legalistic, and constitutional approach of a static and descriptive political morphology to a prime consideration of political dynamics and the processes of decision-making. Hence, the sudden explosion of research in political parties and pressure groups—the main arteries and agents of public affairs today.

The equally important and sudden turn towards comparative studies, reflecting our recent confrontation with contrasting political systems and new political continents makes us realize—what should be axiomatic for all social science concepts anyhow—that the specific nature of parties and pressure groups must be spelled out in time and space. The same concept has a very different meaning in its diverse local representations and, even within the same groups, in its changing historical setting. Any premature generalization only tends to invalidate the genuine character of political forces.

Finally, if we are to take those comparisons seriously, we must also recognize that the political agencies, such as parties and interest groups, are not isolated phenomena but must be evaluated in their interrelations with other political forces. Only such an integrated vista will give a concrete picture of functioning institutions and will bring us closer to a systematic analysis of the body politic.

Interest groups, therefore, must be defined not only within their national and historical frame but also in relation to other political forces at work. Specifically a working definition of interest groups and political parties, tentative and blurred though the borderlines may be, is a necessity from the start. May I suggest such a classification.

Fundamentally, pressure groups are the representation of homogeneous interests seeking influence. The interest group is strong and effective when it has a directed, specific purpose. Political parties, on the other hand, seeking office and directed towards policy-decisions, combine heterogeneous groups. In fact it is one of their major themes to reconcile the diverse forces within a political society. Theirs is an integrative function, which is not in the domain of the interest groups.

Professor McKean: Where would you put minor parties?

Professor Neumann: They are sometimes political groups on the way to becoming major parties, changing in this process from pressure groups to broader political representation, such as the British Labour Party. Sometimes they remain pressure groups of special interests missing out, therefore, on the parties' essential purpose to relate the special interests to the needs of the whole community and to transform the private citizen into a zoon politikon. Indeed, they may get away with such limited aims and in fact may make a temporary success of their one-sided direction. But such an abandonment of their essential political function will turn out to be detrimental for the body politic. The doubtful role played by the German Business Party (*Wirtschaftspartei*) in the late Weimar Republic, may serve as an illustrative warning.

Professor Odegard: Any definition will be arbitrary. The major distinction in Professor Neumann's definition seems to be that interest groups do not openly put up candidates for public office while parties do. When a party ceases to put up candidates, it ceases to be a political party.

Not all groups are interest groups, nor are all interest groups politically relevant. This sociologists often do not understand.

I should like to suggest three areas of inquiry into the forms and functions of interest groups:

(1) The *basis of power* in a society. If political power is restricted to hereditary aristocracy and if universal suffrage is non-existent, the pattern of interest groups will obviously be different from that in a society with universal suffrage.

(2) *Structure of power*. The interest group system is affected by the structure of government. Whether the government is parliamentary or presidential, mayor or city manager, federal or unitary, will have an

impact on the role of interest groups in a society. This is a point which Professor Eldersveld rightly stressed.

(3) *Scope of power.* The characteristic distinction between a totalitarian society and a democratic society is that the totalitarian society identifies society with the state. Under a system in which the scope of power is limitless the group structure will be different from a system in which the scope of power is severely limited. In a democracy the scope of power becomes a major political issue, the debate over public power in the United States being one of many examples.

These three areas have a critical relation to the nature and function of interest groups in the political society.

Professor Leiserson: A premature, formalistic definition of political parties and interest groups might blind us to the fact that they are not the whole but only component parts of the political process. Those who explain everything as the result of pressure group action, tend to confine government to a passive role similar to that of a billiard ball bumped by conflicting pressure groups. Of course, the orthodox liberal conception of the political process that the voters select the parties, the parties select parliament, and parliament chooses the administration is also over-simplified. In fact, each area of public policy has its own aggregation of interest groups.

Professor Heckscher: Although I believe that a conceptual framework is necessary, I wonder if we will get very far by presenting definitions at the present stage. Perhaps it would be better to explore the issue in future discussions, since our definitions may be influenced by the course of our debates.

Professor Ehrmann: I would like to suggest another set of working definitions for parties and pressure groups, both developed by French writers. To Raymond Aron a political party is "a regular and permanent organization of a certain number of people concerned with either conquering power or keeping it." Such a definition is, of course, inspired by Max Weber's analysis of politics.

As to pressure groups Jean Meynaud describes them as "associations of various juridical forms which upon the basis of common goals or attitudes endeavour to impose a certain number of positions and demands by all means at their disposal, but especially by pressure on the public authorities."

This definition of interest groups is in turn almost identical to one formulated by David Truman (and rather widely accepted in the United States): "Any group that, on the basis of one or more shared attitudes, makes certain claims upon other groups in the society for the establishment, maintenance or enhancement of forms of behavior that are implied by the shared attitudes."

Professor Neumann: We cannot draw clear-cut lines between parties and pressure groups. It is indeed very natural that there will be necessary overlappings between both agents. Yet a genuine political party always claims to be an integrating force, and it has in a sense such an educational function at least in regard to its own following. It must constantly present to the individual voter and to the powerful special interest group which it represents, a picture of the collective whole. The party, serving as a broker of political forces, must adjust the wants of the specific interests to the needs of the community and, if necessary, even ask sacrifices from them in the name of the political whole. Even the so-called "class parties," which call upon only a specific part of the population, can not afford to renounce this essential function.

All this does not mean that parties always fulfill that key function of educating the private citizen to political responsibility. Yet wherever the policy making parties do not succeed in this primary task of fitting their specific interest into the framework of the national collective, the modern state is in danger of deteriorating into a neofeudalism of powerful interest groups.

Professor Odegard: In the United States we have seen what happens when parties fail to integrate. I am referring, of course, to 1860 and the American Civil War when parties were unable to resolve the question of slavery. Today the problem of civil rights in the South presents an equally pressing issue, and unless the parties, especially the Democratic party, can resolve it, there will be a time of great difficulty for society.

Professor Finer: If I may turn back to the question of definition, you will see that in my working paper I have defined interest groups thus: "all groups or associations which seek to influence public policy in their own chosen direction, while declining to accept direct responsibility for ruling the country." I do not think this quite distinguishes between parties and interest groups because we have to recognize the existence of borderline cases. Take the case of Colonel Nasser as an example. The *coup d'état* which deposed Farouk was carried out by the army, or as we would call it in this case, an interest group. At that stage the army hoped to be able to govern through the political parties. When this proved impossible, it decided to govern in its own right. At this stage then, I would say that what had been an interest group turned into something more like a political party. However, despite these borderline cases I think the definition I have given will do as a working definition.

Professor Akzin: I agree that we need only a working definition rather than one that covers all fine points. But, even in seeking a working definition, we should hesitate to accept at face value the claims of parties and interest groups as to what they are and do and form our own conclusions on this point.

We should beware of limiting the designation of parties to those large aggregate, non-dogmatic organization such as exist in the United States and in England. Elsewhere there exist small ideological parties, whether we like it or not. We must not call these little parties interest groups. If they put up candidates for office they are parties. Also, our discussion has been confined to states where changes in ruling personnel occur by way of election, but in other societies changes come about by revolution.

An interest group strives for the defense of the interests it represents by indirect influence on the centers of power rather than by openly claiming power. A party attempts to conquer power, either by means of elections, or by violent methods such as a *coup d'état.*

Professor Eldersveld: Perhaps the problem of conceptualization is best solved by a differentiation in functional terms. In our discussion I have noted five functions ascribed to political groups: (1) Setting goals of political policy. (2) Recruiting and selecting personnel. (3) An integrating function *vis à vis* other groups. (4) An integrating function *vis à vis* the government such as policy bargaining. (5) An integrating function in regard to the public, including the group's own membership.

Can we not specify the function which a given group is fulfilling and then decide if it is an interest group or a political party?

Professor Odegard, in his definition, would claim that political parties may perform all of the above functions, but *must* always perform function (2). On the other hand, an interest group may also perform all of the listed functions, but must always engage in (1).

Professor Akzin: I am not sure that all five of Professor Eldersveld's criteria apply to political parties and I would say that only some of them apply to interest groups. In the United States, we have had the "dollar-a-year" men, and more recent developments show further direct participation by interest groups in the governmental process. Perhaps it has become a prime aim of interest groups to get their people into public office, although they will avoid an open claim to rule the country.

Professor Heckscher: Can we now leave the question of definition to which we may come back later and turn to the problems of internal organization? A number of questions arise here whose discussion could prove useful for a further classification of pressure groups.

Professor Ehrmann: Let me list a few of the most significant types of organizations which have been described in the various reports.

There are interest groups characterized by a high degree of bureaucratization and others where membership participation remains strong. As in all organizations an "active minority" seems to be an important factor in most interest groups; but who are the members of that minority—the employed staff or some other "oligarchies"? Is it a general phenomenon that even those pressure groups which may have come into existence as "social movements" turn more and more into "structures of power"? Is there a relationship between the form of organization and between what Professor Eldersveld calls the groups' "ability to unite demands"? In that respect significant differences seem to exist between what one may call primary organizations and the large "peak associations" which provide an umbrella for the groups affiliated with them.

As to membership, does compulsory membership lead to a different type of organization than voluntary affiliation? In some countries the fact that the same persons belong to several groups, and may have divided loyalties, seems to have a moderating influence on group activities. Elsewhere, multiple and overlapping membership is described as forcing the machinery of government to a grinding halt.

Professor Finer: I can give two examples of *de facto* compulsory membership among British interest groups.

(1) The Transport and General Workers' Union is a voluntary organization whose official policy is against "the closed shop." In fact, there are certain areas where members of this union simply refuse to work along side of non-union members; so that, in fact, if one wants to hold the job down in these areas it is obligatory to hold a union card.

(2) Certain of the price rings, which have been examined by our monopolies commission, in some cases would set up a firm as "a fighting organization" to undercut and to drive out of existence independent competitors outside the ring. Here membership in the ring was almost compulsory for any firm that did not wish to be smashed economically.

Now it seems to me that where membership is either legally or *de facto* compulsory, conflicts over the policies to be adopted by the organization will tend to be very sharp indeed. On the other hand, the fact that an organization is voluntaristic and members can quit it whenever they choose, seems to me to make for a lessening of internal conflict. In the last resort dissenting members can vote with their feet and quit. The Federation of British Industries is an example of this. Its membership is voluntary. Frequently it is unable to adopt any line of policy because its membership is so divided, and in such cases its Grand Council will refrain from taking any position at all.

Professor Heckscher: The more directly an organization enters the political scene, the more difficult it becomes to consult the membership. Soon a point is reached when the officers of an organization speak for the group without really knowing its views. They then rely on the cohesion of the membership, hoping that it will sustain their policies. This, of course, raises the issue of bureaucratization of the interest group leadership.

Professor Leiserson: In regard to internal organization, national differences are extremely important. Meynaud's definition appears inapplicable to the American scene inasmuch as in the United States interest groups are highly heterogenous. A primary factor in shaping the form of organization is the degree to which the interest groups acquire and maintain autonomy from governmental responsibilities and control. For example, the American farmer organizations, employers' associations and trade union movements wish to be untrammelled by government interference in their internal affairs. At the same time the need to establish an effective political base from which to deal with elected politicians, parties and government agencies strongly influences their organizational structure.

Professor Chester: The concentration of interest groups around the central government creates particular conditions for their organization. In Great Britain most interest groups have moved their headquarters to London. As in any capital city their officials and government officials may belong to the same clubs, frequent the same habitats, and come in social contact with one another. Important is also the fact that in almost all groups those people rise to prominence who are prepared to give time for work in the organization. Especially in associations without much money this is relevant and helps to concentrate power in a few hands.

Professor Finer: As to the problems of leadership and membership-participation, the English experience shows certain marked differences between organizations of different types. For instance, the common characteristic of philanthropic groups is a great mass of subscribers but few active workers. Indeed, one reason that subscribers offer money is very often so that they may be left alone and not asked to work or campaign actively as voluntary helpers. Here the leaders have to be careful to maintain the goodwill of their subscribers without which the organization could not continue.

There are other organizations which have to negotiate and bargain for their members, e.g., trade unions, the British Medical Association, the National Farmers Union. Since even the smallest member has a direct stake in such negotiations, there is often high membership participation when such negotiations are in progress, and conflict over these negotiations may become both sharp and frequent.

Then again there are large mass organizations whose chief task, as far as the members are concerned, is to offer some kind of technical aid, for instance motoring organizations which provide emergency service, road maps, etc. The members belong almost exclusively to reap these material benefits. They are not very interested in the "high" politics of motoring as such. In these organizations the leadership may possess a very wide discretion to act as it sees fit in its negotiations with ministers.

It is impossible to generalize about leadership and membership participation without distinguishing situations of this kind.

Professor Heckscher: Above all, the members want their leaders to deliver the goods. They are willing to grant authority to the leadership as long as it is successful. May I cite a case in point from the field of labor relations in Sweden. For a time the terms of collective bargaining agreements were put to a membership vote. To this the union leadership objected since the employers were using the obligatory consultation of the union members to water down the demands of the labor negotiators. Therefore, these practices were discontinued at the insistence of the trade union leadership. Since the end result was actually an improvement of labor conditions, the members did not object to their diminished role in the bargaining process.

On the other hand, if the distance between leadership and members widens and if the results of negotiations are not as favorable as the members think they should be, strife within the organization is ripe.

Hence, I would conclude that not only group participation in the governmental process but also certain forms of group activities outside of government favor the development of oligarchical tendencies.

Professor Krusius-Ahrenberg: May I add a few comments which apply to Finland. It must be admitted that in general bureaucratization makes the members less active. But there is not always a strong correlation. Non-economic groups may have little bureaucratization and yet weak membership activity, whereas economic organizations have comparatively active members despite their bureaucratized managements.

Wherever the economic position of a group is at stake and particularly where profits or wages are involved, the rank and file members are eager to be allowed direct participation in the decisions made by their elected spokesmen. As to labor unions the Swedish experience that a consultation of the members may water down claims put forward by the leadership in not true of Finland.

Professor Merle: At the outset I should mention that in France interest groups have not been studied extensively. I know of not more than about five noteworthy studies. One of the reasons for such paucity is the fact that in France pressure groups have not attained the same stage of development as in the United States, probably because they have not yet fully realized their possibilities for action. Nevertheless, the following observations may have general validity.

Groups have a highly anarchic character. Operating on short-range terms and with limited ambitions, they are frequently intermittent. They come and go and replace one another.

The groups are numerous and highly competitive. Hence, they often work against one another or are at least at cross-purposes.

Most groups are organized in a non-democratic and sometimes an anti-democratic fashion. For this very reason few dare show their face. Regular membership hardly exists, for the groups seldom recruit or collect dues. There are some exceptions to this such as the *Association des Parents d'Elèves de l'Enseignement Libre,* the Association of the Catholic Schools. This group appears to be highly organized since it has a journal and a widely-attended yearly congress. However, even there democratic organization does not prevail. There are no real discussions of the Association's work; elections amount to little else than co-optation. The only French interest groups truly based on membership are the trade unions.

Interest groups in France are highly centralized in Paris, since Paris is the place where politics are most important. There are some notable exceptions, such as the Poujade movement, but no one can tell if this will last.

Professor Leiserson: The more an interest group obtains an autonomous base of political power or is given a recognized function in public policy, the more the membership seems to delegate resonsibility to the group leaders and to the bureaucracy. For this reason labor unions in the United States make little use of the rank and file referendum for which the by-laws provide.

What does this do to the individual's conception of the society in which he lives? In a democratic society the citizen joins different associations for different purposes. He evaluates the state largely as the latter enables him to realize his group-affiliated needs and expectations.

Although each association tries to enlarge its scope and to use the formal machinery of government to protect or promote its interests, there are sharp limitations on its ability as long as the state maintains a competitive freedom of organization and communication among complementary, segmental groups and each of them in turn recognize the paramountcy of the public interest by seeking to justify or reconcile their demands and programs in terms of it.

An interesting commentary on the freedom of association granted by the government was provided in one study of an American trade union which showed that the members looked on the union more as a friendly policeman than as an organization of their own.

Professor Finer: If Professor Leiserson means that the greater a group's participation in public life the more bureaucratic its make-up, then I would like to take issue with him. Some British experiences simply contradict this statement.

The National Farmers Union is closely associated with the Ministry of Agriculture and Food, and indeed the County Executive Committees only operate by the goodwill of members of this important union. Yet whenever the annual price review is in question, we find a very active membership participation and with the common farmer playing a potent role.

Similarly the membership of the National Union of Teachers is at times extremely active. Yet that Union is represented on many public bodies and carries out certain minor administrative functions for the Government.

The County Councils Association provides a most interesting example, for on matters affecting regulations which the Government wants it to carry out, it acts almost like a sub-parliament. But on important issues the Executive Council of this association is very anxious to secure the consensus of its member bodies and tries hard to poll their feelings before taking action.

If I may turn to a different matter now. This question of bureaucracy in an association seems to be co-related with the social composition of the body. For instance, compare the Federation of British Industries with the trade unions. The Federation has an admirable Civil Service which numbers nearly 200. This bureaucracy is kept "on tap and not on top" by virtue of the fact that the Federation is composed of very tough businessmen. The trade unions on the other hand have a great distrust for professional officials and have not developed anything so competent as the bureaucracy the employers' organizations possess. However, when they do develop such a bureaucracy, I am inclined to think that they will defer to them considerably more than the businessman in the employers' associations defer to their officials.

Professor Ehrmann: The development of the National Council of Employers in France, the CNPF, provides a good illustration of how the internal structure of a pressure group can be transformed within a short span of time.

When the Council was founded in the immediate post-liberation period, the environment was hostile to business; something like a *furor democraticus* was raging. Modest headquarters and a small staff were at that time characteristic of the organization. Its by-laws seem to promise checks and balances against any active minority. Membership participation was insured to the point of permitting a referendum of the rank and file of businessmen. In fact, such a referendum was held but once at the very beginning of the organization.

Today all this has changed significantly, although only a few words in the by-laws have been altered. The CNPF and most trade associations have sumptuous headquarters and a competent staff recruited from the best schools of the country. What has brought about this change? First, of course, the transformation of the political environment, but, also, the fact that the organizations have proven their worth to the generally diffident French businessman.

To me this example suggests that comparisons do not necessarily always have to involve different countries where the variables may be too numerous to permit valid conclusions. Within the same country the structure of interest groups may change with changes in the party system, modifications of the legislative process, and of public attitudes.

Professor Townsley: I should like to relate some of the experiences in Australia to a number of points that we have been discussing.

Employers and labor have been organized in Australia for a long time and are quite strong. The Australian trade unions have organized a greater percentage of the working class than the British or American unions. As in Great Britain and the United States membership is in fact compulsory. The worker who loses his card loses his job.

As to the peak organizations, the federation of the manufacturers is well organized and has a very strong lobby. When pressure groups have to make quick decisions, there seems always to be someone within the groups who can make them. Nevertheless, bureaucratization in the trade unions and employers' associations is generally still regarded with suspicion.

A distinctive arbitration system has developed in Australia. Disputes are taken to conciliation boards and thence to arbitration courts where judicial review operates. This permits the interaction of unions, employers, and of government acting in the public interest. Of late the government has intentionally developed some counterpressure to offset a labor-management collusion which, in other countries, has tended to cause inflation.

Discussion: THE POLITICAL RELA-
TIONS OF PRESSURE GROUPS;
THEIR INFLUENCE ON PUBLIC
OPINION; THEIR MUTUAL RELA-
TIONSHIP

September 11—Morning Session
Professor Dayton McKean, *Chairman*

Professor Ehrmann: The following problems seem appropriate for discussion at this time, and I am proceeding from the general to the more
specific:

(1) Pressure groups like political parties must come to terms with
their environment.

(2) Since everywhere the patterns of communications emanating from
interest groups are associated with the nature of the political community
in which they operate the strategic position of a given interest group
within the community must be studied.

(3) We may want to discuss the reasons for the contrast which Professor Eldersveld has described: there are pressure groups which, partly
as a result of the public's awareness of their existence, are interested
in maximum publicity; other groups, and sometimes the same groups
at different occasions, prefer secrecy and privacy.

(4) Interest groups often seek to create myths; some of them attempt
to create an opinion about the group's opinions and to influence thereby
their audience.

(5) Most of the time an interest group will boast of the unity that
presumably prevails within its ranks. It has to be examined whether
the solidarity of its membership is real or fictitious and which methods
the leadership uses to manipulate the members.

(6) What is the significance of "fronts" and alliances concluded between interest groups? When are they an asset, when a liability for the
groups or the community? And if there is rivalry between groups what
are its consequences for the governmental process or for the freedom
of the individual?

Professor Blaisdell: Is it correct to say that pressure groups try to come
to terms with their environment? They attempt to affect the climate of
public opinion, using all means of public relations, and these have
grown tremendously in the United States. It is within the normal
activity of all major interest groups to have a highly-organized public

relations staff. However, the interest group does not primarily try to affect public opinion *per se*, but for another goal—to obtain favorable decisions from the executive, legislative or judical branch of government.

Even though pressure groups engage in public relations to change opinions, one cannot assume that in each instance there is a simple cause and effect relationship. Take two examples from the history of labor legislation in the United States, the Wagner Act of 1937 and the Taft-Hartley Act of 1947. From the beginning, management groups opposed the Wagner Act. But despite vigorous activities by the National Association of Manufacturers and other groups, it was not until 1947 that public opinion had changed enough to modify the Act. It is still impossible to determine to which extent the revision was due to N.A.M. publicity.

However, we do know that the American Medical Association launched an effective program to prevent the enactment of a national health program, proposed by President Truman.

We have much descriptive data on public relations, much of it written by public relations firms. As to the analytic side, however, we know much less. Before we can draw conclusions we must understand the whole social context of which politics is but one facet. Discovering causal relationships between environment and pressure groups may lead to an over-simplification.

Professor Webb: The public relations of pressure groups has a special relevance in a *laissez-faire* economy. As you move toward the welfare state, with a tendency of pressure groups to become part of the governmental hierarchy, public relations techniques become less important, and their function is then taken over by other devices.

Professor Heckscher: May I add a footnote here? If a given pressure group is acting through a political party, public relations activities will be moderate, since, otherwise, the group would get little sympathy from an opposing political party. But if the pressure group is operating outside of a party, it will give increased attention to its public relations. Thus the structure of political parties may determine how important public relations are for interest groups.

Professor McKenzie: That a pressure group is closely affiliated with, or even organically linked with one political party does not necessarily mean that its influence on the other major party (or parties) will be negligible. In Britain most of the trade unions are affiliated with the Labour Party; yet with Labour out of office since 1951, the unions have continued to wield great influence (and have by no means muted their propaganda and public relations activities). Ironically enough, some observers have suggested that the main argument in favor of unseating the Conservatives and returning Labour at the next election is that the latter would be less fearful of the unions and more likely to be able to restrain their more irresponsible wage demands.

Professor Finer: I would like to call attention to two other factors:

(1) *The media of public relations.* It is generally considered that radio (sight and sound) is easily the most effective of all media and this has been proved by experience in the U. S. A. Now in Great Britain both sight and sound are politically neutralized by law. This enormously reduces the utility of mass media communications to our interest groups. For the most part they have to operate through the press and this is not a very effective weapon.

(2) *The level of sophistication of public relations in a given country.* Political propaganda has to compete with all other forms of propaganda notably commercial propaganda. The higher the level of commercial propaganda in a given country the higher must the level of political propaganda be, if it is to gain the public's ear. Now, ten times more is spent on advertising in the U. S. A. than in Great Britain and I suspect that this is the reason why political groups and interest groups in the U. S. A. have to put on such a "show." They have to work much harder and spend much more to gain public attention in the U. S. A. than they do in Great Britain.

Professor Eldersveld: When I examined the situation in The Netherlands, I wondered why the Dutch Medical Association had no public relations program. Their answer to my questions might have been a rationalization; however, what I was told let me believe that it was not part of the rules of the political game for doctors to spend money for generating public pressure in their behalf. Perhaps the real reason was that they did not think they needed it. It may be true that, quite generally, the climate of public opinion sets a margin of tolerance within which pressure groups must operate.

Professor Finer: As an addition to this statement: the British Medical Association does not spend any money either for public relations activities. But the National Union of Teachers does. Therefore, another dimension to be considered is the kind of organization or profession with which you are dealing.

Professor Townsley: In Australia, the press is the chief media for all public relations activity and it exercises a profound influence if only by the unofficial censorship which the papers practice when they decide on what not to print. Radio is neutralized. There is neither a national press nor a labor press in Australia. There have been occasions when the press has assisted in bringing down governments, i.e., the Labour Government in 1931, or in establishing them in power. On another occasion, the press exerted great pressure to prevent the nationalization of banks. As a general rule, the press has been effective on critical issues.

Professor McKenzie: I agree with Professor Finer regarding the limited use of the press for public relations purposes. However, let me cite an example to illustrate another function of the press. About four years ago, a teacher's scheme proposed by the Conservative Government was withdrawn under pressure from both sides of the House of Commons. It was highly unusual for a bill presented by a government in power to be, in effect, rejected. In a case study which we ran on the collapse of this Pension plan, we discovered that the reason for the defeat was not so much the lobby of the National Union of Teachers, which was violently opposed to this bill, but the line taken by the responsible journals in England—the *Times*, the *Economist*, and the *Manchester Guardian*. When asked why they opposed the plan, Members of Parliament stated that these journals, which have highly competent research staffs with which an M.P. could not compete, had opposed the plan and that they, the M.P.'s, were impressed by the reasons they have given for doing so. This shows the considerable influence of the serious press on Members of Parliament.

Professor Ehrmann: Who influenced the press?

Professor McKenzie: Our survey did not disclose *how* the press arrived at a decision on a particular issue. We just don't know.

Professor Neumann: The strategy used by pressure groups also depends on the prevailing mood of the country. One may go one step further and state that the recognition of the significance of interest groups and their increasing and open use as channels of policy formation, especially in comparison to political parties, is an indicator of the political climate of a nation. In a period of relative stability and economic prosperity and especially in the follow-up of total war and all-inclusive governmental interventions, one can observe a widespread privatization of interests and "escape from politics".

In the aftermath of the Second World War such a mood has evoked, in the Western World at least, a strong reaction against political parties, reinforcing a traditionally deep-seated skepticism concerning their activities. By the same token, the singleness of purpose and specific concerns of interest groups have often found a ready response and wider respect among the people. Fruitful as such a public awareness of interest group life is (and incidentally our renewed scholarly concern too) it must be related to the whole domain of politics which is not merely a sum total of pressure group activities. Constructive leadership while recognizing their claims must lift the demands of the specific interests to the level of national needs. This is where effective parties come in.

Professor Leiserson: I want to underscore Professor Blaisdell's point regarding the cause and effect relationship between interest group techniques and their success in the political arena.

Public relations are nowadays discussed too much in terms of techniques, much as behavioral psychologists used to talk in terms of conditioned reflexes, as if public opinion were merely "crowd" psychology: a matter applying the appropriate stimulus to secure a desired response. Even the most cynical public relations firms admit that you cannot manipulate public attitudes by pushing buttons. The power of an interest group is not related directly to the size of its membership. An example is the position of organized labor in the United States today.

We should also consider the propaganda activities of revolutionary groups and reactionary groups. Though they are not normally considered as regular interest groups, they are alternative or rival forms of political action-organizations, and for tactical purposes often assume the role of pressure groups.

Professor Heckscher: I believe we shall clarify the different aspects of public relations activities by interest groups:

(1) Some are merely means by which the group communicates with group members or with the public.

(2) Other activities are designed to achieve concrete results. Here one of the most effective media would be interpersonal relationships.

I would like to take issue with Professor Webb's point that in the welfare state interest groups have less need for public relations. That depends on the groups and the issues. Even in the welfare state interest groups may feel threatened when certain issues arise; the groups will then react to such threats.

Interest groups practice public relations in regard to their members as well as to non-members. They must explain themselves and elucidate adopted policies before their membership while they might seek different ends before an audience of non-members. Hence both the content of their campaign and the media employed might be different.

That the use of media will differ with differing circumstances and from country to country is obvious. In Great Britain and the United States, the press is largely independent from political parties. Here, the press may be an effective medium for the interest groups. But in

Scandinavia or Germany where newspapers are identified with political parties, the press will not be as effective a medium. In Great Britain television and radio are not easily available for private groups. In the United States, the reverse is true since you can literally "buy time."

Dr. Hirsch-Weber: There are still party newspapers in Western Germany, but the big dailies and many provincial papers are no longer identified with political parties, though they have certainly definite editorial policies. Thus they are open to statements of a variety of interest groups. Of course, this does not mean that every interest group has an equal standing with every daily. The treatment a group receives depends on the editors', the writers', and the publishers' views and may also depend on considerations motivated by special interests, for instance, those of their advertisers.

Let me add to what was said about the Dutch and British Medical Associations, that also in the Federal Republic, conflicts arose over the income which doctors derive from compulsory medical insurance. The doctors raised protests but refrained from organizing any public campaign. In all probability they considered public relations activities not to be in accord with the standards of their profession. Nevertheless, even without such a campaign their case did get sufficient attention in the press.

Professor Finer: In Great Britain the public relations firms who wish to sell their services have recently made the following distinction:

(1) *"Fire-Brigade" Campaign.* By this they mean a defensive campaign such as was waged by the doctors in the U. S. A. or the teachers in Great Britain or the groups who opposed transport nationalization in Great Britain; the object of such campaigns is to fight off an immediate parliamentary threat to their interests.

(2) *The "Re-insurance"* or (as I choose to call it) *the "in-good-standing Campaign."* This is a campaign designed to prevent such a threat as mentioned above from ever developing. The object of such a campaign is to create in the public mind a favorable image of a firm, or of a cause, e.g. free enterprise. The public relations firms would very much like their customers to spend money for this kind of service but so far they are finding difficulties in selling the idea.

Professor Webb: The general point I wish to make in regard to the public relations of pressure groups in the welfare state was that public relations decline when economic interest groups become part of the hierarchical structure of government. In the welfare state trade unions and farm associations have little or no problem to recruit their members. On the other hand, it is true that when major organizations split on a particular issue public relations activities will be intense

Professor Leiserson: I believe that it would be helpful to distinguish between public relations in general and efforts to defend one's group against aggressive hostility from the outside. This distinction also holds true for the public relations of political parties. Defense against the outside makes the membership self-conscious regarding its affiliations and its relationship to the public order.

In regard to public relations in the welfare state, the situation in the British Commonwealth is quite different from that in the United States. Interest groups in the Commonwealth seem to be responsible in that they seek a recognized role of influence within the governmental system. In America, many interest groups seem to feel themselves apart or above the political order: they look down on government. They look upon themselves as the makers of policy, and on Congress as the mediator between conflicting interests. It has been suggested that in 1952 the seizure of the steel industry was deliberately precipitated by the steel interests which wanted to demonstrate the impotence of government.

Therefore, we need to consider generally whether interests groups think of themselves as playing a limited role within the prevailing order of political values or whether they believe themselves to be above it, outside it, and hence of having a special responsibility of protecting, transforming or displacing that order.

Professor Chester: I would like to add a number of disjointed observations: There is a middle ground between Professor Finer's "fire brigade" and "in-good-standing" campaigns. The fire brigades are called out once a party has taken a definite line. Traditionally the British interest groups say that they can work with either party. However, once a party has taken a position detrimental to the interests defended by a given group, the latter must work with the other party. But on some issues, the parties have not taken a definite stand. Take, for example, such issues as the control of monopolies or the problem of wages. Big trade unions and big trade associations have been playing up to public opinion and have tried to influence it to get the political parties to take their side. In these cases, public opinion has not yet been formed and the interest groups are trying to shape it in a way favorable to their position. Here, as on other occasions, the Trade Union Congress functions as an assembly or an arena to form policy.

There is a difference between persuasion and information. Many groups simply provide information. We must remember that Members of Parliament in Great Britain do not have the same staff assistance as members of Congress have in the United States. Therefore, information from the pressure groups is more important to them. In regard to Professor Heckscher's point as to how strongly you shout, it depends on how you feel. If your life is threatened, you shout loudly, even in England.

Professor McKenzie: The National Farmers Union includes about 90 per cent of the farmers in Britain; it deals directly and intimately with the Minister of Agriculture. The N. F. U. is often able to win the minister around to their viewpoint, and he in turn is frequently able to convince the Chancellor of the Exchequer and other relevant ministers of the wisdom of granting their claims. Thus the process of influencing the decision makers in a unitary state operating as a parliamentary system may be far more simple and direct than in a federal and congressional system such as the United States. An organization like the N. F. U. in Britain, representing almost the whole industry and with direct access to the effective decision makers at cabinet level, need not resort to the raucous publicity activities considered necessary by less well organized American pressure groups which, in order to get their way, will have to bring influence to bear on the administration, congressional committees, state governments, and so forth. It would seem clear that to assess correctly the relative importance of public relations for pressure groups it is necessary to consider the form of government in the country in which they operate and also the extent to which a particular pressure group can legitimately claim to speak for an entire economic group and even for other interests.

Professor Blaisdell: I quite agree. The form of government is controlling the scope of public relations activities in the United States. For example, the press conference is a great instrument of public relations for the Administration.

Professor Lavau: In France the use of public relations to serve long-term goals is relatively undeveloped. However, for the achievement of short-term goals, the French use what they call "Italian Politics," which simply means to establish useful contacts to persons in positions of influence. When recently an important trade association interviewed a potential employee, they asked him if he had a *carnet d'adresses,* an address book with the names of approximately two to three hundred people who can break the ground for important decisions.

An exception to what I have said about the use of public relations for long-term policies is provided by the trade unions, who, whether they know it or not, are engaged in public relations. Especially the

C.G.T. exercises permanent influence on public opinion through its newspapers.

Radio and television in France are government controlled. They are used politically without scruples by the government in power to support its own policies and not infrequently those of interest groups allied with it. The Mollet government used, and abused television and radio to advance the cause of *Force Ouvrière*, the socialist labor unions. Also, the press is an important medium for public relations, especially local newspapers provide service to the government in power and to the groups friendly to it.

In regard to acute critical issues, the French interest groups may become extremely active. They then make great use of the local press. With the exception of the Communist newspapers, all local newspapers in France open their columns to articles by various interest groups such as the veterans, farmers, doctors, etc. However, I believe these articles have little effect, firstly, because they are often excessive in numbers, and secondly, because they appear suddenly at the time of crisis without an adequate long-term preparation of public opinion. For example, in 1957, when Gazier, the Minister of Labor, submitted a proposal for the reform of the social security system, the physicians inundated the press with articles. But the public was unprepared for such a campaign. When the physicians threatened to strike, the public, which had not understood the issue, turned against them and the physicians' resistance fell flat.

Professor Vito: In general, public relations do not have great relevance for pressure groups in Italy. Let me mention, however, that the Confederation of Industrialists, a very powerful group, has organized a National Conference of Economists held yearly for three days at the expense of the organization to discuss important issues of economic and social policy. The participants are persons of importance; the press follows the proceedings closely. The issues are chosen with an eye to problems of particular interest at the moment, so that they will attract the public's attention. This has been so successful a method of spreading a point of view that now the trade unions prepare for similar gatherings.

I have the impression that in Italy the welfare state has created new situations where public relations techniques practiced by interest groups are indeed effective.

Professor Cavalcanti: This is a period of great social and economic transformation in Brazil and in Latin America, generally. Organized groups are of vital importance and their mutual hostility is frequently high-pitched. Action is rapid and forceful. There is a ferocious battle going on between workers and employers.

Organized labor is quite strong in Brazil. It has elected the Vice-President of the Republic from its ranks. In the election campaign the workers had the advantage of strong radio support since the Vargas government had given the unions a radio station. Hence, it was possible to engage in effective and inexpensive propaganda which would not have been possible without the free use of radio. Trade associations are very powerful both in commerce and industry. They have established social service organizations and are supporting schools. This of course is excellent propaganda and opens the way for a public information and education program. The Medical Association, which is very solidly organized, promoted a strike for higher fees two years ago. But its campaign failed, because of the ethical question involved.

The press is free and has a great impact on public opinion. True, some papers are supported by industrialists, but many are neutral. The fall of Vargas and his subsequent suicide might be attributed to the press.

Now the fate of the industries, nationalized by the Vargas government, has become a paramount issue. Private industry clamors for the denationalization of these sectors of the economy. Press and television participate in the battle. Also, the army plays a considerable role. What will be the outcome is difficult to predict, but it is certain that this is very important for the future role of government. In Argentina and Chile the situation is not dissimilar.

Professor Ehrmann: Would you describe the role which the army plays in Brazil as that of a pressure group?

Professor Cavalcanti: The army in Argentina, Brazil and Chile is essentially a conservative force and rarely rises to overthrow the existing authority except to knock out a dictatorship. It sees its task as that of maintaining the traditional government and to avoid a dictatorship, though it is true that Vargas was a dictator twice. Two years ago the army tried a *coup d'état* to forestall, as they said, another *coup*.

The revolution of 1930 was organized not by the army but by other groups acting from within the government. Even in Argentina, the revolution was made by the army against the dictatorship. When I speak of the army, I mean, of course, the Officers' Corps; enlisted men do not make revolutions.

Dr. Hirsch-Weber: Professor Cavalcanti's point about the army cannot have general validity for all of Latin America. In Bolivia, up to the late thirties, the generals made *coups d'état* to obtain political office, i.e., the presidency and ministries, and with it the chance of increasing their personal incomes. Since then the pattern has become more intricate, because also young officers, often siding with fascist as well as with democratic or leftist movements, headed *coups* or revolutions. Similar situations can be observed in other Latin American countries. Therefore, the army should rather be called a political force than a pressure group.

To return to the issue of public relations, I would say that generally business groups are more accustomed to the use of public relations and do a better job of it than labor. One observation concerning the political system as a determinant of the behavior of interest groups: in the German Federal Republic, where the custom of alternative party rule has not been established as in Great Britain, trade unions are more apt to consider strikes as a means to get favorable political action. In Britain they hope for the return to power of Labour. In Bolivia the unions do certainly strike or even start a civil war to get desired political action, or changes in government. Thus, Bolivian unions are really as much a kind of political party as a pressure group.

Professor Townsley: One facet of public relations which we have not yet discussed is the fact that in our pluralistic society government agencies act as interest groups and work on both the public and on groups. There is a two-way flow in public relations. The government provides handouts, communiqués, etc. There are press conferences, and official and unofficial leakage for and to the pressure groups. Such a use of public relations by government agencies is actually increasing.

Professor Inoki: In Japan the army was the strongest interest group before the war—especially from 1931 to 1937. The army could justifiably claim to represent social classes which had no political party or interest groups to represent them, i.e., peasants, small businessmen and workers. These classes were suffering social frustration in many respects; some of their views could be expressed through the army which, because of conscription, had grass roots support.

Today employers' groups are spending a great deal more money on public relations than the trade unions. The leaders of organized labor are almost exclusively non-communist Marxists. Only in 1950 a new trade union movement was founded to oppose Marxist domination. The public relations activities of labor are conditioned by its ideology. Since the trade unions believe in the class struggle they have little understanding for the role of public relations or for public opinion in general. As a result, several strikes in the recent past have widened the gap between the leaders, the rank and file of the unions, and the public. The employers' groups are now taking cognizance of this fact and seek to further separate the union leadership from their members.

Discussion: INFLUENCE OF PRESSURE GROUPS ON PARTIES AND ELECTIONS

September 11—Afternoon Session

Professor Benjamin Akzin, *Chairman*

Professor Ehrmann: In opening this afternoon's discussion I would like to list first some of the factors that are generally mentioned as determining the permeability of political parties to pressure group influence:

(1) The electoral system (this thesis, defended by Duverger, is substantiated in part by the paper of Mrs. Krusius-Ahrenberg).

(2) Existence of a two-party vs. a multiparty system.

(3) The internal structure of a party (disciplined vs. loosely organized parties; parties of program vs. parties of platform).

(4) The social dispersion of the membership between parties and pressure groups (a point developed especially in the paper of Professor Lavau, but also discussed by Professor Heckscher.)

I hope that we may also devote some of our time to discussing the best methods for exploring the relationship between pressure groups and parties. Since there is a constant flow of influence between the two, it may be that concrete case studies comparing the relationship in various countries, but also in the same country at different times, would prove helpful. Such studies would reveal at least the following four historical situations: (a) interest groups are creating a party; (b) a party "adopts" one or several groups; (c) there exists a lasting *"Querverbindung"* between parties and pressure groups; (d) interest groups become the substitutes for parties—a development probably most frequent outside of the Western World.

Professor Blaisdell: What I shall say relates primarily to the third factor mentioned by Mr. Ehrmann, that is, the internal structure of the party, but also to the first (electoral system) and the fourth (social dispersion).

In the United States we must ask which parties we are speaking of because we actually have four parties. Since we have a federal system with a separation of power, there are two Democratic Parties, one in Congress and one out, and two Republican Parties, one in Congress and one out. We could divide still further and would find that in the two Houses of Congress there are two parts of each party. My discussion will concentrate mainly on the Republican and Democratic parties in Congress. For pressure groups work principally on parties in Congress because, at least in the legislative or statutory sense, policy is made there.

Just as parties in Congress try to influence the composition of Congressional committees, pressure groups try to influence committee assignments, especially to the Rules Committee. Beyond that, pressure groups may sway Congressional opinion (1) by testifying before committees, (2) by offering help for the writing of reports, and (3) by the use of outright propaganda when critical points in the legislative process are reached.

If we turn to the relationship between groups and parties outside of Congress, the nominating conventions are of interest. Here we see pressure groups trying to influence the platforms. Why they should do this is obscure as platforms mean little or nothing, and since the Presidential nominee can interpret the platform as he wishes. At the Democratic Convention in Chicago last year, a meeting of the NAACP, the AFL-CIO, and several governors was held, making a strenuous but unsuccessful effort to shape the civil rights plank.

Another interest group activity taking place outside of Congress is connected with the patronage system. Though civil service has grown tremendously through the years and covers most government posts, there are still 1,100 positions in the national government subject to Presidential appointment and Senatorial confirmation. These positions, which in Great Britian are held by the Administrative class, are in the United States reserved to the party faithful. Interest groups are eager to help the chairman of the National Committee in filling such posts.

Professor McKenzie: I should like to add to Mr. Blaisdell's remarks that the meeting of the platform committee at the Democratic Convention in Chicago in 1956 deserves special attention though it has been scarcely commented upon. The Committee met a week before the convention opened to hear interest groups express their wishes in regard to the party platform. This early meeting to prepare the drafting of the platform was an innovation.

Now let me turn to the relationship of interest groups and parties in Great Britain. The parties are particularly sensitive to pressure from interest groups because of the close balance between parties. It would require only a uniform two per cent shift in public opinion to throw the Conservative Party out of power. A one per cent shift would change eighteen seats. Majorities are like snowballs—when they start to melt they go fast.

The position of the trade unions vis-à-vis the parties in Britain is frequently misunderstood. The trade unions are not the sole owners of the Labour Party even though as Ernest Bevin once said the Party "grew out of the bowels" of the trade unions. The trade unions provide only one-half of the total party funds and about two-fifths of the Labour Members of Parliament. In fact, the Conservative Party is also very sensitive to trade union opinion for obvious reasons: one-half of the votes polled by the Conservative Party come from the working class. To stay in power the Conservatives must get at least one-third of the working class vote, but there is only one worker among the Conservative M.P.s in the present Parliament. The middle class followers of the party and the white collar workers often resent the reluctance of the Conservative Party to take a firmer line against the trade unions. Therefore, social divisions within the Conservative Party build up tensions, which to a large extent are due to the Conservative Party's dependence on labour support at the polls.

Professor Iwanaga: The assumption that pressure groups are respectable is not borne out in Japanese politics. Not only Japan, but also other Asian societies are now in a state of flux. All social groups are more or less unstable; many of them are ideologically oriented. The organization of groups is difficult but indispensable in our new democracy, for through the process of group formation and through the groups themselves we can expect emergence of a new pattern of political behavior.

In regard to the relationship between trade unions and the Socialist Party in Japan, it must be stressed that contrary to a widespread assumption, the greater part of the trade unions do not support the right wing but the left wing of the party. Under the impact first of the occupation and now of the worsening international situation, the trade unions have become more and more radical.

Professor Merle: The influence of the Catholic Church on French political parties and elections is sometimes overrated because it is not viewed in the proper historical perspective. Since 1945, for instance, this influence has changed its character and has somewhat decreased. After the liberation, the Church strongly supported the M.R.P. and continued to do so as long as the threat from the socialists and communists seemed great. Now this support for the M.R.P. is greatly weakened and two tendencies are emerging among Catholics taking a political position:

(1) The social (by no means socialist) group which continues to back the M.R.P. and

(2) The conversative which backs rightist parties, the *Modérés*, and does this sometimes against the M.R.P.

I know of a *Département* where, in 1945–46, the Church favored the M.R.P. and in 1951 mobilized forces against the M.R.P. Hence the Church no longer acts as a block, but contents itself to propagate general attitudes. It rarely takes specific political positions even on such matters as the defense of Catholic schools and colonial questions.

The opinions of the Church are passed on to the bishops and archbishops but these can interpret them in their own way. Therefore, positions often differ from one diocese to another. When the Church intervenes, it does so in various forms, sometimes taking a vigorous stand, sometimes remaining deliberately passive. When the Church indicates a preference for a certain party or candidate, such support is seldom explicit. More often the Church merely names the candidates or parties which are unacceptable. A great deal of flexibility might be available to the Catholic voter, depending on the place, the issues and the local situation. Since absenteeism at the polls is believed to profit the Communist Party, the Church always tries to bring out the vote.

Whenever the Catholic Church intervenes, the most important single issue remains the insistence on the freedom of Catholic education. But other factors, such as international issues or social policy, may also play a role without however resulting in a binding directive.

The period of permanent conflict over the Church in politics is more or less over. The Church does not really attempt to create a political party. When the Church wishes to see certain educational, social or colonial policies adopted, it rather acts as an interest group trying to influence public opinion, the bureaucracy, or existing political parties and governmental agencies.

Professor Finer: First may I say how astounded I was to find out from M. Lavau's paper that the *"professions de foi"* exert such tyranny over candidates in France (inasmuch as pressure groups submit questionnaires to the parliamentary candidates). Some groups in England still attempt to influence parliamentary candidates in this way but it is almost wholly ineffective. One reason for this was that in 1950, both the Conservative and Labour Parties appear to have told their candidates never to answer such questionnaires "off the cuff," but instead to reply to them either by citing the appropriate part of the parties' platform or to answer in terms of that program.

If I may change the subject: I would like to make one or two points about pressure groups and parties in elections, because I did not touch on this subject in my paper. The reason is simply that this is not a serious consideration in Great Britain. On the whole pressure groups are disinclined to advise their members to vote for one candidate rather than another, even though one candidate may be more favorable to the pressure group's objective than the other. The membership of most of these organizations is bi-partisan, and a directive to vote for one party rather than another would split the organization along party lines. This is true for instance of the doctors, of the teachers, of the British Legion and of most others.

Professor McKenzie: Neither can such groups influence elections by setting up ancillary fund-raising organizations and election campaign committees to assist the party of their choice. Any such expenditure is illegal under the British electoral law.

Professor Finer: I quite agree, and this eliminates any significant influence by interest groups in parliamentary elections. It is quite true that we do have sponsored candidates, in other words, some pressure groups (other than trade unions, which have a special status) may sponsor a certain candidate; but they will not sponsor a certain *party*. The National Union of Teachers is a typical example. It offers to support the candidatures of a maximum of four people from each of the three main parties. In fact no members of the Liberal Party accepted the offer and at the present moment there are two sponsored candidates of this Union on the Conservative side and four on the Labour side of the House of Commons.

If I turn to the next point, namely the influence which groups exercise on the program of political parties I must admit that this is very obscure. But it seems to work this way: parties tend to draw up their programs in opposition and carry them out when in power. When in opposition, they are deprived of the expert advice of the civil service. True, they have research organizations but these are not technically competent to deal with the administrative detail or even with technical policy required in the construction of a Party program. This is where the "lobbies" come in with all the expert advice which they can offer. The trade unions significantly influence program building in the Labour Party. As to the Conservative Party I could give two classic examples of the influence of lobbies upon the shaping of its Party program. The first is to be seen in L. S. Amery's *My Political Life* Vol. III, pages 19–27, and pages 74 et seq, where he shows how the Conservative Party's protectionist policy of 1932 was drawn up by a Research Committee of the Conservative Party in closest cooperation with agricultural, industrial and commercial pressure groups. The second example is the influence of the Road Haulage Association upon the

Conservative opposition in 1948 by which that Party committed itself to breaking up the nationalized Road Services. In this case the association of British Chambers of Commerce had a different policy from the Road Haulage Association but failed to persuade the Conservatives to accept their policy. Instead the advice of the Road Haulage Association was adopted and implemented in the act of 1953, only to be abandoned (after its failure) in 1956 when an act was passed which largely adopted the view of the Association of British Chambers of Commerce.

Platform drafters try to make their statements vague but as Herbert Morrison said "there is a limit to how vague you can be" and, when a British party makes a pledge, it is expected to keep it.

Dr. Hirsch-Weber: Why?

Professor Finer: What do you mean "why?" *Pacta sunt servanda,* and that's all there is to it!

Finally the question of contributions. There is little doubt that the largest donations to the Conservative Party come from industry. I am not sure as to the legal position of a firm which wishes to contribute to a political party fund—this appears to depend upon the articles or memoranda of association, for according to the way in which these are drafted such contributions will be *intra vires* or *ultra vires*. But recent evidence, publically printed, shows that textile firms in Lancashire have contributed to Conservative Party funds (though they have recently declined to contribute further owing to their disagreement with the present Government's policy in admitting Empire cottons at low rates of duty). Similarly, evidence shows that private firms in the London area have been asked for party contributions.

Professor Leiserson: In the United States, the effect of the governmental system on the party system cannot be overemphasized. Adding to Professor Blaisdell's comments, I should like to point out that the American nominating process, especially the use of the direct primary in state elections, opens the door to the influence of interest groups which sometimes strongly oppose the party organization.

As it functions in fact, Congress acts more frequently as a bipartisan or nonpartisan than a partisan body dedicated to enacting an electoral campaign program into law. This leads to a loose party system, and interest groups tend to operate more directly on Congressmen and the committee system within Congress than on the party organizations in or outside Congress.

Professor Townsley: In Australia some agrarian interest groups represent the large rural holdings; others represent the small mixed farms. Between these extremes are the wool and wheat growers who also have their groups.

There is always organization by up-country groups against the cities; indeed, certain interests in New South Wales go so far as to demand organization into a new state. The government regularly makes concessions to these up-country groups. Also, the electoral systems of some states are biased in favor of country interests.

Most important is the Australian Country Party. Though it claims to be a national party because wool-growing and exporting is so important to the whole nation, it is in reality a party representing special economic interests. Nationally it continues to work with the Liberal Party but on the state level the situation may be different. In Victoria, for instance, the two parties are often in bitter opposition.

In federal politics, the Country and Liberal Parties are allied to keep Labour out. The Country Party fights to keep its identity and bargains hard to determine the distribution of seats in coalition governments. It also effectively controls Australia's overseas trade and currency policies.

Professor Akzin: I wonder whether the time has come to assign respective weight to the various factors mentioned at the beginning of our discussion as determining the influence of pressure groups on political parties. Perhaps we should confine ourselves for the present to an exchange of observations, and leave generalization and conceptualization on the basis of our exchange for a later stage. We may do this at Rome in September, 1958.

Take the question as to whether the pressure groups try to influence parties, or the legislature, or individual legislators, or the executive. The answer depends on the legislative system of the country and/or the pressure group involved. In the United States, the decentralized character of the two parties and their lack of inner discipline, result in the pressure groups centering their attention on those whom they regard as more effective, i.e., individual legislators, legislative committees, and the executive. In France the multiplicity of parties provides a different situation, but leads possibly to similar results. The electoral system may weaken or strengthen parties and may also affect their number. In this latter respect, though, we must beware of exaggeration. France had more parties under the majority system than it has now under proportional representation.

Where the party has great internal discipline, the pressure groups will aim their efforts at the party itself. In Israel, for example, where the parties are extremely strong and influential in national life the pressure groups concentrate their efforts on the party, not because of any "natural law" but because the party largely controls what happens in Parliament, in the cabinet, and in the executive offices.

I also believe that in Israel at least interest groups do influence the choice of candidates to be put up for election by the parties. What is the situation in this respect in other countries?

The pressure groups in Israel can be classed as: (1) inter-party pressure groups; (2) intra-party pressure groups; (3) pressure groups which confine their activities to a bloc of parties (e.g., the trade unions and cooperatives work on the Labor Parties); (4) pressure groups which try to work on all parties. The pressure group seeks out the people with whom it has the strongest ideological or social links. In Israel, a strong link exists between people that have migrated from the same country. In other countries the link might be membership in the same club or past attendance of the same school.

Pressure groups may compete among themselves just as much as political parties. A conflict of interests may occur even when different interest groups share the identical ideological bias and are linked with the same political party. As an example, take the bus drivers who want higher fares, whereas their fellow working men want lower fares.

Professor Neumann: We also must consider the impact which changes in the character of the political system have on the relationship between pressure groups and political parties.

A good case in question is the Bonn Republic. Its characteristic trend towards a two-party line-up and away from rigid *Weltanschauungparteien* means for the interest groups the end of accustomed tactics of concentration on minor parties or the wide use of *Querverbindungen* (extending influence through divided representation in diverse parties). With the concerted efforts on the conquest of power through single-party majority, the parties will also resist the identification with a single though powerful pressure group. This means the end of the typical Continental parties with strict class alignments of straight nationality backing. Interest groups will instead adopt increasingly Anglo-American patterns of playing the role of free-floating vote blocs.

The SPD if it wants to break its traditional 30 per cent limit of the national electorate and thus reach a voting strength of majority proportions must win new followers from non-traditional strata. In short it cannot keep the reputation of being the exclusive spokesman and representative of the working class interests, which in fact it has not been in composition or policy orientation since it has risen to the status of a major national party. However, the special efforts to broaden its social base far beyond its traditional rank and file by reaching out to the middle classes is a typical transformation of the relationship of party and interest groups under the impact of a changing political society. The same phenomena may be observed in the apt strategies of the CDU and its pointed efforts to break the widely accepted image of its identification with a single interest group, the Catholic Church.

Professor Heckscher: May I comment first that much of what Mr. Townsley has said about agrarian parties in his country is true in other countries as well. Let me now turn to two specific areas for investigation: what is the influence of interest groups (1) on nominations; (2) on policy formation?

Nominations: Professor Finer's documentation showing the group affiliations of a great number of Members of Parliament is extremely interesting. One wonders whether this is a coincidence or whether the parties really attempt at the time of the nominations, to give "representation" to various groups. In the single constituency system, it is true, only one or two candidates can be considered, but under proportional representation there are more candidates and it is easier to choose them from among the various pressure groups. Once we have found that influence on nominations does indeed exist the next question to be investigated would be to what extent parties listen to: (1) regular supporters and (2) marginal groups.

Policy Formation: It is probable that interest groups direct most of their efforts towards policy formation in parliament, trying to get promises from the parties and to hold them to their promises; but we must also see whether groups do not appear at conventions and express their wishes there. It is getting increasingly difficult to distinguish between policy formation taking place outside parliament from policies that are developed inside parliament.

To find out to what extent parties take the demands of interest groups into consideration, and whether interest groups attempt to exercise influence at party conventions, would not be too difficult to investigate. We should also promote research on the legislative process and need case studies of important pieces of legislation, while they are considered both inside and outside of parliament.

Mr. Neumann mentioned that the German SPD needed support from ouside of labor. This is true for any labor party in a highly industrialized society where the labor force is decreasing; in such a society the votes of white collar groups and of public employees, not habitually called labor, become indispensable. In mixed economies where more and more local governments own or control services and industries, public employees also have an increasing importance. The trouble here is that most of the support demanding representation comes from non-marginal groups (a point which was made by Professor Finer), but that support from marginal groups is also necessary.

This leads us directly to another question to be examined, namely, whether certain interest groups go along with minorities within the parties rather than with the majority. The tragedy of the SPD in the Weimar Republic was that it did not know what position to take, one strictly serving the interests of organized labor or one furnishing a broader long term policy; it finally lost followers to both sides. But this is a problem which all parties face. From my personal experience as a drafter of party programs during the past 20 years or so, I know that you must put in something for everybody in order to attract the marginal groups. And later you may be stuck with your promise.

Dr. Hirsch-Weber: The point has been raised whether interest groups influence the parties rather than parliament. In 1930 in Germany, the coalition government headed by a Social Democratic Chancellor dissolved under the pressure of the trade unions over a relatively unimportant social security issue. The Socialist trade unions opposed the cabinet's stand on a bill pending in the Reichstag and succeeded in bringing a majority of the Social Democratic M.P.'s, one third of whom were union leaders, to reject the government's proposals. The Socialist chancellor was forced to resign. Many believe that the split of this coalition, a direct consequence of interest group action, was, in the light of later events, a tragedy for Germany.

The reverse happened in 1932. Chancellor Schleicher inquired whether the trade unions would join with him in a common front against the menace of a nazi government. He found some response, but at Socialist party headquarters the leader of the unions was talked out of further conversing with the "reactionary" Schleicher about a government based on trade union support.

We had and still have interplay between the Social Democratic Party and the trade unions. An important issue in the Federal Republic is co-determination. The trade unions proposed co-determination and it has been accepted by the SPD without discussion. The bill on co-determination introduced by the SPD was an exact copy of the proposal which the trade unions had publicized.

At present, the trade union federation could hardly elect a president who would be unacceptable to the SPD; on the other hand, the unions have undoubtedly influenced nominating processes within the SPD. But they do so rather passively as a force to be reckoned with in elections than actively as a group which insists on a right to be represented on party lists. Some observers believe that nowadays the party has a stronger hold on the unions than the unions on the party.

The above indicates, (1) that the relationship between party and interest group may be a two-way affair, (2) that it may be difficult to distinguish between a group's influence on a party and its influence on parliament. Members of parliament are party men. In 1930, and now when the proposal on co-determination was introduced, the unions influenced parliament through those deputies who were union members. At the same time, they influenced the party so that also non-union Socialists voted according to the unions' wishes. But indirectly, this was again an influence on parliament. Parallel to this, one should consider the fact that in several instances interest groups have succeeded in influencing the chancellor and ministers in their double capacity as members of the executive and as party members.

Prof. Beer: When we speak about the goals and doctrines of "interest" groups, we do not mean that they act merely for interest; pure selfishness is as rare as pure altruism. When they claim that their self-interest coincides with the general interest, interest groups may have some degree of justification; nevertheless, by and large, they act, of course, out of self-interest.

Professor Finer drew a distinction between promotional or propaganda groups and interest groups proper. In England during the 19th century, there were many groups with a cause, such as the anti-slavery and the anti-Corn-Law group. Toward the end of the century when the parties grew stronger, these groups tended to decline. The generally accepted explanation is that the parties took over from the groups and that the Reform Act of 1884 marked the end of the "group period."

At the present time there are only a few promotional groups in Britain. The League of Nations Association may have been the last large one (except for the recent group opposing capital punishment). In the United States they are more numerous: we have the League of Women Voters, Americans for Democratic Action, the National Catholic Welfare Council, and others. In France with its many parties the latter carry the burden of propaganda activities; but in Sweden, also a multi-party system, promotional groups abound.

Professor McKenzie: I should like to comment on Mr. Heckscher's remarks regarding the selection of candidates. In the United Kingdom the selection of candidates is in the hands of local party committees, and in three fourths of the electoral districts, nomination is tantamount to election. Although the central office of either party can veto the nominations, this right is rarely used.

The Central Office also has a list of personalities available for nomination by the constituency parties. It encourages selections from this list in order to place an important or attractive personality in a favorable position; but such candidates must still be accepted by the local organization.

On the Labour side, local parties may choose a nominee sponsored by a labor union or a cooperative. Although such candidates can count on financial support from the sponsoring organization in the amount of about 350 pounds, this sum is about half the amount required to defray election expenses.

The Tories do not have such sponsored candidates. That they generally choose middle or upper class candidates is a foregone conclusion. Nevertheless, the Conservative Party headquarters frequently urge local parties to nominate a working class candidate in a "winnable" seat, but almost invariably without success.

Discussion: THE INFLUENCE OF PRESSURE GROUPS ON THE GOVERNMENTAL PROCESS

September 12—Morning Session
Dr. Pendelton Herring, *Chairman*

Professor Ehrmann: It has been proposed that we consider the next two topics of the program together. By discussing simultaneously the influence of interest groups on legislatures and on the administration we may gain a better view of the relationship between groups and the total governmental process. My introductory suggestions will therefore refer to both parliaments and bureaucracy.

(1) The central problem here is obviously that of group "access." The term, while now in fairly common usage, is vague; the variables that determine the ease or the difficulties of group access to the centers of public decision-making need to be analyzed. Only then differences existing between countries or, again, in the same country at various periods, can be explained.

(2) In most countries the role of parliament in the rule-making process has declined, and more particularly so in the field of economic and social legislation. While this has led to a modification of group activities in the legislatures it has not necessarily diminished their interventions in parliament. Among the factors that need to be discussed I mention only the following: (a) Which are the groups that are still particularly interested in contacts with members of parliament? (b) How important for pressure groups are parliamentary committees which of course play a different role in different systems? (c) In parliamentary systems, do the interest groups intervene at the time when cabinets are formed or forced out? (d) Are there significant differences in federal and state legislatures?

(3) We probably want to combine the discussion of economic councils and their role in the legislative process with what is generally called "administrative pluralism," i.e., the participation of interest groups in the activities of regulatory agencies or of similar boards. Especially of the latter the country reports give a very different evaluation. Where Prof. Djordjevic speaks about a "flowering of democracy," Prof. Lavau sees a burdensome interference with the administrative process, and a dangerous diffusion of governmental responsibility.*

* See above, p. 197 and p. 60.

269

(4) Attention must be given to the influence of groups on cabinet ministers as head of administrative departments, and on their "kitchen cabinets" such as the French *cabinet du ministre*. Are there variations when the executive possesses more or less extensive decree powers?

(5) The most important questions determining the relationship between interest groups and bureaucracy appear to be the following: (a) methods of recruitment, training, promotion of civil servants, and, on the other end, what the French call the *pantouflage:* the transfer of civil servants to positions in fields well cultivated by pressure groups; (b) differences which may exist between the access to old-established administrations and to newer, less formalized agencies; some departments, such as those of industrial production, agriculture and perhaps labor, are often described as pleading the cause of special interests within the bureaucracy; (c) the impact of traditions of political neutrality vs. political commitment of the bureaucracy.

(6) In the general field of rule-making the possible influence of organized interests on decisions rendered by the courts and quasi-judicial agencies is largely unexplored but worthy of study.

Professor Blaisdell: May I add to the suggestions for discussion an elementary but important point? We must remember that the participation of interest groups in the political process is at all times tremendously influenced by events external to that process. I am thinking here of the period following World War I and the great depression of the 30's as examples.

Professor Chester: I would like to suggest yet another point for consideration. There is a difference of access depending on the level of government. Contrast, for instance, British local government with the central government. In Parliament there is no committee system equivalent to that of the United States. Access to Parliament therefore must be channelled through an individual Member of Parliament. At the local government level, however, interest groups may have a chance to present their views when a local inquiry is held in town planning cases.

Professor Townsley: In Australia, certain interest groups are directly represented in the legislature, such as the trade unions through the Labour Party, agriculture through the Country Party. But interest groups also apply pressure from the outside. The tendency is to work on the cabinet rather than on Parliament or on an individual member of Parliament. Access to the public service is more difficult to detect. Obviously, when the civil service frames rules that are of interest to groups, the latter find it desirable to contact the administrations concerned. Many informal contacts are established in Canberra, especially at the Hotel Canberra, where most members of Parliament, as well as cabinet ministers, reside. It is generally assumed that numerous and important political decisions are reached on the premises of this hotel.

Professor Heckscher: I would like to ask Professor Chester whether appeals made by pressure groups informally to a minister and those made openly and publicly lead to different results? In the latter case, public opinion becomes involved which means that even if the minister's reaction is unfavorable, the request may still have some weight. Where access is private, possible advantages may be derived from the fact that the cabinet minister could give way more easily.

In Sweden and Finland, we have the concept of "remisses" which is unique and untranslatable and which I have described in my paper.*

Prof. Chester: My point was that inasmuch as the British system provides no direct method of access to Parliament, it is quite natural for a Member of Parliament to say openly that he defends the cause of a certain interest. Especially groups without private access to a ministry or those who want to play on public opinion prefer to have their case presented in this way.

Professor McKenzie: May I add a footnote here? Though it is true that the House of Commons committees do not listen to interest groups, political party committees do hold private hearings so that there is a chance for each group to put its case before both parties. These hearings are strictly secret and are covered by the Parliamentary Privilege.

Professor Finer: The party meetings are indeed *very* secret. But in general, it seems to me, that observers outside Great Britain do not pay enough attention to the fact of bills in the standing committee stage. By examining the proceedings of the committees one can readily see that interest groups are responsible for many changes in the bill. This role of interest groups is not regarded as sinister but rather as important and necessary.

Professor Akzin: When the celebrated village idiot was asked how he had managed to find a stray cow, he replied, "I asked myself where I would go if I were the cow." What we have to do is to put ourselves in the place of the interest group. If you had the ear of the minister involved, would it not be simplest to make use of that? On the other hand, when the interest group goes before the public, great effort and great expense are involved, and the opposition has an opportunity to present counter arguments.

I might be introducing a value judgment here, but I would say that

---

* See above p. 96.

from the point of view of democratic government we ought to prefer the system of public access to the informal or private access.

Professor Heckscher: I can see some reasons why interest groups would like to have publicity even when they have the ear of the minister: they may want public action for future reference so that they can refer back to a promise or the like. Interest group leaders also often wish to show their members what they have been doing. Of course, if it is a small group, word can be passed informally but if a large group is involved, publicity may be an important device of informing the membership.

Professor Beer: I would like to raise a question regarding the access of organized interests to elected representatives.

In any modern society, many interest groups which are concerned with policy will be involved in the governmental process in one way or another. I suggest that this problem of access is most easily settled where the influence of the Rousseauean theory of representation is least developed. And I am using Rousseau merely as a symbol, for in the United States the Populist or Jacksonian theory is rather similar.

When we compare the House of Commons with Congress, we see that in the former many interest groups are directly represented, while in Congress few have such representation. Lawyers predominate in Congress. The difference of attitudes of Members of Congress and Members of Parliament in regard to interest groups emerges from an analysis of the biographies which the representatives contribute to official publications both in the United Kingdom and the United States. The House of Commons' biographies stress the Members' interest group affiliation. The members of Congress, however, mention their membership in fraternal organizations, their law degrees or other studies, but seldom interest group affiliation. In this respect the United States resembles France.

A typical statement reflecting the American attitude towards interest group representation was a remark which Harry Truman made recently to reporters upon his return from a trip abroad. When asked for his comments on the present administration in Washington he said something like: "It's time to take the government out of the hands of the pressure groups and put it into the hands of the people." This standard American cliché is typical for our attitudes towards interest group representation.

If we compare such an outlook with that held in Sweden—and I would ask Professor Heckscher whether that is true—it seems that there the Rousseauean view concerning the evilness of the "little societies" does not prevail.

Dr. Hirsch-Weber: Distrust of interest groups emanates not only from Rousseau's theory of representation, but also from other theories of the state. In Germany the myth of a superhuman state facing the individual is not yet dead. Such a conception of the state leaves little room for the activity of interest groups. On the other hand, there is the view, which has found expression in the Basic Law of the Bonn Republic, that in a democracy the parliamentarian is "responsible only to his conscience," wherefore he should not be subject to party discipline or any other kind of pressure. Others regard pressure group activity, admittedly or not, as an expression of class interests and find it legitimate, especially if it emanates from their own class. You even find remnants of the medieval corporatist theory of the state, which would give interests their constitutional representation if they fit into the desired pattern.

How do members of the Federal Parliament themselves feel about the pressure from interest groups? Two examples I know of personally may provide some insight, but they are perhaps untypical:

(1) One deputy, a Socialist and Professor of one of the social sciences, was outraged by pressures from a pharmacist who threatened to induce his association to have its membership vote against him if he did not take a favorable stand on a certain issue. He asked the lobbyist to leave his office.

(2) A prominent industrialist who has been a member of parliament refused to be a candidate again, partly because he felt that the influence of interest groups in public life was becoming too great.

Professor Krusius-Ahrenberg: There is much prejudice in Finnish public opinion against interest groups, partly because of the heavy pressures of post-war years but partly because of the old ideas of representative government which are still going strong. Many people also object to the strict party vote in parliament and there are deputies who share this opinion.

We too have the system of "remissers" referred to by Mr. Heckscher, but the frequent hearings of pressure group representatives by parliamentary committees are far more important. Any member of a Committee may suggest that a certain interest organization be heard, and this suggestion will be accepted. In addition to the hearings there are other forms of contact—travels arranged for the Committee members' information, etc.

Professor Almond: I wonder to which extent over-lapping membership in interest groups, parliament, and government agencies can truly be defined as "access" to parliament and to these agencies. This raises an important problem for research. In the past, when it has been found that memberships did in fact overlap, this was interpreted as indicating interest group representation in Parliament or in a given agency. I do not believe this can always be so construed. Even a trade union member who is a member of parliament has to distinguish between his two roles.

Professor Neumann: The present discussion illustrates the difficulty of genuinely comparative observations. A reference to developments in Germany may serve as an illustration.

Here the after-effects of an authoritarian system are still felt. The persistent theory of the all-powerful state is reflected in the attitude toward bureaucracy, which is regarded as the safeguard of neutrality and the national interest above the party factions. Such an attitude has also prevented a proper recognition of the interrelations of interest groups and political parties. In fact it has created a schizophrenia of accepted beliefs and political practices. The best illustration could be given in Weimar's constitutional definition of the parliamentary deputy as being the free representative of his conscience alone (article 21), while in reality he was not at all elected as a free individual but via Proportional Representation in fact very often put on the party list as a representative of specific interests. Indeed, the concrete character of "representation" in the different nations must be spelled out, if one is to define clearly the intricate intermeshing of politics and political interest groups.

The same *caveat* may be in order in respect to the diverse role of Economic Parliaments, in accordance with the place assigned to them in the different national systems and ideologies. Though such bodies may be useful as supplementary advisory councils for national legislation, wherever they are introduced in place of political parliaments, they decree the end of democracy. The "expert" character of occupational representatives limits their authority and naturally suggests the creation above them of a political apex which claims to represent the whole of the nation. Bismarck and Mussolini were not accidentally the champions of a chamber of corporations and the declared enemies of political parties.

Dr. Herring: I believe an underlying theme has been provided by Professor Beer when he referred to the various theories of representation. In our further discussions we might keep in mind the importance of these theoretical implications.

Professor Webb: When considering different theories of representation, we must not lose sight of the prevailing economic climate. Both in Australia and New Zealand, a Member of Parliament might pridefully identify himself as a member of a trade-union or a grazier association but he would be reluctant to admit connection with a manufacturer's group.

Professor Cole: To return for a moment to a point raised by Professor Neumann, I would agree that often the motivation for the establishment of an Economic Council or other types of functional representation stems from a desire of the "authoritarian" to check or limit the role of parliaments and to extend the competences of government. But sometimes such forms of interest representation are suggested in order to make more effective the work of parliaments and to limit the role of the state. I believe that the history of Germany from Bismarck's abortive effort to set up a permanent economic council for the whole of the empire to the present day will provide examples of both types of motivation.

Dr. Hirsch-Weber: In the Federal Republic there is presently some aversion to "direct" democracy because the use Hitler made of the referendum. Also the Weimar Republic's experience with the referendum is generally considered to have been unfortunate, though I personally would take exception to such a conclusion.

Similarly many people in West Germany feel that the government should have sufficient authority and that Parliament as a representative of the people should not be subjected to outside pressure.

The debate on cartelization provides a good example of camouflage of interest group tactics in the German Parliament. Everyone knew that the most influential sectors of industry wanted cartels, and that the Federation of German Industry had used pressure to have them legalized; however, an amendment favoring cartels was introduced not by a representative of industry but by a member elected from a Bavarian rural district who had no particular knowledge of nor interest in cartels.

As to an Economic Council (*Wirtschaftsrat*), the trade unions would like to see it established in a more efficient and powerful form than it existed under the Weimar Republic. The employers' association are not opposed to the creation of such a council, and the chancellor too expressed his willingness to have it established. However, as he would not grant the unions as strong a representation in the council as they would like it, the unions are not enthusiastic to have a *Wirtschaftsrat* called into existence under present conditions. Because it is feared that the council might try to dominate parliament, opinion in general is not too enthusiastic to have a *Wirtschaftsrat* which would be more than a mere forum expressing the groups' views.

Professor Vito: The function of Economic Councils can be interpreted in a number of different ways:

(a) We have Professor Neumann's description of how they have been planned in Germany in by-gone days to reduce the political power of parties and parliament. I believe this has little present application.

(b) The Economic Council can also be conceived as a means of reducing the direct intervention of the state in economic policies, as Professor Cole mentioned. Interest groups are invited to express their views and to collaborate with governmental agencies.

(c) A third concept has its basis in the changing economic structure of the contemporary world. The decline of laissez-faire and the rise of the welfare state have made it more and more difficult for parliament to legislate rationally on economic matters. Under such conditions the Economic Council can be useful as a device:

(1) to enable the government to draw on people with experience,

(2) to provide an opportunity for the government to recognize the legitimacy of interest groups and to encourage them,

(3) to control pressure groups not by legislation but by making their activities public. The Economic Council can help integrating groups into the economic life. For when an issue arises, these groups are obliged to state their views publicly, which makes a certain control over them possible.

The theory of Rousseau would be justified only if you ignore groups and consider governmental action in a social vacuum. Recognizing rather than ignoring the legitimacy of groups will result in an effective discharge of its economic functions by the state.

Though pressure groups have been studied scarcely in Italy, there is a widespread belief that the more extensive the legislation on economic matters, the more legitimate interests are endangered and must be given the possibility to state their views. The Italian Economic and Social Council, provided for in the Constitution, will start operating in a few months and will consist of representative of employers, employees, agricultural, commercial, banking, insurance and many groups which have an interest in the economic activity of the state. This type of Council could be used to control pressure groups and to clarify many controversial questions.

In conclusion, I believe the real danger of such councils is not that they will strengthen pressure groups, but that they may not work.

Professor Heckscher: I would like to make several points: In any country with a strong party system, the ability of groups to exert influence on parliament or the cabinet is limited.

There exists, I believe, a significant difference between countries where those pressure groups have been in the foreground that are dominated by non-democratic or even anti-democratic interests such as banks and industry, and between countries where the more "democratic" interest groups, such as the trade unions, have a significant role. Perhaps studies would show that at least in the past in the United States the greatest pressure has come from undemocratic business groups. Differing national experiences would then account for different national attitudes in regard to interest groups.

Though there is a long tradition of civil liberties in the Scandinavian countries, genuine democratic representation in parliament is of rather recent date. Previously unrepresented groups have won a hearing in parliament through such organizations as the trade unions. In the 19th century, when the parliament represented rather narrow special interests, the trade unions could justifiably say they were the spokesmen for the people to a far greater degree than parliament. In many other European countries during the same period even the bureaucracy was more representative of the people than parliament.

One can cite three important ideological attitudes: (1) The old *conservative* attitude was based on the principle that the State had a mythical personality and could negotiate with the Estates which were representative of interests. Here the individual is relatively unimportant. (2) The *liberal* attitude claimed that the individual could enter into direct relations with the state by means of parliamentary representation as well as through an increasingly liberal economic system. (3) The *Socialist* or *Marxist* attitude, denouncing both of the above as buncombe, claimed that economic power alone is of real importance and that neither individual representation nor political devices can obliterate that fact. According to this view, trade unions and cooperatives would acquire not only economic but also political power and face the state as equal partners. (Of course, in Marx's theory the state will eventually disappear). This view was at the basis of much reform legislation in Western Europe.

Professor Leiserson: May I comment on the method of our discussion. We started out by considering interest group representation in the legislatures in descriptive, behaviorist terms. A historical perspective was introduced by Professor Beer. I suggest a third level of analysis for which political science is groping in the present atmosphere of tension between the behaviorists and the traditionalists. We are discussing here the institutional assumptions of a given political system. In the United States the theory of representation underlying the Constitution of 1787 never adopted the Rousseauean nor the medieval nor the early Whig-

Tory views, but rested on a mechanical basis. The President was conceived as an expert, a nonpartisan magistrate, who would impartially enforce the law on behalf of the community as a whole. In the making of law, the Senate would represent the propertied, professional and better-educated classes, the House of Representatives the masses of people. The relationship between these elements in the formal governmental structure was supposed to be regulated by the "checks-and-balance" equilibrium principle, modified of course by the powers of the states under the federal system. The closest approximation to an explicit theory of representation at that time, which was never really agreed to but comes very close to explaining the American conception of how group interests in society can be expressed was James Madison's famous No. 10 paper in the *Federalist*. The complexities of Madison's formulation of the relations between social structure (factions) and the governmental processes of lawmaking (the Constitution) have never been satisfactorily unravelled in political theory.

Professor Finer: Popular beliefs about the way a government operates, or should operate, are themselves political forces which will buttress (or disturb) the political system and the distribution of power and authority. It does not matter whether such beliefs are philosophically false—what is important is whether they are accepted. The concepts of Rousseau or of Jackson are such beliefs and form a kind of political "myth."

Now, parts 1 and 2 of my paper* are purely factual descriptions of the interest groups at work in the British system; but I felt that if I ended my paper there I would leave the quite false impression that total anarchy prevails. Therefore, I added part 3 which discusses the "Lobby and the Public Interest".

Groups do exist in every political system, but they never operate entirely in a vacuum. They operate within the network of institutions, procedures and shared beliefs. In some countries these institutions and procedures have struck little root; and the shared beliefs are shadowy or non-existent. Here the consensus that integrates society has dissolved with a result that the pressure groups are free to pursue their divisive policies without restraint. In such cases—e.g., in the Middle East—they are genuinely disintegrative. In Western countries, and certainly in Great Britain, one prevailing myth, or shared belief, is that there is a "public interest" which is different from and transcends sectional or group interests. The question is, what are the *criteria* of such a "public interest"? I have made the habit recently, whenever I have met a former

* See above, p. 117.

minister to ask what criteria he used in deciding that such and such a decision was "in the public interest". I have not yet met one who has been able to clearly describe these criteria.

The truth is that there are two extreme positions as to the nature of these "public interests". In the first place there is the notion of Rousseau that the public interest is quite distinct from the sum of particular interests. It transcends them, is different from them, and if it happens to coincide with the sectional interest of any one group this is purely accidental. On the other hand we have the theory of Bentham. The notion here is that the public interest is the aggregate of the maximum satisfactions that can be afforded to each particular interest. Calhoun merely carried this Benthamite view to its extreme conclusion when he argued that each sectional group must agree before any common policy might legitimately be pursued. I am inclined to believe that although the British public firmly believe in Rousseau's view that the public interest transcends any particular interests, the practical administrator and minister tends *in fact* to work in the manner of Bentham and tries to reconcile the clashing interests of particular groups in such a way as to make all of them as happy as they can possibly be, given the fact that they have to co-exist with their competitors and rivals.

Now in Britain there are, of course, many groups which vie with each other for political advantage and the larger ones may attempt to crush the smaller. The administrator tries to reconcile these conflicting claims. "Little birds in a nest must agree" (an English nursery slogan) is characteristic of empirical Benthanism. When he tries to conciliate group claims, the British administrator is motivated by Bentham's view of the public interest.

Professor Lavau: While Rousseau's influence on French politics has been great, I believe that there has been a tendency to exaggerate it. We must distinguish between the theoretical contribution furnished by Rousseau to French politics and between his impact on the functioning of the political system. Political ideology is strongly marked by Rousseau. In theory all political institutions rest on Rousseau's concept and are supposedly organized to represent the general will. Theoretically the French deputy is not simply the representative of his constituency but the voice of a larger community. Yet, however important the ideology, it is contradicted by reality. The drama and indeed the tragedy of French politics is that we live under a theoretical myth which everyone must accept but that the political facts have nothing to do with this myth.

French parliament expresses and represents sectional claims and the needs of various groups. The administration is more or less the guardian of the general interest actually resisting the sectionalism and the demagogery of parliament. Even the deputies themselves count on the administration to provide a brake on excessive demands made by parliament. Not the deputies but the administrators can afford to be Jean-Jacques' disciples. It is true that since almost every deputy is elected by the most diverse elements he cannot function as the exclusive representative of a single group. Therefore, parliament does not represent exactly the social classes or the various interest groups in France. In order to correct this inexact representation, the Economic Council and the multitude of consultative boards have been created.

But all this could not satisfy the organized interests so that pressure groups have now infiltrated the governmental process on all levels: parliament, cabinet and administration. Parliamentary committees are an important channel for group influence, also because operations are mostly secret and because it is sufficient to exercise influence on the few actually active committee members.

It is commonly said that there are two types of cabinet ministers in France: (1) the lawyer-administrator who represents his administrative subordinates, and (2) the politician who attempts to excerize pressure on the administration. While this is generally exact, it is somewhat oversimplified. Also the *cabinet du ministre* lends itself to pressure group activity. To give but one example about which I have personal information: the so-called Pinay Accord dealing with Franco-Moroccan affairs was entirely negotiated not by Pinay but by a dozen young men in different ministerial cabinets and the representatives of the associations particularly interested in this agreement.

Generally speaking the classical and traditional administrations have been more or less impervious to group action. They are willing to receive information but are not vulnerable to pressure. However, a new development has made some administrations more accessible to interest groups. Special committees have been formed and been attached to such ministries as Agriculture, Public Works, National Defense, etc. to advise the appropriate minister. These committees, which operate secretly, have provided an opportunity for pressure groups to make narrow interests prevail.

Discussion: THE INFLUENCE OF PRESSURE GROUPS ON THE GOVERNMENTAL PROCESS
(Continued)

September 13—Morning Session

Professor Chester, Chairman

Professor Akzin: I propose that we open this morning's discussion by raising the following question: To what extent do interest groups converge on the professional bureaucracy rather than on the political heads of the executive?

Professor Blaisdell: According to our original agenda we were to discuss the influence of pressure groups *on* the bureaucracy. More accurately we should consider the influence of pressure groups on *and in* the bureaucracy.

Bailey's case study of the passage of the Employment Act of 1946 contains interviews with Congressmen. In one case Bailey concluded that pressure from interest groups was felt not so much *on* as *in* the congressman.

Pressures are channelized because of the growth of rule-making by regulatory agencies. These agencies hold open hearings and the whole process of listening to interest groups has assumed a high degree of respectability. The legal profession has an important place in this process. There are, in addition, other channels through which an appeal can be made if the interest groups are not satisfied with the decision of the regulatory agency. The White House can be approached, informally and unofficially. A group can take its problem to an individual member of the House or Senate and try to persuade him to put pressure on the agency. An appeal can even be made to the courts.

A different way of interest groups working *within* the bureaucracy is to have a group representative appointed to the board of a regulatory agency. Interestingly enough, a former Congressman who is now on the board of such an agency was complaining recently about pressures on board members by Congressmen. Another episode involved the State Department's negotations with the Netherlands regarding civil aeronautics regulations which eventually permitted the Dutch Airline to operate to certain American cities. The air lobby complained that if they had just had some clue during the proceedings of what the Department was considering they would have known *how* to lobby.

I have differentiated here between administrative agencies and those regulatory agencies with rule-making power. In the United States this is an important distinction to draw because the second category has a great deal more discretion.

This whole matter has been systematized through the Bureau of the Budget, the budget preparation, and the entire appropriation process. Our colleague from Japan has pointed to the existence in his country of a "sub-system"; such a system also operates in the United States. There is a community of interest between the Congressional appropriations subcommittees, business in the executive branch, and the pressure groups concerned with the same subject matter. One example of this is so-called "pork-barrel" legislation. Such legislation provides a good example of all these groups working together and the combination is called the "lobby that can't be beat." Another example of "systematization" is to be found in the Defense Department budget. Two-thirds of the federal budget are allocated to this Department and the system is so intricate and complicated that the congressional committees just do not have the time to study the matter carefully. Since World War II interest groups with primary or secondary interest in defense appropriations have proliferated. Hence, one observer has stated that Congress has lost control over the part of the budget that goes into defense appropriations.

Professor Leiserson: A consideration of the relationship between interest groups and the bureaucracy should actually precede that of the relationship between pressure groups and the legislature. We delegate to interest groups the problems of handling a great deal of our economic life. There exist, therefore, today public government and private governments each with its own bureaucracy.

In response to Professor Akzin's question as to whether non-governmental pressure groups approach the bureaucracy first or the political heads first, I would say that if an interest group has a limited objective, it is likely to prefer the legislature and establish relations with the committees of Congress. In normal times, each public department or agency tends to develop its more or less autonomous structure of power relationships with its own clientele groups. However, in periods of economic depression (1933–35) or international crisis (1941–45) government of necessity tries to unify these private and public bureaucracies into a more closely-coordinated structure of official public action (N.R.A.; W.P.B.). Dr. Griffith has characterized these sub-systems as a number of separate whirlpools of policy formation; the legislative or congressional committee structure heightens this tendency toward dispersion; one of the more vital functions of the political executive is to try to bring them together.

Dr. Hirsch-Weber: It is difficult to formulate one clear-cut answer to Professor Akzin's question. Would it not be logical to suppose that the addressees of interest groups are the persons to whom they have access, and on whom, if need be, they can put pressure? Their access may be equally easy to the political head and to the professional bureaucracy; but when it comes to using pressure, one can imagine that the political head of the administration and political appointees are more receptive than the regular civil service.

Professor Townsley: In Australia two aspects of government determine the working of pressure groups: one is the cabinet form of government and the other is the federal system.

The cabinet system makes the executive dominant within the legislature. The executive has physicially invaded the Parliament building and the cabinet ministers dominate everything. The interest groups, therefore, concentrate their efforts on the cabinet, and since we have highly disciplined parties, the elected representatives go along with the leaders of the party who are cabinet ministers.

Among the six states of the Australian federation New South Wales and Victoria are dominant to about the same degree. When interest groups do not get what they want from the federal government, they concentrate on the states because the federal government is sensitive to state opinion and political parties are dependent on their state organizations.

As far as the public service is concerned, it has a reputation for integrity and immunity from at least the evil aspects of pressure group activity. Much, of course, depends upon personal relations built up between senior public servants and representatives of groups.

Professor Heckscher: Most people think of pressure groups as working on the state, but actually the bureaucracy will also work on pressure groups in order to get their support. Therefore, Professor Akzin's question as to whether pressure groups converge on the bureaucracy rather than on the political heads is almost impossible to answer.

When there is a clash between special interests and the common good, the state first through the bureaucary and perhaps later through the ministers and the cabinet will try to get all interests groups to work together.

Professor McKenzie: What Professor Heckscher says of the collaboration between interest groups and the bureaucracy is also true in Britain. But one must remember that "ease of access" to the effective decision makers on either the executive or the bureaucratic level may carry with it certain obligations and responsibilities. The minister or civil servant may readily listen ot the views of powerful interest groups and he may in turn burden them with "confidential information" and urgent pleas for cooperation in the national interest. It is sometimes hard to say who is influencing whom.

It has been suggested that in practice the job of the elected decision-makers is merely to reconcile divergent interests, or to put it another way, that the direction in which the executive decides to move is merely the result of a parallelogram of forces (i.e., of the pressures that play upon the decision makers). But this is a grossly over-simplified view. In Britain, and I suspect in most democracies, there is at least tacit acceptance of Burkes proposition: "Your representative owes you not his industry only, but his judgment; and he betrays instead of serving you if he sacrifices it to your opinion. . . . " In our preoccupation with the legitimate role of pressure groups we should not ignore completely the importance of political leadership and of decisions taken "in the national interest".

Professor Akzin: Society is made up of interests. In considering the interrelations between interests and bureaucracy the political scientist should perhaps inquire into the reputed disinterestedness of civil servants. We investigate critically many other areas but tend to accept at its face value the doctrine of the disinterestedness of the bureaucracy. I do not mean to imply that civil servants are grafters. I accept their financial integrity. But is there really an absence of interest? Is it not likely that a sectional or some other special bias is exploiting the attitude of the civil servant? That was the sense of my original question.

Professor Almond: How are we to compare interest groups and bureaucracies in different countries? One problem is the poverty of our vocabulary to handle these questions. For example, "access" and "penetration" are good words, but inadequate to handle all the problems involved. "Access" can vary all the way from making an appearance at a hearing to a close participation in the decision-making process.

Another problem, raised by Professor Akzin, is that in making comparisons we cannot effectively isolate the bureaucracy-interest group relationship. The raw claims of interest groups are affected by what the party does and by what the legislature does. Since there is so much variety in what the parties and legislatures do in different countries, there is bound to be a difference in the impact of group actions on the bureaucracy.

Professor Beer: The point made earlier by Professor Akzin regarding the influence of pressure groups on the bureaucracy is well-taken. The story is told that when Churchill was Chancellor of the Exchequer, he stated as a categorical view of the Treasury that the government could not provide additional employment and so nothing was done to meet the growing problem of unemployment. The United States' system was more subject to pressure from interest groups and during the depression, fortunately, public loans were frequently made.

The public interest is not something that floats above human beings. If a society is highly divided, you have rival concepts instead of common premises regarding the public interest, and these rival views make reconciliation difficult. In France, for example, compromise is so arduous because of the different notions of the public interest. Under such conditions even "mere interests" are not reconciled easily.

Professor Chester: I should like to make a number of points. It must be emphasized, somewhat in opposition to what Professor Akzin has said earlier, that the bureaucracy in Great Britain does take a leading part in the formulation of policy when it advises ministers. If, however, the minister rejects the views of the civil service, the latter carries out loyally the policy of the cabinet.

In Britain at least interest groups and civil service use somewhat the same organizational terminology. Each has in its bureaucracy its own levels with the "appropriate level" chap in the ministry contacted by the "appropriate level" chap in the interest group. They talk the same language, perhaps go to the same clubs. I am speaking, of course, of the well-organized interest groups. There is thus a danger that the bureaucrats in both the interest groups and the ministry will be more influential than the elected representatives, except on matters of policy of great interest to the public.

Two illustrations regarding nationalization in Britain are of interest. The nationalization program of the Labour government caused very intense feeling in Britain as is well known. When, however, it became obvious that the Coal Nationalization Bill could not be defeated and would pass Parliament, the Coal Owners Association cooperated in the drafting of the bill by providing the particulars and the technical detail necessary to carry out the nationalization. On the other hand, when the nationalization of the iron and steel industry was in process, which of course was a much more closely contested Bill, the Iron and Steel Association refused to cooperate in the drafting. Some thought this refusal not to be "cricket", not "playing the game".

Professor Cole: I should like to raise several questions in order to broaden our discussion. What are our criteria for comparison here?

We have limited our discussion more or less to political systems with a common cultural background and have omitted governments where other kinds of access exist.

Is this concept of "access" the most useful one for comparative purposes in both "western" and "non-western" countries?

In addition, can some mention be made of "access" to the courts which we have not considered? Because of their composition the German labor courts might provide an instructive example.

Dr. Hirsch-Weber: The Prussian civil service was quite liberal up to the Bismarck era. From then on and until 1918, the civil service was in the hands of the ruling groups of Prussia; pressure groups, therefore, had to operate on a conservative bureaucracy, and one could expect that agrarian groups were successful in their demands on the bureaucracy. There is the famous case of the *Kanalrebellen*, high civil servants who were at the same time elected members of the Prussian Diet. Against the instructions of the cabinet they voted against the building of a canal, proposed by the government but opposed by agrarian interests. They were first discharged but later reinstalled and, most of them, promoted.

During the Weimar Republic, the civil service in its majority was more conservative than governments formed by the SPD and other democratic parties. To a certain extent they constituted a particular political force upholding monarchical traditions. Yet in 1920 during the Kapp Putsch, the civil servants remained loyal to the government and, by refusing to work with Kapp, they helped to save the Republic.

Today it is difficult to discern the complexion of the civil service in Western Germany. A number of law professors, for instance, criticise severely the fact that trade unionist and other members of interest groups have entered the civil service. To these critics the civil service is the only stronghold of the state, and in their views the state can be safe only with a strong civil service which owes nothing to political appointments. I personally believe that political appointments by democratic parties can help to strengthen the democratic state.

Since Professor Cole mentioned the labor courts it may be useful to say a word about their composition. On the highest court, the professional jurists are in the majority. On the lower courts, representatives of labor and management are more numerous. The presiding judge, as a rule, is a learned jurist; the two co-judges are one representative each of labor and employers. In examining some decisions, I have noticed that the lower courts are more "progressive" than the Federal Labor Court. This may be due to its composition, but it may also be a question of personalities.

Dr. Herring: I am impressed by the agreement reached in our discussion and I hesitate somewhat to raise questions that may break into the happy circle of common discourse that has been established. However, since we are all striving to understand better the nature of political relationships and of political processes, should we not ask ourselves whether interest-group analysis provides a broad enough basis for examining the problems of politics in the present-day world? Certainly it is an approach that seems well suited to the study of how men are governed, particularly in "open societies", and it also holds great promise for the comparative analysis of political processes in different countries. I think this approach by focusing attention on the interaction of interests groups—particularly organized groups—tends to take for granted the institutional setting. Is not the prevailing ideology regarded as a climate of opinion within which the political process is observed? I would suggest the hypothesis that in situations of rapid change the interest-group configuration, to the extent that it has become organized and hence bureaucratized, might not accurately reflect all the factors that should be brought under observation. For example, the significance of science in the political process should be examined not only as an interest group by noting the activities of organized scientists but also as a potent emergent institutional development, and a force that likewise has important ideological implications. How can interest-group analysis cope with such developments? Moreover, the role of individual leadership seems to be greatest in times of crisis. Both the cultural and institutional settings within which interest groups operate are highly relevant in efforts at explaining political behavior, and modern technology may be effecting the cultural context in ways not immediately reflected in traditional patterns of political interaction.

Professor Almond: In our discussion of politics, our language has been the language of structure or of institutions. The short-comings of our language become clear even when we attempt to compare pressure groups in the same culture, for example, in France and Great Britain. But when we move to the politics and the interest group situations of non-Western countries, we find our confusion compounded if we consider such situations as though they were the same as in the West. My suggestion for a solution to the problem of comparison is to think in terms of *functions* or activities. We might ask what kind of institutions perform what kind of activities: parties, pressure groups, the bureaucracy, or what? Our present political concepts are more than one and a half centuries old. The American classifications dividing government into the legislative, the administrative and the judicial branches, may not be helpful to explain mechanisms outside the culture of the West. Here is a fruitful area for a theoretical contribution and I believe that the comparative study of pressure groups might very well make this contribution.

Professor Heckscher: This is a fundamental rather than just a conceptual difference. Our discussion of interest groups pertains only to those societies where an accepted set of values exist.

Professor Iwanaga: I am much impressed with Professor Almond's point. We need a new vocabulary to cope with new problems. We in Japan often use foreign languages when we try to express new ideas and approaches. How far we could go, I am not sure. However, Professor Almond still faces the problem of how to distinguish and clarify the differences in quality of apparently similar functions arising from fundamentally different political cultures.

Professor Leiserson: I too agree with Professor Almond that the vocabulary we use does not always correspond to political reality. We do need new concepts and his suggestion that we use a functional analysis seems promising to me. What matters is that we keep clearly in mind the political function of responsibility as well as the consultation or representation of economic and social groups in the process of decision-making.

Professor Chester: May I remind the group to remain on the subject of relations between pressure groups and the bureaucracy.

Professor Lavau: When I talked of occasional resistance of the bureaucracy to government, I had in mind actual occurrences. In theory of course the administration executes the wishes of the cabinet and of parliament. But in practice, the civil servants sometimes feel that they have to prevent the fantasies of the Assembly from being translated into policies.

Despite the structure of the French system, civil servants are often in direct contact with interest groups. In some ministries, such as Agriculture, Public Works or National Defense, interest groups find more outright support than in others.

In budget discussions, a minister may defend the position of "his" particular interest group, which leads, at times, to a battle between two ministers representing different interests. But even when the administration defends special interests, the position of the groups is not presented in undiluted, but rather in moderated and mitigated form.

Professor Blaisdell: To compare the situation described by Professor Lavau with the attitude of civil servants in the Unitel States is difficult. I know of some instances where the civil service has taken action contrary to the wishes of the President or Congress. But this is by no means the rule; possibly it occurs only in exceptional cases.

I am concerned by misleading statements that pressure groups have become part of the administration. Though the groups are certainly powerful in the United States, I would hesitate to call them part of the administration. Perhaps one could say that they are part of the administrative process.

Professor Leiserson: Traditionally the bureaucracy in the United States does not consider it its political function to define the public interest. They are concerned with the political consensus at a higher level.

As to the political role of the administration in the United States, it simply does not enjoy the same status as the other formal political institutions. Therefore, a bureaucrat would be extremely careful about setting himself up against the politician, the elected representative.

Professor Macpherson: Professor Leiserson, you said that the American administration had no *tradition* of the concept of the public interest. Can one develop?

Professor Leiserson: Maybe what I said could lead to a misinterpretation. We do have conflict of interest laws negatively defining certain types of official conduct as not conducive to the public interest.

Professor Chester: In Great Britain the civil service is thought to have a different, a longer term, point of view and not to be swayed by momentary interest to the same extent as politicians.

Professor Finer: May I tie this to an institutional point? In the British parliamentary regime the minister takes a personal moral responsibility for any decision. It would never do for him to blame—or to praise—either the civil servants or the interest group from whom the idea was said to have emanated. To try to shelter behind these would be to commit political suicide.

Discussion: THE OVER-ALL EFFECTS OF PRESSURE GROUPS ON POLITICAL CONSENSUS AND DECISION MAKING—RESULTS OF A COMPARATIVE STUDY OF PRESSURE GROUPS FOR THE ADVANCEMENT OF POLITICAL THEORY

September 13—Afternoon Session
Professor James K. Pollock, *Chairman*

Professor Ehrmann: If we compare, during this last session of our debates, the questions raised in the working paper with the manifold observations made in the country reports and during our discussions, we may conclude that, although many questions remain unanswered, our data have become far more concrete. We are, it seems to me, at least closer to a conceptualization of interest group activities and therefore on the way to a more meaningful and more rigorous comparison.

The following remarks are meant to serve as an introduction to a discussion both of the over-all effect of interest group activities and of the value which the comparative study of groups may have for political theory.

When trying to determine "over-all effects" we must ask whether the influence exercised by pressure groups can at all be measured. Our friend Eldersveld, it is true, has called for a research design that would permit such a measurement on a comparative basis, and we may wish to discuss his suggestion. I personally would like to register doubts whether power and influence can ever be analyzed quantitatively and whether groups can even be assigned a "power quotient".

Am I mistaken if I have noted throughout our proceedings the multiform but definite expression of a political postulate which at the same time has important theoretical implications? The activities of interest groups, most of us seem to think, can hardly be curtailed; yet the processes of democracy should not be impaired by group pressures.

Certainly, the classical theories of representation have been found insufficient for a realistic study of politics. The interest group "system" is with us whether we want it or not and demands at least equal attention to the party system. In Professor Heckscher's analysis group activities may in fact introduce desirable elements of "direct democracy" into an otherwise representative system. But the decisive question still requires an answer, namely whether political institutions conceived in an age of individualism and liberalism are able to counter-balance strongly organized interests, and to ensure the prevalence of the "public interest."

Much of what has been submitted here is based, I believe, on the assumption that an equilibrium, a parallelogram of forces, as some have called it, is desirable. But does its emergence not rather depend on factors such as consensus, moderation, the "countervailing power" of unorganized interests, the courage of politicians, the resilience of administrators, in short on factors compared to which the behavior of groups themselves is only secondary? It might also be necessary to ask whether and under which conditions the constantly renewed quest for a precarious equilibrium could actually result in negative immobilism.

In terms of political theory does the emphasis on a comparative study of interest groups merely herald a return to pluralism? Certainly the very kind of material we are working with suggests the acceptance of much of what is characteristic of analytical pluralism. But are we willing to espouse also that brand of philosophical pluralism which considers the state just one association among others? Moreover, on the European continent pluralism has frequently traveled in corporatist clothes. We should at least be aware of the political implications of such an approach.

All this raises numerous questions of methodology on which we have touched but which need much further elaboration. In the words of Professor Almond, should we (and I would add, are we able to) seek generalizations about human behaviour and social institutions which are not culture-bound? Can we test a generalization developed in one culture by examining to which extent it holds true in another? However, that may be, we need to obtain the maximum of comparable data. We also need to add to the material gathered in Western countries the experiences of non-Western cultures; we must know more about the impact of pressure groups on international politics.

The Executive Council of the International Political Science Association has already decided that some of the sessions of the Congress to be held in Rome in 1958 should be devoted to a further discussion of pressure groups studies. An appropriate title might be: "New Dimensions for Comparative Research and Political Theory by the Study of Interest Groups."

Professor Webb: There are two words Professor Ehrmann has used as if they were the same, namely "consensus" and the "public interest." These terms will always crop up together in discussion of this kind and I suggest that the two ideas while interrelated are nevertheless distinct. We have a set of existing value judgments about the political system and the political process which we can regard as consensus. Public interest as a specific context is distinct from this. Consensus gives a broad framework within which pressure groups work in the political system. The term "public interest" is used extensively by the courts and involves the process of creating an equilibrium between group conflicts. An example of what I mean can be found in the Australian Broadcasting System's announcement that it would treat all pressure groups equally. But Parliament said the churches were in a special classification and should have free time. This was a decision by which Parliament expressed "consensus."

Professor Djordjevic: I wish to make some general remarks on the problem of the political significance of interest groups. I hope that what I have to say may prove of some importance to cooperative efforts aimed at advancing political theory. I will not repeat what I wrote in my paper and, of course, I am not able to give answers to every question formulated by our rapporteur.

The systematic but rather empirical study of interest groups is of relatively recent date; it was initiated in the U.S. some fifty years ago. But the interest in interest groups is as old as human society. From Aristotle to Marx, all great political and social philosophers have given us insight into the existence and role of interest groups as well as into the relationship between them and between power and politics. This is not surprising. Nor have these writers invented interest groups, which are in truth the very essence of political power and policy. Their existence and role are not a matter of social pathology, but of social and political anatomy and physiology. However, of course, pathologic developments are not excluded from any body, including the body politic.

It is true that this very fact was more or less concealed during the history of human society. First it was hidden by the simplistic and relatively static character of non-developed societies. Afterwards and until our days either the absolutist and totalitarian structure and ideology of the state, or a metaphysical and idealistic political philosophy, or finally formalist and legalistic theories proved unable to reflect the reality of the social structure, to analyze the essence of power and to grasp the real meaning of political society.

Modern society is a dynamic body, complicated and diversified in its structure, full of conflicting and even antagonistic interests. Consequently, the political affirmation, the role and influence of different interest groups are the general tendency of human society. The form of that affirmation, the degree of influence and the political importance of interest groups vary from one country to the other and within the same country, under changing historical conditions. But the growing political role of interest groups is a general trend. I would say that what is involved here is not only a question of pressure on formally constituted power, but the very structure of political society and power. We have interest groups operating from the outside and from within. Who would assert that parliament and government, even when based on the classical theory of political representation are assemblies of angles inspired by the Hegelian "general idea" or the general interest of solidaristic philosophy?

We have to distinguish, of course, between the direct and indirect, open and hidden, rationalized or mythical, developed or non-developed influence of interest groups. It is also necessary to stress that we must carefully avoid any generalization which is not based on a thorough and unbiased study of the social basis and the political premises cf a given political system.

In Yugoslavia we may say that the political affirmation and the growing role of interest groups within the producers' and workers' councils and other organs of social self-government attest today to more or less effective but immanent trends of a socialist political system, based on the common ownership of the means of production. This society is not, as some think, "monolithically" harmonious and homogeneous, but in fact heterogeneous and full of contradictions. Among the contradictions, that between general and individual interests remains the most important. Building the self-government of producers' and the decentralized social self-government in the framework of a socialist society involves the more or less recognized necessity of checking both the bureaucracy and the monopolistic position of the ruling political organizations. What we have is merely the framework of a socialist society and only under these concrete social and political conditions can the institutionalization of definite interest groups be considered as leading to democracy.

Starting from these asumptions I believe that the study of interest groups on a cooperative basis is necessary and possible: I am suggesting that concrete and empirical studies of pressure groups be continued; but these studies, instead of being solely pragmatic, have to be guided by certain general assumptions based on previous studies and on a more comprehensive conception of the nature of political society. In connection with this, I think that identification or, better to say, conceptualization of interest groups is only one of the tasks. The functional approach, suggested by Professor Almond, is a sound idea.

While it is to be expected that a comparative study of interest groups would make some contributions to political theory and to a better knowledge of society, state and politics, the importance of such results depends for a large part on the quality of our work. But on the basis of already known results, this study is promising. I have emphasized in my paper some positive theoretical implications of an inquiry into interest groups for the study of the political process.

The study of interest groups has already contributed to a better understanding of the failure of all metaphysical, idealist, fetishist, apolitical and formalistic theories concerned with state and politics. Here lies, in my opinion, the real contribution which American political science has furnished. We have to be constantly aware of the fact that many of us are more or less under the influence of traditional theories and old stereotypes. Ideas too are mental or, if you wish, intellectual pressure groups of their own, prying on our mind and consciousness.

The recognition of the place and the political role played by the conflicting interests of various interest groups has been of great value for the creative development of socialist political theory—to long sterilized by the absolutist and fetishist Stalinist dogmatism. Such a recognition has opened the road to free and daring socialist thinking in Yugoslavia and to the democratization of the socialist society. Many speculative generalizations on the relationship between the study of interest groups and the advancement of political theory are possible. My paper submitted to this conference has engaged is some such generalizations. After the successful meeting which we are closing today, I have learned to be more cautious. The only scientifically valuable generalizations are those arising from concrete knowledge and data; as Hegel said, only the concrete and not the speculative generalizations can be truthful.

Fruitful generalizations, however, are to be expected from a comparative study using the methods which I have outlined. That such expectations are justified this meeting of 14 nations, organized by the International Political Science Association, has once more proved.

Professor Finer: Coming back to the question with which Professor Ehrmann opened today's meeting, I would like to ask whether it is even desirable to *try* to measure the influence of groups. There are two chief difficulties in the way of such measurement, one of which is statistical and the other philosophical. As to the first, what I mean is that we have no quantitative index of power or pressure. As to the second, it is very hard to find any scientific proof that a particular measure is *due* to the particular pressure of a specific group. In general no such causal relationship can be established. And even if we did establish the relationship (by asking the people concerned) we would have to know whether the group was merely "stating its case" or whether it went so far as to threaten sanctions. Nor do we know how much of what the group wanted it actually got. Furthermore, sometimes many groups exercise pressure simultaneously and it proves impossible to identify which of the many pressures was the effective one.

I have been working on the politics of transport nationalization for some time now and I can cite an example from this. In the original bill of 1946 the Labour Government proposed to restrict the right of private industry to carry its own goods in its own vehicles. The Government was put under great pressure to omit this restrictive clause. The Trade Unions concerned split, some being for the restriction and some favoring its removal. Likewise, the Labour Party was split on this matter. Industry of course wanted the restrictive clause deleted. And it is said that the Co-operatives also wanted it deleted and that they brought pressure in this direction. I have made very extensive inquiries but the net up-shot is that the decision to remove this clause from the bill was a cabinet decision. The reasons are not precisely known and in these circumstances it was impossible for me to show which of the many pressures decided this outcome.

This raises the whole question of method. For, even in the above case, a well informed guess can be made, but the best way of reaching this kind of informed guess is the technique of the case study as used by Stephen Bailey in his *Congress makes a Law* and this is the technique I myself am trying to use.

Now in my particular study the results are rather interesting from a methodological point of view. Despite pressures the truckers got no concessions; the shippers on the contrary got nearly all they wanted despite Trade Union opposition and despite the fact that they were "capitalists" and that the Labour Government was in power. Again the local authorities also received most of what they wanted, although they applied practically no pressure in the normal sense of the term. Despite all my research I find it almost impossible to determine why some of these groups were successful and why some of them were not. As I say, at the best I can make some informed guesses.

May I add one final point. If, as I suggested, the case study technique is the appropriate one to determine questions of this kind, we are abandoning strictly "scientific" proofs and are in effect using the historical method.

Dr. Hirsch-Weber: We may not be able to "measure" the influence of pressure groups, yet in some instances we can trace it by case studies. For instance, we can compare the government draft of a bill with its shape after its first, second and third reading before a legislature. There may be fundamental changes, and these changes may be in accord with demands of interest groups. One will also find that deputies, from one reading to the other, shift their vote on a specific issue, either when their party, or when they as individual members are won over by an interest group. This method of comparison can be supplemented by interviews with parliamentarians and lobbyists. Naturally, whether pressure was applied can seldom be found out unless it was pressure "in the open", for instance, the menace with a strike.

Returning to Professor Ehrmann's remark on equilibrium, I think that there are two problems involved in it. Just as in economic theory, in political science one often finds an underlying assumption that equilibrium is desirable. This would be a hidden value judgment, which should be stated clearly.

Leaving aside the question of value judgments, we also find that we are doing static or, at best, comparative static analyses, to borrow a concept from the economists. We assume a political system in equilibrium (which need not be identical with an optimal state!) and investigate the place of interest groups in that system. When studying the enactment of a bill, we analyse the impact of interest groups as forces disturbing the equilibrium. Once the act is passed, a new equilibrium has assumedly been reached. I believe, however, that we should go much further and seek for a more dynamic approach. Should we not try to do process-analysis taking into account the social changes brought about by interest groups? Our society is not static. The outcome of the activities of interest groups, the changes they work in the social system are as meaningful for understanding the governmental process as the things we have hitherto studied.

Professor Blaisdell: I agree with Professor Finer on the difficulty of measuring influence. An interest group is not always a pressure group. A more satisfactory term than the concept of influence is the term Bentley used fifty years ago: "Activity". Activity is the key to pressure group influence and the lack thereof.

I agree with Professor Almond that the better we can define what we are looking for, the more successful we will be. Pressure is only one form of influence, and influence is only one form of activity. We would learn more by substituting a "functional-activity" test for the test of "influence".

I also agree with Professor Cole that we should broaden our inquiry to include the courts. We tend to concentrate on the legislature, as did Pendleton Herring's early work entitled, *Group Representation Before Congress.*

In the United States, we are up against a special difficulty because we are struggling with a narrow definition of "pressure group". The courts define lobbying as exerting influence upon Congress. This is entirely unsatisfactory. As a more satisfactory definition, I would suggest "any effort to influence any governmental decision."

Professor Leiserson: If we had better tools we would use them. Do we not confuse two levels of analysis? What we are reaching for is to get beyond tracing purely empirical patterns of inter-personal relationships and to start making assumptions about relationships between public and private groups. We hope to develop the analytical process rather than having to rely wholly upon the descriptive. The problem is to find certain strategic, critical variables that will provide guides or indices to relevant facts. Scientific understanding of the political process depends upon our ability to make significant hypotheses about relationships between variables. In this process case studies, such as Odegard's study of the Anti-Saloon League, and Garceau's of the American Medical Association, provide suggestive starting points for broader analysis.

Professor Finer: Isn't this really the approach of Pareto? It gives us a set of equations, or of functional relationships consistent of a number of variables, but we can not quantify any of these variables. They remain abstract.

Professor Almond: The activities of interest groups are more complex than just the transmission of influence or pressure. One of their most important functions is the integrating or aggregating role by which narrow interests are assimilated into more general ones. The party is the main integrative agency in the political process. The interest group plays the role of an articulator of interests, but it also has an integrating function.

An example of an issue in American politics which is integrated least is the tariff problem. On other issues interest groups screen narrow interests, but this is different in regard to tariff legislation.

There are definable kinds of activity of interest groups. The functional-activity approach tries to define and to distinguish them. The particular value of this approach is that it can be used in other than Western societies and even in "underdeveloped" regions.

Professor Heckscher: How do you translate these functions from one society to another? One could show groups integrating and transmitting demands in one society, but the objects of their requests might simply not exist in another society. For example, in our society one group would integrate and transmit the ideas and aims of manual labor, but in another society the influence of manual labor might be negligible.

Professor Almond: The problems you raise are certainly pertinent. But we must consider the functional approach merely as a forward step, not as a solution. I believe that in a non-Western society you will find maybe not the same but other kinds of groups. Some societies may not have landowners as a formally-organized association, but rather a landed aristocracy, family groups, or other kinds of cliques which own land.

Professor Finer: If we use Professor Almond's functional approach taking Cyprus in the 19th century as an illustration, we would find that there were no political parties, but that the Church performed acts which elsewhere we associate with parties. The same role was played by the Church in Bulgaria under the Turks. One reason for the Church and the Army holding a political role in Spain and Portugal in the 18th century was that they were the only organized and hierarchial organizations there. They were the only possible integrating agencies and performed the functions we would seek out when using Professor Almond's approach.

Professor Almond: That is a good example. In other societies this group might be a bureaucracy.

Professor Hirsch-Weber: Are not also the functions which interest groups perform different from system to system? Certainly values, such as what constitutes "public interest" etc., and the degree of consensus about them, change. In any conclusive analysis using the functional approach we have to take into consideration the values held by interest groups as well as the functions actually performed by them.

Professor Ehrmann: Maybe at some point the study of interest groups will become secondary to the study of interests.

Professor Inoki: We in the Far East can profit by a study of pressure groups in the West. There are many parallels. For example, if in Japan the trade unions persuade the workers to surround the parliament building in a street demonstration, we know from studies that these things have happened in Western countries too.

Professor Akzin: We seem to be evolving toward a general pattern of the political process in which two fundamental units operate in the

East as well as in the West, in the present as well as in the past. (1) The individual striving for power; (2) the group striving for power. The group is united by ideological aims or by interests, whatever the connection between the two. It has money, kinship, and internal discipline as binding forces. Certain groups have developed into political parties, striving for influence in specific ways. This brings us to the question: when parties crystallize, what is the role of noncrystallized groups?

Professor Townsley: Political theory has advanced least of any area of political science in recent years. We still rely on the old philosophers and on the old concepts. These concepts are not wrong, but they need to be re-expressed in terms of our society. The greatest contributions in the last century, outside of the Marxists and the Benthamites, have been made by jurists. Today we need to re-formulate the meaning of power, of sovereignty, of law, of consent, of representation, and of the nature of society in general. The study of interest groups can make a substantial contribution to such a re-examination.

Are sovereignty and law to be found in the reconciliation of conflicting interests? Or do we find, in the Hegelian sense, the true sovereign above the conflicting interests? We still use the old-fashioned term of the public good. It there continuing validity in the concept of a higher law?

The ideas of J. S. Mill about consent and representation are no longer adequate. What we have been saying this week points the way to a re-examination, without which dated concepts may forever lose their value. Also, on the nature of power within society ideas are changing. A recent book by C. Wright Mills, *The Power Elite,* though not highly regarded by some, presents nonetheless a new approach.

Professor Chester: Professor Leiserson has talked of variables. So do the economists and they too expect them to change. I am afraid we will not make much progress until we narrow the field. What we need is an agreement on how to break the area up into segments so as to get comparisons.

Professor McKenzie: Mr. Almond's idea of using the functional approach for the comparison of groups acting in different societies is very useful indeed. But in many countries, in which almost no groundwork has yet been done in this field, we also need a great deal of straightforward descriptive and historical material.

Professor Cole: I agree with Mr. McKenzie and Mr. Chester on the need for descriptive analysis. When we search with Professor Almond for functional equivalents I believe that the bureaucracy is a most promising field which has been given little attention outside the United States. The activities of and the influence brought upon the bureaucracy lend themselves to a cross-cultural comparison as well as to descriptive and historical studies.

Professor Almond: Quite right; also for historical research the functional approach would prove helpful.

Professor Leiserson: Although factual, descriptive and case studies are needed, we must nevertheless emphasize analytical work. Notwithstanding Mr. Townsley's plea for a re-examination of old philosophies and old concepts, I would say that we must hypothesize a bit and not simply review historically the old values. Mr. Hirsch-Weber raised a question which deserves an answer; namely, whether or not pressure groups are working for the "public interest". Problems of value are of paramount importance.

Professor Pollock: Speaking about the need for "purely" descriptive work, may I add that many of our younger scholars are held back when they note how refined and sophisticated such studies are in fact. They hesitate to carry on, feeling that they may not be able to keep up to the high standards. I would never want to see the value of descriptive studies depreciated, just as I would not want to see any international study befuddled by an obscure methodological terminology.

Professor Blaisdell: What is the effect of the operation of pressure groups on the public interest? Already at that point we get into the question of values. Do they all serve or promote the public interest, or only some of them? Government committees which look into this subject tend to be partisan. In one study of "lobbying" a few years ago, the committee divided on the question of values along partisan lines.

Fortune Magazine has made the statement that some of our worst legislation has resulted from pressure group activity which, of course, is also a value judgment. George B. Galloway, during the consideration of the Reorganization of Congress Act, said that the public interest is more than just the sum of sectional or economic interests of the country. We must indeed go beyond mere analysis and delve into the question of values.

Mr. Ehrmann made the point that in certain situations the action of pressure groups may become secondary. When should the groups be ignored or by-passed? When the safety of the state is at stake? Even in a crisis some of the government's actions are of course inspired by pressure groups. In each of such major events as the New Deal, the Foreign Aid Program, Korea, pressure group activities were overshadowed by the emergency, but the groups continued to act and to fill in "gaps" left open by governmental policies. In the foreign aid program, for instance, pressure groups worked within the larger decisions, which they had not made, in order to obtain privileges.

Professor Macpherson: It seemed to me that Mr. Hirsch-Weber, in an earlier intervention, was not pleading for the value judgment, but rather that he warned against reading our own values into our studies.

Dr. Hirsch-Weber: I was merely saying that value judgments underly many of our pressure group studies, and that we should be conscious of that. This does not mean that the analyst should suppress his value judgments, it only asks for awareness. Besides, I pleaded for taking into account the values held by the pressure groups we study.

Professor Vito: There is always the danger that each scholar tries to put into his work his own particular premises.

Professor Akzin: Should not pressure groups have the same status as parties and individuals? The democratic state demands freedom of organization and propaganda for parties. Should not pressure groups enjoy the same right?

Professor Finer: It seems to me that it is possible that pressure groups may well accrete far too much power and that this may well be a threat to British parliamentary government. Take the general secretary of the Transport and General Workers Union. Once elected, he holds office during good pleasure and therefore does not continually have to seek re-election like M.P.s. His Union controls about 16 per cent of the votes at the Labour Party Annual Conference, and something like 17 per cent of the votes at the T.U.C. Also it has 14 members in Parliament. The general secretary of this Union is today more powerful than a Cabinet Minister. Indeed, he resembles one of the "over mighty subjects" of the English Middle Ages.

Nor is this all. Some pressure groups are larger or have more social-economic leverage than others. Some citizens are not organized at all or are organized in weak associations. There is a continual danger that these may be squeezed out by the pressure of the bigger.

Professor Webb: There is still the distinction between interest and consensus which I discussed earlier. This came up again when we talked about value judgments. The state demands adherence to public policy although the groups can disagree with the policy and seek to have it altered. Indeed public policy may alter. For example, the activities of the Jehovah's Witnesses were contrary to public policy during the War, but are not so now. It is obligatory to *follow* public policy, but nobody is compelled to *believe* in it.

Professor Pollock: I believe that for the balance of the afternoon, we should make an effort to discuss the question of where do we go from here. We should especially outline plans for future research since we will be taking up the subject of interest groups again next year in Rome.

Professor Heckscher: As far as Western countries are concerned, we have reached a considerable amount of consensus, using more or less the same concepts. Here we will only need to continue the work upon which we have engaged. But the job of getting outside the Western orbit is far more difficult. Mr. Almond's functional approach is intriguing. It will serve the study of interests as well as that of interest groups.

There are two types of countries outside the Western orbit. One is the underdeveloped countries anxious to follow the West but not sufficiently industrialized. Fruitful comparisons between such countries and the West could be made by contrasting industrialized Western countries as they are at present and as they were about a hundred years ago. The other type are the countries following socialist or communist patterns. Their economies are different and so are the ways in which interests proceed to assert themselves. Much depends on whether or not the country is industrialized. Mr. Djordjevic has shown that sectional interests exist in his country. We should try to find out whether and how they arise, how they make themselves felt and heard in other communist countries.

In our efforts to widen our study of groups, Western and non-Western scholars should cooperate and the International Political Science Association has an important role to play in this field.

Professor Almond: What Mr. Heckscher has said in regard to the communist system could be applied to authoritarian systems as well. There is a kind of latent, pluralist interest group system even in totalitarian countries. In authoritarian countries such as Spain and Portugal there is a legitimate, overt interest group system.

We tend to put the Communist countries and the West poles apart in comparisons. However, especially since the end of the Stalin era, it is legitimate to consider the place of pluralism in these countries. I would support an extension of our studies to include totalitarian, authoritarian, and non-Western countries.

Professor Merle: I should like to point out how important it is in my opinion that we study international pressure groups. We have concluded here that a study of political systems leaving out the role played by pressure groups would be completely unrealistic. But this holds true, also, for the study of international relations which needs to be reconsidered drastically in the light of our studies on domestic pressure groups. I add that methodologically speaking we should not only concentrate on the groups accredited with the United Nations, but use the term in the larger sense and study all pressure groups which affect the international scene.

Professor Akzin: I would go even further. Not only groups organized on an international level observe attention, but also national groups whose activities have an international impact.

Professor Pollock: We have been talking here this afternoon about some ambitious projects and yet no one has raised the question of how to improve the equipment which is at the disposal of political scientists when they attack these questions.

We have a great deal more cooperative research and more aid for research than formerly, but we need more of both. While our needs are more modest than those of the natural scientists, they are real indeed. We must call for more assistance in conducting more searching, broader, and more clearly defined research projects. Many of them can and ought to be done on an international basis.

As President of this group, I am glad to see new faces here and younger people. This is an indication of the widening influence of our organization.

Before bringing this final session to a close, I should like to express our thanks to the Ford Foundation, the University of Pittsburgh and the Falk Foundation which made this meeting possible. We are grateful to the Secretary-General for the indispensable arrangements and to the Committee on Local Arrangements for its hard work. We also appreciate the careful and painstaking work of the Rapporteur. This is in my opinion the best meeting we have ever had and this, I am sure, is due to a large degree to the careful preparation of papers and questions by Professor Ehrmann. This meeting like others has made me proud of our profession.

Professor Heckscher: We have all learned much here. It is good to come to America for the first time. When the plans for this meeting were made, I was, in view of the short time at our disposal, uncertain as to how successful it would be. It has been an excellent meeting, I was happy to see the high degree of sophistication and learning and I hope that our Association will come back to this country again.

I would like to repeat the thanks of our President to all he has mentioned. Most especially, I should like to move at this point for a vote of thanks from all the members of the Executive Board and of the Association to our President, Mr. Pollock. Much of what was accomplished here was due to his fine work and his arrangements. He is the best president we have had in this organization, and I propose that we express our gratitude to him. (Applause)

End of the Fifth Round Table of the International Political Science Association

INDEX

INDEX

INDEX

67

833